FORTRESS

Introduction to
the Lutheran Confessions

Title page of the Book of Concord, *1580.*
From Erwin Weber, From Luther to 1580: A Pictorial Account

FORTRESS

Introduction to the Lutheran Confessions

Günther Gassmann

Scott Hendrix

Fortress Press ◆ Minneapolis

FORTRESS INTRODUCTION TO THE LUTHERAN CONFESSIONS

Scripture translations from the Revised Standard Version of the Bible, copyright © 1946, 1952, and 1971 by the Division of Christian Education of the National Council of Churches of Christ in the United States of America, are used by permission.

Cover design: David Meyer
Cover graphic: *Graphics for Worship* copyright © 1996 Augsburg Fortress.
Frontispiece: *From Luther to 1580: A Pictorial Account* copyright © 1977 Concordia Publishing House. Used with permission.
Map (pg. 198): *From Luther to 1580: A Pictorial Account* copyright © 1977 Concordia Publishing House. Used with permission.

Library of Congress Cataloging-in-Publication Data

Gassmann, Günther, date
    Fortress introduction to the Lutheran confessions / Günther
Gassmann and Scott Hendrix.
        p.   cm.
    Includes bibliographical references and index.
    ISBN 0-8006-3162-5 (alk. paper)
    1. Konkordienbuch. 2. Lutheran Church—Doctrines—History.
3. Lutheran Church—Creeds—History and criticism. I. Hendrix,
Scott H. II. Title.
    BX8068.G37 1999
    238'.41—dc21   98-52258
                                                              CIP

The paper used in this publication meets the minimum requirements of American National Standard for Information Sciences—Permanence of Paper for Printed Library Materials, ANSI Z329.48-1984.

Manufactured in the U.S.A.   AF 1-3162

*To our students in courses on
the Lutheran Confessions at*

The Lutheran Theological Seminary at Gettysburg

The Lutheran Theological Seminary at Philadelphia

Lutheran Theological Southern Seminary

The Theological Faculty, University of Tartu, Estonia

CONTENTS

◆————————————————◆

PREFACE

The idea for this book came from our experience of introducing the Lutheran Confessions to people who previously had little exposure to them. These audiences include students at Lutheran seminaries who were studying the confessions for the first time and Christians from many traditions who were discovering the documents in ecumenical conversations. The Lutheran tradition has produced many worthy treatments of the Book of Concord (1580) and of the individual confessional writings that it contains. These treatments include insightful theological analyses of the documents and detailed studies of the historical context. Over the years we have greatly benefited from these studies and we continue to use them in our work, including the preparation of this book.

As we taught the confessions in recent years, however, we felt that a basic introduction should be available in addition to these more extensive works. This book is our attempt to provide that kind of introduction. It is for students in college and seminary who are taking courses on Lutheranism, but it is also for people in the churches who want to sharpen their knowledge of the Lutheran tradition.

The focus of our study is the Book of Concord itself, where it came from, what it contains, and how it has defined Lutheran identity. It treats the Book of Concord as both a historical landmark and a theological foundation despite the fact that it is subject to the conditions of its century, one of which was a strident polemical atmosphere that we no longer share. Chapters one and two place the confessions in their historical framework by providing introductions to the Reformation in general and to the rise of Lutheranism in particular. Chapter three discusses the concept and the importance of confession and introduces each document in the Book of Concord. The next three chapters deal with the theology of the confessions: chapter four explains the pillars on which the structure of that theology is built; chapter five treats the sacraments, the ministry, and the nature of the church; chapter six, on the Christian life, embraces the issues of sin, the human will, election, the two reigns of God, good works, and eternal life. Finally, chapter seven calls attention to the significance of the confessions for Lutheran identity, for the expansion of Lutheranism to every continent, for the foundation and work of the Lutheran World Federation, and for the emergence and ecumenical commitment of a worldwide communion of Lutheran churches.

The writing of this book has itself been a dialogue between the authors. One is American and one is German. One is a church historian who has taught at several seminaries and has written mostly about the Reformation. The other is a systematic theologian who has held several ecumenical positions and has written widely on Lutheranism and on ecumenical topics. We do not have exactly the same position on all the themes of this book and we have made no attempt to harmonize our theologies. The chapters are not a conglomeration of our ideas: Hendrix is the author of chapters one, two, six, and the first two sections of chapter four; Gassmann is the author of chapters three, five, seven, and the last two sections of chapter four. Nevertheless, we have read and discussed all the material together and we have learned from each other in the process. As a result, we have made some changes in what we have written along the way and we have been forced to restate our ideas with more precision. We hope that our book can illustrate the way in which Lutherans from different backgrounds and disciplines can live in dialogue with one another within the framework of a common confessional identity.

To make this book useful as an introduction and as a reference, we have included a glossary of important theological and historical terms that appear in the text with an asterisk. At the end of each chapter we have suggested questions that might guide discussion of the material and further reflection on it. Endnotes have been left to the discretion of each author, but together we have supplied a bibliography that indicates the length and breadth of research on the confessions to which our study is also indebted. Although we have consulted and occasionally invoked the critical edition of the confessions published in Germany, we have regularly cited and quoted texts in English from the Tappert edition of the *Book of Concord* that was published in 1959. In these quotations we have amended the text insofar as it was necessary to employ more inclusive language. Our references to the Book of

Concord cite the same paragraph numbers that are used in both the critical and the Tappert editions; references to the Formula of Concord (FC) are to the Solid Declaration unless otherwise noted. For stimulating, shaping, and probing our thinking over the years we wish to thank the many students and colleagues in whose midst we have taught and discussed the history and the meaning of these documents. In particular we would like to thank the class in Lutheran Confessions that we taught together at Gettysburg Lutheran Seminary during the fall semester of 1997. The students gave helpful feedback to the first draft of this material and cheerfully cooperated with our experiment. We also appreciate the interest and support of our Gettysburg colleagues. A sabbatical grant from Lutheran Brotherhood facilitated the preparation of the final text. Ursula Gassmann and Emilee Hendrix provided spiritual, editorial, and material nourishment for the project and we thank them for it!

Günther Gassmann
Scott Hendrix
December 1998

ABBREVIATIONS

Ap.	Apology of the Augsburg Confession
BC	*Book of Concord* (ed. Tappert, 1959)
BSLK	Bekenntnisschriften der evangelisch-lutherischen Kirche
CA	Augsburg Confession (Confessio Augustana)
Clemen	Luthers Werke in Auswahl (ed. Otto Clemen)
CR	Corpus Reformatorum
FC	Formula of Concord
FC-Ep	Formula of Concord – Epitome
FC-SD	Formula of Concord – Solid Declaration
LC	Large Catechism
LQ	*Lutheran Quarterly*
LW	Luther's Works. American edition
LWF	Lutheran World Federation
NPNF	Nicene and Post-Nicene Fathers
OECT	Oxford Early Christian Texts
OER	*Oxford Encyclopedia of the Reformation*
PL	Migne, *Patrologiae cursus completus*, Series Latina
SA	Smalcald Articles
SC	Small Catechism
Tr.	Treatise on the Power and Primacy of the Pope
TRE	*Theologische Realenzyklopädie*
WA	Luthers Werke, Kritische Gesamtausgabe (Weimar edition of Luther's Works)
ZThK	*Zeitschrift für Theologie und Kirche*

CHAPTER ONE

Setting the Stage

The Reformation
in Historical Context

◆

Politics

When the Reformation began in the early 1500s, Christianity was almost fifteen hundred years old and had spread to northern and western Europe from its origins in the Mediterranean world. By mid-century the Reformation was causing a restructuring of Christianity in Europe that would define the shape of the faith in the modern world. By 1580, the year in which the Lutheran *Book of Concord* was published, the bishop of Rome was no longer the supreme religious authority in western Europe and the Church of Rome was no longer the only church. Anglicans loyal to the English crown made up the majority of Christians in England. Followers of the French reformer, John Calvin* (1509–1564) and of his Swiss predecessor, Ulrich Zwingli* (1484–1531), were prominent in Switzerland, Scotland, the Netherlands, southern France, and in parts of western Germany and eastern Europe. They were called Reformed Christians and adhered to various Reformed confessions produced locally where they were strong. Lutherans dominated Scandinavia and half of Germany where they had originated. Their confessions, all produced in Germany as the Lutheran movement defined itself, were brought together in the *Book of Concord*. Roman Christianity, now reduced to one among several confessions in Europe, defined its new identity as Roman Catholicism through the canons and decrees of the Council of Trent* (1545–1563).

This restructuring of Christianity was in large part a political process. During the Middle Ages, church and state had become more and more intertwined. Europeans saw themselves as a Christian society ruled by two powers, one spiritual and the other temporal. At the top of the spiritual hierarchy was the bishop of Rome, the pope, who exercised jurisdiction over all the archbishops and bishops who ruled the provinces and dioceses of Christendom throughout Europe. The chief civil authorities were the kings, queens, and princes of Europe, plus the emperor of the Holy Roman Empire, which mainly comprised Germany as it was then. The pope was not only a spiritual power. By virtue of his claim to territory in Italy, called the papal states, the papacy was also a temporal power that played politics and occasionally sent troops into battle. By the same token, the rulers of Europe also considered themselves spiritual powers. They felt responsible for the church in their territories and had the right to appoint certain clergy and to influence religious life in their domains.

Frequent conflict between spiritual and civil authority marked the Middle Ages and continued during the Reformation. No permanent restructuring of Christianity would have happened without the support and engagement of secular rulers against the bishops and the popes. In England, for example, the Reformation owed its sanction to queens, kings, and their advisors. In 1534 King Henry VIII declared himself the supreme head of the English Church because Pope Clement VII refused to annul Henry's first marriage to Catherine or to approve his secret marriage to Anne Boleyn. Reformed Christianity would not have gained a foothold unless city councils in Zurich and Geneva had supported the reform programs of Zwingli and Calvin. After several wars of religion between Catholics* and French Calvinists, the conversion of King Henry IV to Roman Catholicism in 1593 guaranteed that Reformed Christianity would not take over France. Under the Edict of Nantes* (1598), a vigorous minority of French Calvinists called Huguenots enjoyed another eighty-seven years of toleration in a predominantly Catholic country.

In Scandinavia, rulers and parliaments gradually recognized official Lutheran churches. In Germany, Lutherans would not have succeeded unless the princes and cities that favored them had resisted the efforts of the Catholic emperor, Charles V, to restore the Christian unity of the empire on his terms. Although the Edict of Worms* declared them outlaws in 1521, Martin Luther and his followers survived because they were protected by the electors of Saxony, where Wittenberg was located, and by other rulers who supported the evangelical* movement and formed alliances in its defense. Political reasons also prevented Charles V, who remained loyal to Rome, from squelching the evangelical movement in the 1520s and 1530s. The eastern border of the empire was threatened by the Ottoman Turks, and the emperor needed money and troops from the evangelical princes to fend off the Turkish threat.

This political standoff lasted until 1547. By that time, when Charles V finally decided to move against the evangelicals, they were strong enough to survive the onslaught. The Peace of Augsburg* (1555) granted those cities and territories that adhered to the Augsburg Confession legal status in the empire. According to the principle *cuius regio eius religio* (i.e., a ruler determines the religion of the territory), city councils and the nobility decided whether their territories would be Catholic or Lutheran (the latter now officially defined as adherence to the Augsburg Confession). As a result, territories like Saxony, Hesse, and Württemberg, along with cities like Nuremberg, Magdeburg, Strasbourg, and Braunschweig, all made Lutheranism their official confession. About half of Germany, the Baltic countries, and all of Scandinavia eventually became Lutheran. Lutheranism also survived oppression in small pockets of east-central Europe, but political forces eventually produced a stronger Reformed presence amid the Roman Catholicism and Eastern Orthodoxy of that region.

◆

Society

The Reformation happened at a time when European society was undergoing rapid change. The most important change involved the expansion of cities. The population was growing and people were moving from the countryside into towns, which dotted the landscape. Cities in Europe were still small by modern standards. A large city contained thirty to fifty thousand people, while the university town of Wittenberg numbered several thousand inhabitants at the most. The large number of literate people who lived in towns made them the center of politics and ideas.

Luther's new theology was spread by pamphlets printed in the towns of Germany. His tracts were snapped up by people who also read them out loud to others at home and on the job. In just six years, from 1517 to 1523, Luther became the most popular religious author of all time in Europe. For the first time in history, the invention of printing with movable type made it possible to spread new ideas quickly among a wide audience. This print revolution had an effect on communication in the sixteenth century comparable to the impact of television and computers on the late twentieth century. Without the printing press the Reformation either would not have happened or would have happened more slowly.

The Reformation first took hold in towns and cities. By 1500 city councils were already in charge of some religious institutions and appointing clergy to their positions. These actions often led to conflict with the local bishop who was loyal to Rome. The first evangelical preachers tried to persuade city councils to permit evangelical worship and the teaching of Luther's theology in the churches of the town. They were successful in notable cases like Wittenberg (1522) and Nuremberg (1525). In Germany a number of cities were independent of the territory that surrounded them. That independence made it easier to adopt the Reformation even though opposition still came from the local bishops and intermittently from Emperor Charles V.

Reformation in the cities and in the countryside did not always come from the top down. Sometimes a more democratic or even revolutionary process was at work. The earliest supporters of evangelical preachers often came from the lower class rather than from the elite of the town who controlled the council. Public demonstrations in favor of the gospel (i.e., evangelical preaching and worship according to Luther's theology) pressured the council to admit backers of reform to their chambers. Sometimes violence erupted. One way or another, many councils gave in to popular support for the Reformation and adopted it as the legal form of Christian faith and practice in their towns.

Popular enthusiasm for Luther's ideas also led to a revolution in the countryside. Many serfs and peasants seized on Luther's notion of Christian freedom and demanded more rights for themselves as Christians and as subjects. At first, preachers and some townspeople rallied to their cause and organized them into political and religious bands called Christian associations. When they resorted to random violence and military campaigns, however, they lost the support of Luther and other reformers. The most notorious revolutionary leader was the evangelical preacher, Thomas Müntzer* (c. 1491–1525), who viewed the Reformation as the chance to realize the kingdom of God on earth. He challenged Luther's leadership in central Germany and died in 1525 as the leader of a peasant army that was slaughtered by the princes. Although the Revolution of 1525* in Germany failed (it is also known as the Peasants' War*), the evangelical movement continued to attract people at every level of society, and more towns and territories adopted the Reformation.

◆

Church

The Reformation caused a revolution in the church and among the clergy. Before the Reformation, there was a widespread desire for change and many attempts were made to reform the priesthood and the administration of the late medieval church. The most promising efforts came from two general church councils that met in Constance* (1414–1418) and in Basel* (1431–1439). These councils succeeded in healing the schism of Western Christianity; in the fourteenth century this schism had led to competing popes, one living in Rome and the other in Avignon. The councils, however, were not able to achieve more power over the papacy or to improve significantly the life and learning of the clergy. Although the rulers of France and England asserted more control over the church in their lands, the popes of the late Middle Ages were able to consolidate their authority. The Fifth Lateran Council* (1512–1517) had just approved Pope Leo X's claim of papal sovereignty over councils when Luther drafted his Ninety-five Theses* in 1517 (see pp. 11–12). After Luther was condemned by Pope Leo in 1520, he appealed his case to a council. Later, many people wanted a neutral council of the church to settle the religious conflict in Germany, but such a council was never called and the Church of Rome lost control of Christianity in much of Europe.

At the same time, the late Middle Ages experienced a notable upswing in piety. Monastic orders were growing; pilgrimages to shrines of saints were popular; laypeople, individually and in religious auxiliaries, gave large sums of money to endow masses for their own souls after death and for the souls of their loved ones. The interest from these endowments paid the stipends of additional clergy who said private masses in countless chapels, cloisters, and cathedrals around Europe. People also attended public mass, especially on numerous festival days, where they paid special reverence to the elevated host (the wafer consecrated during the Eucharist as the body of Christ). A special festival named Corpus Christi (Latin for "body of Christ") became a popular part of late medieval piety. The consecrated host was held high in a monstrance (a clear vessel for viewing) and carried in procession through a town or village for the people to revere. Religion was intensely visible in the lives and in the communities of the laity.

So many clergy were added to the rolls that in the German city of Hamburg there was one priest for every ten laypeople. Most of these clergy possessed little formal education. They had never studied at a university, and whatever theology they knew came from popular books on the lives of saints and from manuals on how to perform the sacraments. A wide gap existed between the upper and lower clergy. Most bishops and their assisting clergy came from wealthy, even noble, families, and they sometimes built careers by paying fees to occupy more than one ecclesiastical office at a time. While the upper clergy benefited from several salaries, the lower clergy sometimes received no salary at all and had to live off the land attached to their church and from the gifts of their parishioners. Understandably, the evangelical movement attracted more priests than bishops because the bishops had a great deal more to lose. In addition to the grand master of the Teutonic Knights, who became the Lutheran Duke Albert of Prussia, and Archbishop Hermann von Wied, whose attempt to bring the Reformation to Cologne failed, only two German bishops joined the evangelical movement: the bishops of Samland and Pomerania, also in Prussia.[1]

The money to finance clerical livings, small and large, came from tithes exacted from laypeople. They also had to pay tithes to local monasteries if the monastery had traditional rights to the land that they worked. Although inhabited by the religious (a term for monks, nuns, and clergy) who had vowed to live in poverty, cloisters of both men and women, monasteries and convents, grew quite wealthy from income off their cash endowments and their properties. No wonder, then, that anticlerical sentiment among the laity was high and contributed to the popularity of the evangelical movement. Over and above the financial disparity, laity were angered by the immunity from civil taxes and jurisdiction enjoyed by most clergy, who could be tried only in church courts over which the laity had little influence. Furthermore, enough clergy lived with concubines and had children by them to cause public scandal. The vow of celibacy* prevented clergy from marrying, but some bishops winked at the practice of concubinage and allowed it to go unchallenged if the priest paid a fine. It is fair to say, however, that living with a concubine troubled the consciences of some priests and their partners as much as it offended their parishioners.

For this reason as well, the Reformation was phenomenally popular among monks and priests. As the evangelical movement began in Germany, monks left the cloisters in droves and priests married as soon as they could. Despite the charming story of Luther's future wife, Katharina von Bora* (1499–1552) being rescued from the convent in a herring barrel, the Reformation was less popular among nuns. The convent was a safe place for women in which they could exercise the authority and responsibility denied them in a civil realm dominated by men. Although some nuns were glad to turn Protestant* whether they married or not, many others remained in their convents and offered stout resistance to the Reformation. Still, the struggle of many religious with their vow of celibacy made the evangelical movement, which encouraged the marriage of clergy, all the more attractive.

◆

Theology

The late Middle Ages was a rich theological period. Theology was highly regarded as an academic discipline and respected scholars taught it at most universities. This scholastic* theology, as it was called, was divided into different schools of thought that took their names from distinguished teachers of the thirteenth and fourteenth centuries like Thomas Aquinas* (c. 1224–1274) and William of Ockham* (c. 1285–c. 1349). Luther, for example, learned theology at the University of Erfurt from teachers who belonged to the school of William of Ockham called Nominalism*. When Luther joined the faculty of theology at the University of Wittenberg in 1512, he found colleagues trained in other scholastic traditions.

All scholastic theology was under attack, however, by the time Luther arrived in Wittenberg. A new intellectual movement called Christian humanism was in full swing and was influencing how theology was taught. Born in the fourteenth-century Italian Renaissance, humanism was the recovery of the texts of Greek and Roman antiquity. Christian humanists paid special attention to the Bible (in the original Greek and Hebrew) and to the writings of the early church theologians. They criticized scholastic theologians for not going back to those original Christian sources and for repeating unfruitful debates that came from their medieval textbooks. The cradle of the evangelical movement was Wittenberg, where Luther and his colleagues attempted to focus the study of theology on the Bible and on theologians of the early church. The evangelical movement was eagerly supported by young humanist scholars like Philip Melanchthon* (1497–1560), who arrived in Wittenberg in 1518 to teach Greek.

Other kinds of theology also enriched the setting in which the Reformation began. Monastic orders handed down the traditions of their teachers and instilled a theology of humility in the minds and habits of their members. In this way the young Luther learned the theology of Augustine* (354–430), the early Christian bishop and theologian after whom his order was named. From his mentor and superior in the order, John von Staupitz* (c. 1469–1524), Luther received both theological and pastoral advice filtered through von Staupitz's well-trained and broad theological mind. Mystical theologians were also read and studied even though they were not officially represented in the universities. As a student and young instructor, Luther acquainted himself with the works of John Tauler* (c. 1300–1361) and Jean Gerson* (1363–1429). In 1516 and 1518 he published a sample of German mysticism from the fourteenth century called *A German Theology*, from which he said he learned more than from any book except the Bible and the works of Augustine.[2] Finally, as a young instructor, Luther often reacted positively to theological opinions contained in the biblical commentaries that he consulted for his lectures.

For the beginning of the Reformation, however, all that academic theology was less important than the theology that governed popular piety. This theology revolved around the sacrament of penance* and was taught mainly in sermons and devotional literature. Basically it told people the following: You should use the sacrament of penance frequently. You should feel genuinely sorry for your sins and confess as many of them as you can remember. After confessing, you will be absolved of your sins if you promise to atone for them (called "making satisfaction" for sin) according to the religious task imposed on you by the priest. These religious works, also known as good works, varied from simple assignments like giving alms or praying the rosary to bigger challenges like undertaking a pilgrimage. If penitents did not perform these works, the penalty of their sin would have to be worked off in purgatory, a state between death and resurrection in which the purification of the soul could be completed. On special occasions penitents might gain release from the assignment by acquiring an indulgence letter in return for a contribution. These indulgence letters had arisen over the centuries to make penance more tolerable, but they had also come to be used, like the papal indulgence of 1517, to raise money for special projects like the building of St. Peter's Basilica in Rome.

It is easy to see how both clergy and laity could abuse the penitential system. Although designed to assure people of forgiveness and salvation if they took their sin seriously and made satisfaction for it, the system left many people either uncertain of forgiveness or skeptical of the church's sincerity. Even when prompted by priests using manuals, people were not sure they had confessed every sin or done enough good works to make up for the sins they were truly worried about. Other people wondered how seriously the church took either sin or forgiveness when it encouraged people to acquire indulgences in support of building projects instead of completing their penance.

The Reformation began when a new theology drawn from the intensive study of Scripture and early Christianity clashed with the popular theology behind this penitential piety. The center of this new evangelical theology was the certainty of God's forgiveness to those who repented of their sin and trusted in Jesus Christ alone as the way of salvation. It made some use of scholastic, monastic, and mystical theology, but it rejected the parts that did not fit its evangelical emphasis. It did not regard itself as a new theology but as the recovery of the gospel message for a church that had lost its center. Most important of all, it was not a school of theology to be debated but a practical theology to be proclaimed and lived. It sought a new and more genuine Christian faith, piety, and community for people who, although quite religious, had been led astray and had lost Jesus Christ as the center of their faith and life. The recovery of that center—with the freedom, consolation, and assurance it brings—was the goal of the Reformation and its theology.

Questions for Discussion and Further Study

1. Indicate some of the developments that shaped the historical context within which the Lutheran Reformation and its confessions emerged.

2. What were some of the elements that formed the theological background of the Reformation?

3. Describe some of the diverse historical contexts in which Lutheran churches live and witness today and compare these contexts to the setting of the Reformation.

S. H.

CHAPTER TWO

The Development of Lutheranism

Defining a Lutheran Movement

1. The Indulgence Controversy

Lutheranism arose out of the evangelical* movement that began with the indulgence controversy between Martin Luther and the clerical hierarchy of the late medieval church. In the fall of 1517, Luther heard that outlandish claims were being made for the St. Peter's indulgence (see p. 9) that had been authorized by Pope Leo X and was being offered near Wittenberg. Preachers were claiming that the acquisition of an indulgence letter would grant complete remission of sin. In order to protect people from this deception, Luther wrote ninety-five theses for a debate on the power of indulgences and the pope's right to offer them. The theses were formulated in Latin and were probably posted on the door of the Castle Church in Wittenberg as a notice of the debate. Luther also sent copies to some friends and to Archbishop Albert of Mainz* (1490–1545), the highest church official in Germany, who was promoting the sale of the indulgence. Before long, the theses were translated into German and greeted with enthusiasm around the empire. Albert of Mainz sent a copy to the curia, the central government of the church in Rome, which opened an investigation of the little-known Augustinian professor in Wittenberg. Within a year, Luther's invitation to a scholarly debate had become a legal process in which he was the defendant.

Luther's legal conflict with the Roman curia went through several stages from 1518 to 1521. Despite attempts on both sides to avoid a showdown, Luther was finally excommunicated in a papal bull dated January 3, 1521. In May of the same year he was proclaimed an outlaw in the Holy Roman Empire after appearing before Charles V at a diet (i.e., a convention) of the empire in Worms. At this diet, Luther refused to recant his writings because his conscience was bound by Scripture. This famous speech made clear that Luther was also fighting for the consciences of all believers who felt oppressed by the church's laws.[1]

Indeed, by the time of his appearance at Worms, Luther had become a hero to countless people in Germany who believed he was fighting for their cause. Not all of his supporters had the same cause, however. Some were attracted by his attack on the papacy and were hoping that Germany could rid itself of fiscal exploitation by Rome. Others supported his criticism of clerical privilege and the sacramental system of the church. Luther's objection to a superior spiritual status for clergy in favor of the spiritual priesthood of all believers appealed to widespread anticlerical sentiment. Some people liked the simplicity of Luther's earliest explanations of the Lord's Prayer, the Apostles' Creed, the Ten Commandments, and the sacraments (1519–1520). They showed how Christian life was grounded on faith in God's promises and on charity toward the neighbor. Others were taken with the notion of Christian freedom, which Luther explained in a popular treatise that appeared in late 1520. The claim that Christians were free in faith reverberated widely among people who felt themselves to be in social, economic, and religious bondage.

This early support for Luther would be tested between 1521 and 1530 as the evangelical movement expanded. In 1522 Luther was still defining a common evangelical cause as the cause of Christ:

> I ask that people make no reference to my name; let them call themselves Christians, not Lutherans. What is Luther? After all, the teaching is not mine. Neither was I crucified for anyone. St. Paul, in 1 Corinthians 3 [:22], would not allow Christians to call themselves Pauline or Petrine, but Christian. How then should I — poor stinking maggot-fodder that I am — come to have people call the children of Christ by my wretched name? Not so, my dear friends; let us abolish all party names and call ourselves Christians, after him whose teaching we hold. The papists deservedly have a party name, because they are not content with the teaching and name of Christ, but want to be papist as well. Let them be papist,

then, since the pope is their master. I neither am nor want to be anyone's master. I hold, together with the universal church, the one universal teaching of Christ, who is our only master.[2]

This vision of a common evangelical movement against the "papists" was not to be realized. His followers would not all agree on what belonged to the genuine cause of Christ, and not all of his sympathizers would end up in the Lutheran movement that was eventually limited to those cities and territories that adhered to the Augsburg Confession of 1530.

2. The Wittenberg Movement

The first serious steps toward an evangelical form of Christianity were taken in Wittenberg in the fall of 1521. While Luther was safely in hiding at the Wartburg Castle after being subjected to a friendly kidnapping by the agents of Elector Frederick*, his followers went ahead with concrete reforms. In October Augustinian monks in Luther's own monastery stopped saying private masses and began to leave the cloister. Andrew Bodenstein von Karlstadt* (1486–1541), Luther's faculty colleague, wrote theses against clerical celibacy* and monastic vows. Then, on Christmas Day, 1521, against the elector's wishes, Karlstadt celebrated the first public evangelical mass, pronouncing the words of institution in German and distributing Communion in both kinds* (i.e., both bread and wine were offered to communicants). Karlstadt, himself a priest, practiced what he preached. First, he married; then, in January 1522, he persuaded the city council to adopt a church order* for Wittenberg that required that the evangelical form of Mass be celebrated and that statues and pictures be removed from the churches.

Matters now came to a head. When Elector Frederick tried to restrain the city council, it summoned Luther back to Wittenberg to help settle the crisis. On the first Sunday in Lent, 1522, he mounted the pulpit in the parish church and delivered the first of eight sermons, often called his Wittenberg or Invocavit sermons, which repudiated Karlstadt's attempt to implement evangelical reforms by force. Although he supported the reforms, Luther argued that the same people who had just been freed from the "laws of the pope" should not be coerced against their consciences to make changes before they were ready. As a result, reform was implemented gradually in Wittenberg and Karlstadt's leadership was discredited.

Karlstadt's model of evangelical Christianity was too different from Luther's to become part of a Lutheran movement. That difference involved not only the pace at which reforms were implemented but also the purpose of external rites like sacraments. In his new role as pastor in Orlamünde, Karlstadt ceased to administer baptism to infants. Under the influence of mysticism, Karlstadt also argued that the bread and wine of Communion did not contain the body and blood of Christ but pointed the communicant instead to the saving body of Christ on the cross. Luther, however, argued that the forgiveness of sin that Christ obtained on the cross had to be distributed to believers through the external (i.e., outside the mind of the believer) means of Word and Sacrament. The faithful were not dependent on their spiritual meditation upon the cross; they could count on receiving forgiveness whenever they heard the gospel proclaimed and participated in the sacraments. This necessity of external means became a hallmark of the Lutheran movement.

3. The Lord's Supper Controversy

A second, similar controversy helped to define the Lutheran Reformation. It occurred between Luther and Ulrich Zwingli* (1484–1531) over the presence of Christ in the Lord's Supper. Zwingli based his reform on the authority of Scripture in which he, like Luther, had discovered the gospel, but his view of the sacraments differed from Luther's. Both reformers emphasized the role of faith in receiving the forgiveness of sin. According to Zwingli, however, the Lord's Supper recalled the saving death of Christ in such a way that faith brought Christ into the sacrament as food for the soul. Zwingli also adopted the suggestion of a Dutch theologian, Cornelis Hoen (c. 1460–1524), that bread and wine signified the body and blood of Christ but did not actually become that body and blood. In contrast, because the words of institution said so, Luther continued to believe that bread and wine were in fact the body and blood of Christ, although he rejected the medieval doctrine of transubstantiation*, which explained how the change occurred. Zwingli's view seemed to deny the full presence of Christ, often called the real or bodily presence, because only the spirit or the divine nature of Christ — but not his human nature — seemed to be required for Christ to become food for the soul.

In late 1524 Zwingli's view began to influence evangelical preachers in Switzerland and southern Germany, and by 1529 a split of the evangelical movement seemed imminent. To forestall a schism, Philip of Hesse* (1504–1567), the German prince most interested in Protestant* unity, convoked a meeting of leading evangelical theologians at his castle in early October 1529. This Marburg Colloquy* was the only time that Zwingli and Luther met face to face. Zwingli insisted that the words "This is my body" meant "This [bread] signifies my body." To make his counterpoint, Luther reportedly chalked the words ("This is my body") on the table, covered them with a velvet cloth, and then, when he was accused of lacking proof from Scripture, removed the cloth and declared "Here is our Scripture passage."[3] Although they agreed on thirteen other theological articles, the gathering could not reach agreement on the mode of Christ's presence in the Lord's Supper. The discussion was sometimes heated, but the articles concluded with the desire that "each side should show Christian love to the other side insofar as conscience will permit."[4] Little did they know it then, but this formal disagreement was the beginning of separate Reformed and Lutheran confessions.

4. The Diet of Augsburg (1530)

A Lutheran confession was first defined as such at the Diet of Augsburg in Germany in 1530. This Augsburg Confession, as it came to be known (see pp. 38–40), was the product of more than a month's work under the direction of Philip Melanchthon* (1497–1560). From the Coburg castle, where he remained under Saxon protection as an outlaw of the empire, Luther enthusiastically endorsed the document. He told Melanchthon that it pleased him very much,[5] and he remarked in another letter that he rejoiced to see the day when Christ was publicly preached in such a beautiful confession.[6] Nonetheless, Catholic* theologians prepared a refutation of the confession and persuaded the emperor to endorse it. This Roman Confutation* of the Augsburg Confession was read before the diet on August 3, 1530. The Lutherans refused to agree that their confession had been refuted and asked for a copy of the confutation. It was denied them.

Meanwhile, behind the scenes unofficial negotiations had involved Melanchthon with Catholic officials and theologians. Melanchthon indicated that Lutherans might recognize the jurisdiction of Catholic bishops if Rome would concede the right of communicants to receive* both elements, the right of clergy to marry, and the abolition of private masses and monastic vows. Mindful of his original purpose to reunite the dissenting parties, Emperor Charles decided to make the negotiations official after the Augsburg Confession was rejected. Despite earnest efforts by Melanchthon, John Eck* (1486–1543), and others, however, agreement could not be reached. The claim of the Augsburg Confession that the "dispute and dissension are concerned chiefly with various traditions and abuses" (BC 48.2) turned out to be too modest. Melanchthon could not give up the changes advocated in the second part of the confession because the abuses they corrected either contradicted Scripture or were "contrary to the gospel and the teaching about faith in Christ" (CA 15.3; 26.4, 8; 28.50–52). On the Catholic side, to concede such changes would have been to impair the authority of bishops and to alter Christian worship and piety.

On November 19, 1530, the failure to reach agreement was formally recognized in the Edict of Augsburg*. The evangelical cities and territories were given until April 15, 1531, to inform the emperor if they would return to the faith and practice of the Roman Church. By this time, Melanchthon had completed his response to the Roman Confutation that is known as the Apology (i.e., defense) of the Augsburg Confession (see pp. 40–41). At the end of the diet, the Saxon chancellor attempted to show a draft of the Apology to Emperor Charles, but as he reached for it, the emperor's brother, King Ferdinand of Austria, whispered in his ear and Charles withdrew his hand. In spite of this symbolic refusal to consider the debate still open, discussion and conflict would continue for twenty-five years before the matter was settled. Nevertheless, when the Saxon party left Augsburg for home in September 1530, a Lutheran movement had been defined.

◆

Expanding the Lutheran Reformation

1. Church Orders and Catechisms

While Lutheranism was being defined politically at Augsburg, evangelical preaching and practice were being installed locally by means of visitations*, church orders, and catechisms. Visitations were inspection tours of parishes carried out by clergy and public officials. The first

visitations in electoral Saxony were prompted by the Peasants' War*
(1525), which had devastated parts of Germany including areas in and
around Saxony. Some parishes were also left without pastors when
priests had departed and not been replaced. At the instigation of
Nicholas Hausmann, a pastor in Zwickau, Martin Luther requested
Elector John* to arrange for an inspection of parochial conditions in
Saxony. The first survey in 1526 brought back dismal results. Barely
half of the pastors were judged to be preaching the gospel. Thereupon
two professors, one of them Melanchthon, and two electoral officials
were appointed to a commission of visitors. Melanchthon also wrote a
set of guidelines called the *Instruction for the Visitors of Parish Pastors in
Electoral Saxony* (LW 40:265–320). In his preface to the *Instruction*,
Luther justified the prince's initiative by pointing out the failure of
bishops to perform their ministry of oversight. According to Luther,
Elector John was acting out of Christian love and out of concern for
the gospel and the "welfare of the wretched Christians in his territory."[7]

The *Instruction* was one of the first attempts to define a Lutheran
church order. It contained an important statement of evangelical theology; sections on prayer, the sacraments, and marriage; guidelines for
daily worship and the Christian calendar; and outlines for the office of
superintendent of the clergy and for school curricula. The *Instruction*
also influenced the content of the Augsburg Confession. Soon other
evangelical church orders were being adopted in every place the new
form of Christianity became official. Two of the earliest were written
for the cities of Braunschweig (1528) and Hamburg (1529) by John
Bugenhagen* (1485–1558), a colleague of Luther and Melanchthon
and pastor of the parish church in Wittenberg. These orders were used
as models for Lutheran churches in many parts of northern Germany
and in Denmark. Gradually, some church orders began to name the
Augsburg Confession as a standard of doctrine and practice. For
example, in his 1536 church order for Hannover, Urbanus Rhegius*
(1489–1541) listed sixteen points taught by the "holy gospel," and then
added: "All that and what our side confessed before his imperial
majesty at the diet in Augsburg is ever the truth."[8]

The same motivation that led to the visitations also prompted
Luther to write his catechisms. "The deplorable conditions which I
recently encountered when I was a visitor," he wrote in the preface to
the Small Catechism (1529), "constrained me to prepare this brief and

simple catechism or statement of Christian teaching."[9] The need for pastoral care and instruction was extreme: "The common people, especially those who live in the country, have no knowledge whatever of Christian teaching, and unfortunately many pastors are quite incompetent and unfitted for teaching." Nicholas Hausmann, the same pastor from Zwickau who suggested the visitations, also requested help in catechizing young people.[10] Luther responded by composing two forms. The Small Catechism, its original five parts printed on separate posters, was designed to teach the evangelical faith to everyone, including children. The Large Catechism, originally called the German Catechism, was to a certain extent the companion for the German Mass composed by Luther in 1526. Based on his sermons, it was directed toward regular preaching and teaching of the catechism "from the pulpit at stated times or daily as may be needed."[11] Both catechisms belong to a much larger body of instructional manuals that flew off the presses in Wittenberg and other towns. From 1522 to 1529 thirteen different booklets were printed in Wittenberg, including the earliest catechism (1525), which was not written by Luther but was based on his works.[12] Many evangelical preachers would write their own catechisms, but only Luther's would attain the status of confessional documents (see pp. 42–44). Next to the Augsburg Confession, they exerted the greatest influence on the process of defining the growing number of Lutheran churches.

2. The Smalcald League

Despite the rejection of its confession at Augsburg, Lutheranism underwent rapid expansion during the 1530s thanks to the Smalcald League*. This league was formed as a defense against the Edict of Augsburg by evangelical cities and territories in December 1530, at the small town of Smalcald in Thuringia. The league became a Lutheran alliance because adherence to the Augsburg Confession was required for admission. As important cities like Strasbourg and Hamburg and large territories like Württemberg joined the league, most of German Protestantism became Lutheran. By cutting off the Zwinglians* who would not subscribe to the Confession, the Smalcald League sealed the split between Swiss and German Protestantism and spurred the evolution of Reformed and Lutheran confessions.

Until it was defeated by Charles V in 1547, the league provided a secure political framework for the development of Lutheran churches in Germany. This development was assisted by an important agreement on the Lord's Supper known as the Wittenberg Concord*. In late May of 1536, this agreement between Wittenberg and south German theologians produced a definition of the presence of Christ that would become definitive for Lutheran theology and reappear in the Formula of Concord (1577).[13] This definition expressed a temporal over a spatial understanding of the presence of Christ and chose the concept of sacramental union, endorsed by Melanchthon and Martin Bucer* (1491–1551), to describe it. Luther may have preferred a local inclusion of Christ's body in the elements; but he accepted the sacramental union, which located the presence of Christ primarily in the action or "use" of the sacrament. After agreement was reached, the theologians present and about fifty townspeople took Communion together on Ascension Day.

The concord came just in time. A week later, on June 2, 1536, Pope Paul III called a council of the church to meet the next year in Mantua (Italy). Since Emperor Charles had given the Lutheran cities and territories breathing space until a church council was called, the Smalcald League now had to respond. Elector John Frederick of Saxony* charged Luther to draw up a statement identifying those theological articles that could be negotiated at a council and those that could not. Luther started to work but had to dictate part of the articles after he fell ill a week before Christmas in 1536. He was still recuperating at the end of December when a conference of theologians met at Wittenberg to debate and revise the articles before signing them and sending them on to the elector. In part II, Luther said that "the papacy is of no use to the church because it exercises no Christian office" and that the pope would never give up his claim to be head of the church by divine right (i.e., by God's express will declared in Scripture).[14] As in the past, Melanchthon wanted to hold open the possibility that the papacy might "allow the gospel," and that the evangelical party, in such a case, could grant the pope superiority over other bishops by human authority alone. Melanchthon attached such a statement to his signature under Luther's articles.

To make a decision about whether to attend the council, the league then met in February 1537 at Smalcald. Since theologians were also summoned to appear with their princes and city delegates, it became the largest gathering of Lutheran theologians to date. Elector John Frederick planned to present Luther's articles for adoption by the diet, but two developments prevented it (see pp. 41–42). Instead, the Smalcald Articles were signed voluntarily by many of the theologians present. As part of their reaffirmation of the Augsburg Confession, the theologians at Smalcald also signed the Treatise on the Power and Primacy of the Pope composed by Melanchthon (see p. 42). The diet at Smalcald then officially accepted the treatise and decided not to send representatives to the council called by Pope Paul III.

3. The Failure of Dialogue

The council was not convened after all. Instead, Charles V pursued the religious reunification of Germany through a series of colloquies in 1540 and 1541. The first colloquy met at Hagenau in June 1540 and determined that the Augsburg Confession and the Apology would serve as the basis of negotiations. When they resumed at Worms in late October, Melanchthon prepared a revision of the Augsburg Confession that took account of the unity between the Wittenbergers and the south Germans that had been reached in 1536. Alongside the public negotiations, a series of private conversations were initiated in Worms by the emperor's chancellor, Nicholas Granvelle (1486–1550), who strongly supported the peace policy of Charles V. These conversations produced a common text much faster than the official talks, and Granvelle adjourned the Worms colloquy until the next meeting of the diet at Regensburg in April 1541. Despite objections from John Eck and Melanchthon, representing the Catholic and Lutheran sides, respectively, Granvelle declared that the basis of discussion at Regensburg would no longer be the Augsburg Confession but the document that had been forged in the private talks at Worms.

This so-called Regensburg Book* was a collection of twenty-three articles discussed by six theologians who were appointed by the emperor himself. They included Eck and Melanchthon, Bucer, and John Gropper* (1503–1559), a reform-minded Catholic theologian from Cologne whose ideas had influenced the book. Before talks started, twenty-one additions were made by the papal legate, Gasparo Contarini* (1483–1542), a prominent cardinal who had chaired a 1537 commission investigating abuses in the church.[15] Contarini also insisted on including transubstantiation in the article on the Eucharist because the church had decreed it in 1215. Lutherans objected to this addition and to other positions taken by the Catholics on the sacraments, clerical celibacy, the invocation of saints, and the authority of the church to interpret Scripture. The tenacious conflict over these issues overrode the agreement that was reached on the doctrine of justification. That agreement tried to meet the concerns of both sides by accepting two kinds of righteousness involved in justification: (1) the righteousness of Christ freely imputed to believers as the sole basis of forgiveness; and (2) the inherent righteousness of believers that produced good works worthy of reward. Neither Melanchthon nor Eck liked this statement, and responses from Luther and the Roman curia judged it to be misleading, but Contarini avidly defended it as "very catholic*."[16]

The Regensburg Colloquy of 1541 did not resolve the religious schism. Although thoroughly political, the colloquies did show that some opponents could acknowledge each other as Christians in a search for common ground. Besides that, little had been gained except, perhaps, the realization that an agreement on the concept of justification without agreement on its implications for practical issues like the sacraments, the saints, and church authority was fruitless. After twenty years, the principal antagonists in the drama of the German Reformation were little changed and still at a standoff.

4. Scandinavia and Other Lands

In the meantime, Lutheranism was expanding beyond Germany. To the north, the Reformation came to Scandinavia through itinerant German-speaking preachers who brought their message to German merchants in the coastal market towns. In connection with political upheaval the rulers of Scandinavia then installed the evangelical movement as the official form of Christianity. Subscription to the Augsburg Confession eventually made the churches Lutheran, but the process was gradual and varied from country to country. For example, Denmark received a Lutheran church order in 1537 but Sweden did not adopt its first Protestant ordinance until 1571.

Political movement toward the Reformation was precipitated by the bloodbath of Stockholm in November 1520. Trying to expand his power, King Christian II of Denmark (1481–1559) executed eighty members of the Swedish aristocracy in Stockholm. The bloodbath produced a rebellion led by Gustav Vasa* (1496–1560), whose family had been among the victims and who then ruled the newly independent country from 1523 until 1560. Although scarcely Lutheran, Gustav quickly made the church in Sweden subordinate to the crown.

The Lutheran Reformation in Sweden resulted primarily from the efforts of two Petri* brothers, Olaus* (1493–1552) and Laurentius* (1499–1573). Both brothers had been educated in Wittenberg under Luther and his colleagues. As a pastor in Stockholm during the 1520s, Olaus Petri translated the New Testament into Swedish, wrote a manual for evangelical clergy, and issued both a Swedish hymnbook (1530) and a Swedish mass (1531). Also in 1531 Laurentius Petri became the first evangelical archbishop of Uppsala. Because one of the bishops who consecrated him, Petrus Magni, had himself been consecrated with papal approval in 1524, the Lutheran Church of Sweden preserved continuity with the historical episcopate. Under the leadership of the Petri brothers, the evangelical movement gained strength, but not without setbacks. Before his death in 1560, King Gustav curbed their power by importing a German Lutheran professor, George Norman, to become superintendent of the church with jurisdiction over the clergy.

In 1571 Laurentius Petri finally achieved his goal of an evangelical ordinance for the church in Sweden, but it did not require subscription to any Lutheran confessions. In fact, the ordinance was compromised by a ceremonial liturgy called the Red Book (1576) published by King John III, who secretly converted to Roman Catholicism and allowed the Society of Jesus* to operate a theological college in Stockholm. Before he would declare his Roman allegiance publicly, however, John insisted that Pope Gregory XIII allow Swedish clergy to marry, Mass to be said in the vernacular, and both elements to be distributed at communion. The pope refused and tried to force his hand, but John then denied his conversion and expelled the Jesuits* from Sweden. When it looked as if Catholicism would have another chance after John's death, his brother Charles convoked a church assembly (Uppsala, 1593) that required future monarchs to subscribe to the Augsburg Confession.

Both Sweden and Wittenberg influenced the Reformation in Finland. It was ruled by Sweden and consisted of one diocese that was occupied from 1528 to 1550 by Bishop Martin Skytte, a Dominican monk and a humanist. Skytte was sympathetic to reform, but the young Finns whom Skytte sent to Wittenberg became the vanguard of the movement, especially after they returned to become teachers in the cathedral school at Turku. The star among them was Michael Agricola* (1510–1557), whose Finnish translation of the New Testament, published in 1548, made him the father of written Finnish. His *Biblical Prayer Book* (1544), a unique manual for clergy, and a Finnish order of the Mass (1540), based on Olaus Petri's Swedish order, were also essential resources for the Finnish Reformation. After Skytte's death, Agricola became bishop of Turku. His traditional piety and conservative liturgical stance left an enduring mark on Finnish Lutheranism.

In Denmark the Reformation proceeded quickly during the 1530s under King Christian III* (1503–1559). The most committed Lutheran of all the Scandinavian rulers, Christian declared that only evangelical Christianity would be allowed in Denmark and deposed all the Catholic bishops. John Bugenhagen was called from Wittenberg to preside over the Reformation. He crowned the king and queen and ordained the new Lutheran superintendents. Chief among them was Peter Palladius, who had studied for six years in Wittenberg and became not only a conscientious bishop but also a scholar of renown at the reopened University of Copenhagen. The new Latin church ordinance, approved by Luther and revised by Bugenhagen, was proclaimed by Christian III on the same day, September 2, 1537, that Bugenhagen ordained the superintendents. The ordinance, officially adopted in Danish in 1539, required adherence to the Augsburg Confession. Both Christian III, who corresponded regularly with the Wittenbergers, and his son, Frederik II, made sure that the church in Denmark remained steadfastly Lutheran.

Christian III also tried to introduce the Reformation into Norway and Iceland, which came under the sway of Denmark after 1536. In Norway the Danish church order was adopted in 1539 by diets in Oslo and Bergen, but the Reformation proceeded slowly because there were no religious texts in Norwegian and few evangelical preachers to reach people in the parishes. In Iceland official opposition to the Danish church ordinance was not broken until 1552, and Lutheranism became an effective force only during the last third of the century.

By contrast, the Reformation was firmly established in major Baltic cities by 1530. Evangelical preachers from Germany occupied pulpits in the towns of Reval (Talinn), Dorpat (Tartu), and Riga, which lie in modern Estonia and Latvia. Although opposed by Roman prelates, the Reformation was tolerated by the political authorities. After a period of radicalization in the mid-1520s, the evangelical movement was stabilized in Riga by John Briessmann* (1488–1549), who came from Prussia to serve as pastor of the cathedral from 1527 to 1531. The grand duchy of Lithuania, even before it was united with Poland in 1569, was a much larger and religiously diverse territory, with many Eastern Orthodox Christians. There the Reformation took hold slowly and a small Lutheran presence was firmly in place by midcentury. Lutherans were soon outnumbered by the Reformed (Calvinist) Church of Lithuania, which organized in 1557 and convened in Vilnius. It had established a foothold among the upper nobility and survived the Catholic Counter-Reformation* better than the Lutherans did. By the end of the sixteenth century, Lutheran churches in Estonia and Latvia were larger and sturdier than in Lithuania.

A pattern similar to that of Lithuania, but on a larger scale, marked the course of Lutheranism in Poland, Bohemia, and Hungary. During the early years of the sixteenth century, evangelical preaching was embraced mainly by German-speaking communities that later became the backbone of new Lutheran churches in all three countries. A prominent example was the Lutheran Church in Transylvania (Siebenbürgen), a part of southeastern Hungary settled heavily by Germans. By the 1550s the towns in this area had adopted a Lutheran church order and were choosing their own clerical superintendents to preside over the churches. Soon, however, Lutherans faced competition from Calvinism, which appealed to members of the non-German Hungarian and Polish gentry or to indigenous reform movements like the Unity of the Brethren* in Bohemia. Both Lutherans and Calvinists then had to withstand the efforts of the Counter-Reformation to reassert the primacy and influence of Rome in all three countries. Despite those efforts, the Lutheran Reformation retained a significant presence in eastern Europe.[17]

◆

Consolidating a Lutheran Confession

1. The German Settlement

Luther died in 1546 prior to a series of events that decided the outcome of the German Reformation. Charles V concluded that the religious division of the empire would not be solved by peaceful means at all and he prepared for war. In 1546 the time was right. A council of the church finally convened at Trent in 1545, ending the respite enjoyed by the Protestants. The Smalcald League had been weakened by the bigamy of Philip of Hesse. Already married since 1523, Philip was smitten by a young woman whom he also married in 1540. Since bigamy was a capital crime in the empire, Protestant politicians and theologians tried unsuccessfully to keep it a secret. Its disclosure neutralized Philip's leadership of the league and caused serious dissension in its ranks.

In late April of 1547, the army of Charles V defeated the Smalcald League at Mühlberg on the Elbe River southeast of Wittenberg. Both Elector John Frederick of Saxony and Philip of Hesse were taken prisoner, and Wittenberg itself capitulated on May 19, 1547. The city was not plundered, but witnesses reported that Charles V entered the Castle Church and stood on Luther's grave. John Frederick had to give up his electoral title, which was assumed by Duke Moritz* (1521–1553) of the other Saxony,[18] who had supported the emperor in exchange for this prize. The German Reformation appeared to be over and Lutheranism defeated.

Instead of pressing his advantage, however, Charles decided to impose a temporary religious solution at the next diet held in Augsburg from September 1, 1547, to June 30, 1548. This solution, called the Augsburg Interim*, was a Catholic document that threatened to revoke the changes introduced by the Reformation.[19] Its twenty-six articles reinstated the jurisdiction of Catholic bishops, seven sacraments, the medieval Mass, festivals like Corpus Christi and All Saints that Protestant areas had abolished, and traditional fasting regulations. The only changes conceded to Lutherans were the distribution of both elements at Communion and marriage of the clergy. Justification was defined in terms of a twofold righteousness similar to its treatment in the Regensburg Book. In southern Germany the interim was resisted by hundreds of evangelical pastors who either hid from Charles's troops or went into exile.

To the north, the new elector, Moritz of Saxony, was troubled by the agreement, and his advisors asked the Wittenberg theologians to work out a milder form of the interim.[20] Their revision allowed the reinstatement of some practices, called *adiaphora** (Greek for "indifferent things"), because they did not contradict Scripture or affect one's salvation. Such adiaphora included confirmation and ordination by bishops, extreme unction, the celebration of Mass "with the ringing of bells, with lights and vessels, with chants, vestments, and ceremonies," the celebration of Corpus Christi without processions, and fasting on Fridays and Saturdays. Rejected were prayer to the saints, private masses, and the canon of the Mass*. The document contained a lucid statement of justification by faith drafted first by Melanchthon as a critique of the Augsburg Interim. It affirmed that good works produced by faith could be called righteousness, but it denied that these works replaced or supplemented faith in Christ as the righteousness that saves. Although this milder document never became law in Saxony, Lutheran theologians who insisted on a complete rejection of the Augsburg Interim dubbed it derisively the "Leipzig Interim,"[21] and accused Melanchthon of betraying Luther.

As it turned out, the interims had little to do with the political outcome of the Reformation. Other northern princes persuaded Elector Moritz to join them in a new campaign against the emperor. They struck an alliance with King Henry II of France and succeeded in pushing Charles out of Germany and forcing him to negotiate with the Lutherans. In the Treaty of Passau (1552), Charles agreed to lift the Augsburg Interim in most of south Germany. The next Diet of Augsburg in 1555 legally guaranteed the coexistence of two Christian confessions in the empire: Catholics and the adherents of the Augsburg Confession. Besides Lutherans, therefore, all other Protestants were excluded. The right of determining the religion of their subjects was granted to secular rulers. Catholic bishops who governed territory were allowed to become Lutheran at the cost of forfeiting their land. Although intended to be provisional, the Peace of Augsburg settled the Reformation in Germany politically and legally. After thirty-four years of trying to uphold the religious unity of the empire, Charles V felt the compromise was a failure. He abdicated his rule and retired to a monastery in Spain, where he lived out the last three years of his life.

2. The Quest for Lutheran Identity

For Lutheranism the Peace of Augsburg* was a political victory, but it was not yet a theological settlement. Theologians who resolutely opposed the interims unleashed a savage attack on Melanchthon and his colleagues in Wittenberg. Their chief spokesman was Matthias Flacius Illyricus* (1520–1575), originally from Croatia, who arrived in Wittenberg in 1541 and became professor of Hebrew just before Luther died. Flacius then left Wittenberg for Magdeburg, where he joined forces with Luther's old colleague Nicholas von Amsdorf* (1483–1565) in fighting the interims. They formed the nucleus of a Gnesio-Lutheran* (from a Greek word for "true" or "genuine") party, which delivered more than ninety polemical pamphlets from the "chancery of God" (as they called Magdeburg) against the so-called Adiaphorists in Wittenberg. For the Gnesio-Lutherans, no ceremonies were harmless adiaphora if they were presented to the people as necessary parts of worship and piety. Flacius feared that ceremonies allowed by the Leipzig Interim would be celebrated in their most Catholic sense and that evangelical laity would lose the freedom of the gospel. For Melanchthon, however, it was better to allow such ceremonies to be practiced than for the laity to be deprived forcibly of their evangelical pastors. He protested that he had successfully resisted the canon of the Mass and never allowed any alteration of doctrine.

After 1552 the controversy over adiaphora became irrelevant, but it had already damaged the pursuit of Lutheran identity. The authority of Melanchthon and the Wittenberg faculty was diminished and they were nicknamed Philippists* (after Philip Melanchthon) by their detractors. During the 1550s, the Gnesio-Lutherans expanded their campaign for genuine Lutheranism by accusing Philippist theologians of betraying Luther's theology of good works and of the human will. These accusations, which reignited old reservations about Melanchthon's theology, turned into bitter controversies that were later resolved in the Formula of Concord (1577; see pp. 44–47). Nevertheless, the University of Wittenberg blossomed during the last decade of Melanchthon's life. In 1560 student enrollment surpassed that of the years preceding Luther's death. After returning from examinations of candidates in Leipzig that spring, Melanchthon died in Wittenberg on April 19, 1560, and was buried in the Castle Church not far from Luther. Before he died, Melanchthon had made parallel lists of reasons why it would be better to remain alive or to die. One reason he gave for preferring death was that it would finally release him from the madness (*rabies*) of the theologians.

Indeed, the pursuit of Lutheran identity provoked other controversies. One of these involved Andrew Osiander* (1496–1552), the long-time leader of the Reformation in Nuremberg. In reaction to the interim, he moved to Königsberg (in East Prussia) and published a unique view of justification, which he attributed to the indwelling of the divine nature of Christ. This view met with nearly unanimous rejection by other Lutheran theologians and by the Formula of Concord (article 3). Another controversy involved the theology of John Agricola* (1492–1566). One of Luther's earliest students, Agricola had clashed with Melanchthon in 1527 over the place of the law in the Christian life. When the conflict resumed in the late 1530s, Luther labeled Agricola antinomian* and he was banished from Wittenberg. Agricola's argument that the law neither brought Christians to repentance nor taught them how to do good works was revived in the 1550s. It was again rejected as antinomian by Philippists and some Gnesio-Lutherans.

The quest for Lutheran identity also involved conflict over the Augsburg Confession. Melanchthon's revision of the confession for the 1540 Colloquy at Worms (called the Altered Augsburg Confession* or the *Variata**) was a thorn in the Lutheran side. During a meeting of Catholics and Lutherans at Weimar in 1557, the Gnesio-Lutherans insisted that any theological positions that deviated from the original (unaltered) Augsburg Confession of 1530 had to be condemned. When Melanchthon and his supporters refused to give in to this demand, the Catholic side professed confusion over which Lutherans were the true adherents of the confession.

The issue came up again at a meeting of evangelical princes at Naumburg in 1561.[22] Elector Frederick III of the Palatinate, a territory along the Rhine that had been Lutheran, wanted the princes to approve the *Variata* (1540) as a legitimate interpretation of the unaltered version (1530). This effort was part of his strategy to have John Calvin's* theology officially accepted in Germany so it could be taught in the Palatinate. Calvin, reformer of Geneva and chief theologian of Reformed Protestantism, had indeed subscribed to the Augsburg Confession as part of the Strasbourg delegation to the religious colloquies in 1540 and 1541.[23] Elector Frederick III now thought that article 10 of the *Variata* was close to Calvin's view of the presence of Christ in the Lord's Supper. Therefore, if the *Variata* could be accepted as a legitimate version of the Augsburg Confession, then the teaching of Calvin's theology in the Palatinate would also be legal in Germany. Although this strategy failed at Naumburg in 1561, Elector Frederick went ahead with his plans anyway. The Palatinate became Calvinist and adopted the first German Calvinist confession: the Heidelberg Catechism* of 1563.

The conflict at Naumburg intensified the suspicions of the Gnesio-Lutheran party that theologians in electoral Saxony (the Philippists) held a Calvinist view of the presence of Christ in the Lord's Supper. These suspicions first arose in the early 1550s when Calvin appealed to Melanchthon and the Wittenbergers for support against the attacks of Joachim Westphal* (1510–1574), a Lutheran pastor in Hamburg. Although Melanchthon and the Wittenbergers remained silent, their adherence to the *Variata*, rejected by the Gnesio-Lutherans, increased those suspicions, and soon they were accused of being Crypto-Calvinists*. The exasperation caused by this conflict and by the conversion of the Palatinate to Calvinism finally prompted two Lutheran princes to seek an end to the controversies over Lutheran identity.

3. The Road to Concord

The two princes were Duke Christoph of Württemberg in southwestern Germany (Swabia) and Duke Julius of Braunschweig-Wolfenbüttel in the north. Duke Christoph had been pursuing reconciliation in the south since the 1550s with the help of his chief theologian, Jacob Andreae* (1528–1590). In 1568 he agreed to help his cousin, Duke Julius, who was just introducing the Reformation into his territory with the help of theologians Martin Chemnitz* (1522–1586) from the city of Braunschweig and Nicholas Selnecker* (1530–1592) from electoral Saxony. Christoph sent Andreae north to join the team assembled by Julius, but their first efforts on behalf of concord failed. Then, in 1573, Andreae wrote *Six Sermons on the Divisions among Theologians of the Augsburg Confession*.[24] The preface described his purpose as "restoring through God's grace wherever possible Christian unity among the theologians of the Augsburg Confession without any compromise of divine truth."[25] That unity seemed to be near as the *Sermons* received a favorable response from north German theologians, especially David Chytraeus* (1531–1600) of Rostock, who suggested the sermons be reformulated as theses and antitheses. Andreae's revision was then reworked by Chemnitz and Chytraeus into the Swabian-Saxon Concord (1575), a document that reflected the agreement of theologians in both north and south Germany. In order to succeed, however, the drive for concord needed the backing of princes as well as of theologians. A crucial factor was the support of Elector August of Saxony* (1526–1586), in whose land the Philippists were dominant. Although Andreae had not exclusively taken the side of the Gnesio-Lutherans, he and the Philippists had become alienated in 1570 over the issue of the ubiquity* of Christ's body. According to this doctrine, the human nature of Christ was present everywhere (*ubique*) that the divine nature was present owing to the union of natures in the person of Christ. On this basis, Luther had argued, the human nature of Christ (i.e., the body and blood) could be present in the Lord's Supper. The leading reformer of Swabia in the generation before Andreae, John Brenz* (1499–1570), had argued for ubiquity as a doctrine that distinguished the Lutheran theology of a real bodily presence* from the Calvinist teaching of a spiritual presence of Christ in the Lord's Supper. In electoral Saxony the Philippists had consistently refused to accept ubiquity because it had not been part of Melanchthon's theology. In the early 1570s, however, a group of radical Philippists took over in Wittenberg and moved beyond Melanchthon's theology toward a view that seemed to deny any real presence whatsoever. After they were discovered to be in correspondence with Calvinist theologians, Elector August arrested them as Crypto-Calvinists and threw his support behind the campaign of Andreae.[26]

Elector August now became the driving force behind Lutheran unity. He called in Nicholas Selnecker, an advisor he still trusted, and they invited Andreae to come north again. At a conference in 1576 arranged by August at Torgau, Selnecker and Andreae met with Chemnitz, Chytraeus, and two theologians from Brandenburg: Andreas Musculus* (1514–1581) and Christoph Körner* (1518–1594). Within ten days (May 28–June 7) they had agreed on a new text in twelve articles that appeared to resolve the controversial issues. They held a service of thanksgiving at which Selnecker preached, and then this Torgau text was sent to other theologians and officials throughout Germany for their criticism. On the basis of their responses, the Torgau Book was revised at two meetings held at Bergen Abbey near

Magdeburg in March and May of 1577. This Bergen Book became the Solid Declaration of the Formula of Concord, while a summary of the Torgau Book, already prepared by Andreae, became the Epitome. On May 28, 1577, the Formula of Concord was presented to Elector August.

From 1577 to 1580, Andreae campaigned in Germany on behalf of its acceptance. Instead of making further revisions or holding a synod to approve it, he recommended that the Formula be published as part of a broader collection of doctrinal standards that would replace the collection of each territory known as its *corpus doctrinae** (body of teaching). The primary document in this collection would be the Augsburg Confession, since it was the legal criterion of Lutheranism in Germany and had been the object of so much controversy. In the preface Andreae let it be known that the signers of the Formula were committing themselves exclusively to the original version of the confession from 1530 and that only this version was being included in the *Book of Concord* (*BC* 8–9). Andreae also defended the Formula against some of the objections that had been submitted. He emphasized that the agreements reached in the Formula were based on Scripture and comprehended in the creeds, the Augsburg Confession of 1530, its Apology, and in the Smalcald Articles and catechisms of Luther (*BC* 13–14). On June 25, 1580, fifty years to the day after the presentation of the Augsburg Confession to Emperor Charles V, the *Book of Concord* was published in Dresden. Andreae's preface was signed by three electors, over fifty additional rulers from the nobility, thirty-five city councils, and over eight thousand pastors.

Those signatures primarily indicated agreement with the Formula of Concord as the true interpretation of the Augsburg Confession. Not all Lutherans were convinced. King Frederick II of Denmark had already opposed the Torgau Book and, after he received an ornate copy of the *Book of Concord* from his sister Anna, the wife of Elector August of Saxony, he threw it into the fire. In 1672 Denmark accepted the Formula. The dukes of Pomerania refused to sign because they felt it did not do justice to Melanchthon's theology. The biggest surprise came in Wolfenbüttel. Although Duke Julius gave his signature in 1580, a quarrel between him and Martin Chemnitz eventually prevented the Formula from becoming an official standard of doctrine in his territory. Nevertheless, the reception* of the *Book of Concord* was widespread enough to mark those churches that adhered to the Augsburg Confession as one of four distinct Christian traditions arising from the European Reformation. The other confessions, as these traditions were called (see pp. 33–35), were Roman Catholicism, Calvinism, and Anglicanism. Lutheranism took its place alongside them in the new confessional landscape that left its imprint on Christianity in the modern world.

Questions for Discussion and Further Study

1. What were the deeper theological issues underlying the indulgence controversy?
2. Give a short account of the Diet of Augsburg (1530) and of the writing and the aim of the Augsburg Confession.
3. In what sense can one characterize Luther's catechisms as theology for the people?
4. Select and describe two or three of the inner-Lutheran controversies to which the Formula of Concord responded.
5. "Defining a Lutheran Movement" — how does one do this today in terms of both continuity and change?

S. H.

CHAPTER THREE

The Lutheran Confessions

The Texts

◆

Confessing and Confession as Fundamental to the Church

Confessing one's faith is a constitutive part of the identity and life of those who follow Christ. People cannot remain silent once they have received God's free grace for Jesus Christ's sake and have been enabled by the Holy Spirit to believe in this life-changing gift. This gift elicits their response in words and in life, a response that also includes their confession of faith. To confess what one believes is necessary in moments of decision or crisis. Confession is required if believers are to manifest their communion as members of the body of Christ, if they are to respond in worship to God's grace and love, if they are to resist forces that threaten or deny life, if they are to express together their joy and thanksgiving, and if they are to witness to their faith and invite others to join them.

The personal and corporate confession of faith was, according to the biblical witness, already an essential element in the life and worship of the people of Israel and of the first followers of Christ and their communities. In the Old Testament the saving act of God in the exodus formed the basis of Israel's identity and was summarized in creedal form in Deut 6:4-5 and Exod 15:1-18. In the New Testament the significance of God's new saving action in Jesus Christ is expressed in confessing statements (like Matt 16:16-17; John 20:28; Acts 4:8-12; Rom 1:3-4; Eph 1:3-14; Phil 2:5-11). In them belief in Christ's resurrection becomes the heart of faith (Rom 10:9; 1 Cor 15:15). Some christological statements are expanded to include reference to faith in God (1 Cor 8:6) and by becoming trinitarian in form (2 Cor 13:13).

The formulation of confessional statements multiplied in the early church. Such confessions were used in worship, proclamation, and teaching, especially in the instruction of candidates for baptism (e.g., the predecessors of the Apostles' Creed). They also served as a means to defend the faith against heresies (e.g., the creed of the Council of Nicea* in 325). The impulse to develop statements and confessions of faith continued throughout church history and reached its climax at the time of the Reformation, when a large number of such confessions were produced by different Reformation churches and groups. Within present-day Christianity creeds and confessions are an essential element in most churches. The role and authority of such texts is, however, defined differently.

The term and the concept of confession can mean different things. It can refer to:

1. spontaneous or formalized acts of confessing in which individuals or communities confess their sin or their faith and hope;

2. a short formalized text, usually a creed or confession of faith, that has been received through the tradition of the church or has been formulated in the present;

3. a confessional text or document, most commonly known as the confessional writings or confessions of Reformation churches, like the Anglican Thirty-nine Articles of Faith, the Lutheran Augsburg Confession, or the Reformed Westminster Confession. These documents define and express the self-understanding of a church in terms of its fundamental convictions of faith.

What are the significance and function of these creeds and confessions? They have:

1. a self-defining or self-identifying function for a Christian community by stating its binding doctrine, that is, the fundamentals of Christian faith and life to which a community subscribes and by which it is constantly reminded of its foundations and central calling;

2. a normative function by giving direction and orientation, under the supreme authority of Holy Scripture, for the faith, life, worship, and mission of the church;

3. a critical function by helping to distinguish between true and false teaching;

4. a community-building function by gathering believers around shared convictions, providing them with a common basis and orientation, and serving them in times of difficulty or persecution as signs and means of solidarity;

5. a kerygmatic function by announcing the Christian faith in and to the world;

6. a doxological function by providing a liturgical response that acknowledges and praises the one God who is the fountain of all confession;

7. a hermeneutical function by pointing to the center of Scripture, the gospel, and by helping to distinguish fundamental doctrines from theological interpretations;

8. a catechetical function by being instruments and guidelines for Christian education;

9. an ecumenical function by serving as a common bond for worldwide Christian communions of churches of the same confessional tradition and as an essential expression of Christian unity between churches of different traditions.

The Lutheran confessions are a particular expression of this wider reality of Christian confession that is fundamental for being a Christian and a Christian church.

◆

The *Book of Concord:*
The Corpus of Lutheran Confessions

1. The *Book of Concord*

The *Book of Concord* (BC) of 1580 is the authoritative collection of confessional texts that received official recognition in churches of the Lutheran Reformation. Its shape has its roots in the idea of a collection of authoritative documents, a body of doctrine (*corpus doctrinae**), that goes back to the 1530s. At that time so-called church orders were introduced by evangelical territories and cities to provide coherence and stability for their churches. It was soon recognized that such church orders* had to include doctrinal norms as a binding orientation for the faith, proclamation, and teaching of a particular church. The first church order to contain such doctrinal provisions was that of Pomerania in 1535, which was finalized and published by John Bugenhagen*. It prescribed that evangelical* preachers should teach and preach according to the Augsburg Confession (CA), together with its Apology (Ap.), and that they should use Luther's Catechism. From then on the Augsburg Confession received a central place in many church orders that were introduced during the following decades and that included a great variety of confessional documents along with writings of individual theologians.

After the middle of the sixteenth century, controversies with Roman Catholicism became more intense and theological differences among the churches of the Augsburg Confession weakened their coherence and the political position of their territories. It was thus in the interest of princes, city councils, and their leading pastors and theologians that greater unity be established among the churches. They wanted, and this was an urgent matter, to safeguard the confessional settlement of the Peace of Augsburg* (1555) and to preserve the pure teaching of the gospel in Lutheran lands. After plans for a broader Protestant* alliance had failed, several Lutheran territorial churches began to establish common bodies of doctrine. The collection agreed on by six north German cities at Lüneburg in 1551 listed the Augsburg Confession and, as its authentic interpretation, the Apology, the Smalcald Articles (SA), the Small Catechism (SC), and other writings of Luther. In 1570 Saxony also included Luther's Large Catechism (LC), and another body of doctrine agreed on at Lüneburg in 1576 enumerated for the first time, with the exception of the Formula of Concord (FC), which was still to come, all the texts of the future *Book of Concord*: Three Creeds, Augsburg Confession, Apology, Smalcald Articles with the Treatise (Tr.), Small Catechism, and Large Catechism.

From 1573 onward the ecclesiastical, theological, and political efforts at inner-Lutheran unity and consolidation pursued two aims in one interrelated process: (1) to establish a common and binding body of doctrine in the form of a collection of confessional documents; and (2) to work out a concord that would settle inner-Lutheran theological controversies (see pp. 44–47). Accordingly, the series of texts aiming at theological concord included proposals for a body of doctrine that in some form (the 1575 proposal suggests one book) should consist of: the Bible (the 1575 proposal makes it the primary, decisive norm), Creeds, Augsburg Confession, Apology, Smalcald Articles, Treatise, Small Catechism, and Large Catechism. Proposals for such a body of doctrine were made in the 1574 Swabian Concord, the 1575 Swabian-Saxon Concord, the 1576 Torgau Book, and the 1577 Bergen Book, which, in fact, became the Formula of Concord. The Bergen Book no longer used the term "body of doctrine" (*corpus doctrinae*). It was replaced in the Formula of Concord by "The Summary Formulation, Basis, Rule, and Norm" and in the title of the *Book of Concord* simply by "Concord." A detailed preface for the Formula of Concord, which had been prepared between 1578 and 1580, became also the preface for the *Book of Concord,* of which 6,000 copies were printed by January 1580. The official publication of the *Book of Concord*, with the original signatures of electors, princes, and estates and more than 8,000 signatures (both to the *Book of Concord* and the Formula of Concord) of pastors, theologians, and teachers, took place on June 25, 1580, the fiftieth anniversary of the Augsburg Confession. This date was chosen to underline the explicit purpose of the *Book of Concord* and also of the Formula: to serve as an authentic interpretation of the Augsburg Confession and to be thus a summary of evangelical teaching that is a true explication of Holy Scripture and that is in continuity with the faith of the church through the ages.

The *Book of Concord* of 1580 with its ten texts—Three Creeds, Augsburg Confession, Apology, Smalcald Articles, Treatise on the Power and Primacy of the Pope, Small Catechism, Large Catechism, and Formula of Concord—has not been accepted in its totality by all Lutheran churches in the world, but all have accepted the Augsburg Confession and the Small Catechism as the primary confessions of Lutheranism.

2. The Three Ecumenical Creeds

The Lutheran reformers held in highest esteem "the three catholic or ecumenical symbols" (Latin heading in the *Book of Concord*) and included them in the *Book of Concord* in order to show that the emerging Lutheran churches were in continuity with the ancient church and its faith and were not inaugurating a new faith or a new church.

The Apostles' Creed has its roots in the many short trinitarian baptismal confessions that were formulated during the first centuries. It goes back specifically to the ancient Roman baptismal creed already used in the second half of the second century. The present form of the creed seems to have emerged in the fifth century. Between the seventh and ninth centuries it was received into the liturgy of the Western church, where it still occupies a central place.

The Nicene Creed originated in the context of the struggle against heresies and for preserving the unity of the church. The Council of Nicea in 325 adopted a creed in which the divine origin and nature of Jesus Christ were confessed against the teaching of Arius* that the Son was inferior to the Father. The creed was expanded by the Council of Constantinople* in 381 to refer also to the personal and divine nature of the Holy Spirit. The Niceno-Constantinopolitan Creed, which is its proper name, was received by the Council of Chalcedon in 451 and then by both the Eastern and Western churches. It is, on the one side, an important bond of unity between the Eastern Orthodox and the other Christian traditions, while, on the other side, the Western insertion (widely in the ninth century) of the phrase that the Holy Spirit proceeds from the Father "and the Son" (*filioque*) has contributed to the division between East and West.

The Athanasian Creed was not formulated by the great theologian Athanasius* (c.296–373) but emerged most probably during the fifth or sixth century. It presupposes and confesses the development of dogma in the fourth century about the Trinity and in the fifth century about the two natures of Christ. It gained an important place in the medieval church in the West and was thus also received by the reformers. It is not much in use today.

3. The Augsburg Confession (CA, 1530)

In January 1530, Emperor Charles V summoned an imperial diet to take place that same year in Augsburg, Germany. He asked the princes and the representatives of free cities in the empire to establish a united front against the Turks by overcoming the religious division of the empire. The emperor promised to listen to both sides and to seek a settlement of the conflict. In order to prepare for the diet Elector John of Saxony asked his Wittenberg theologians to explain and justify the changes that had been introduced in the church of his territory. These

Torgau Articles of 1530 were taken by the evangelical party to Augsburg. Luther was banned from coming to Augsburg, and the other leading evangelical theologian, Melanchthon*, was asked in May 1530 to prepare an "apology" (a defense) with the help of the Torgau Articles. In the face of Roman accusations the evangelical party soon realized that a defense of changes and reforms was not enough but that a basic doctrinal statement was also necessary in order to repudiate the accusation of heresy. For such a statement Melanchthon was able to use the Schwabach Articles of 1529, which had been written with strong input by Luther and drew heavily on his so-called confession of 1528, an appendix (LW 37:360–72) to his *Confession Concerning Christ's Supper* against Zwingli.

Combining these two aims, Melanchthon worked on a comprehensive text that was no longer a simple defense but became a true confession. The Schwabach Articles formed the background of the first part of what was to become the Augsburg Confession with its "Articles of Faith and Doctrine" (1–21), while the Torgau Articles formed the background of the second part of the Augsburg Confession about "abuses which have been corrected" (22–28). On June 25, 1530, the German text of the Augsburg Confession was read in front of the emperor, the princes, and the representatives of free cities. Copies of the German and Latin versions were submitted. The present text of the Augsburg Confession has been carefully reconstructed from several copies of the year 1530 because the originals had been lost. The Augsburg Confession was gradually accepted by the Lutheran estates and, finally, at the 1537 convention of the Smalcald League*. From the beginning it was considered to be the central statement within the collection of Lutheran confessions. In 1555, in the Peace of Augsburg, the Augsburg Confession received imperial legal status as the basic document of one of the two Christian religions legally recognized in the empire: the Churches of the Augsburg Confession and the Roman Catholic Church. Together with Luther's Small Catechism, the Augsburg Confession is today the most widely accepted Lutheran confession.

The Augsburg Confession of 1530 consists of two parts with altogether 28 articles. Both its German and Latin versions, which are not identical, are regarded as authoritative, though the German text has priority. The Augsburg Confession, true to its historical purpose, is an irenic, ecumenical confession aimed at preserving the unity of the church. In this spirit it emphasizes the agreement of the evangelical teaching with the biblical witness and the tradition of the church throughout the centuries. It reconfirms the condemnations of old heresies, repudiates the new errors of radical movements, and in some cases takes issue with the emerging Reformed movement. It avoids some highly controversial topics like the papacy, which was then taken up in the Treatise of 1537 (see p. 42), and it pleads for liberty in non-fundamental issues. Though it bears the marks of its origin, it is a Christian confession and not simply a Lutheran one.

4. The Apology of the Augsburg Confession (Ap., 1530/31)

On August 3, 1530, the response of the Roman party at the Diet of Augsburg was read in the same hall where the Augsburg Confession had been read. The emperor had rejected the first draft of this confutation because of its excessively polemical character, but he considered the revised version to be a convincing rebuttal of the Augsburg Confession and demanded its acceptance by the evangelical side. The evangelicals refused and promised an answer to the Roman Confutation* even though the other side had refused to provide a copy of the text. Melanchthon was asked to get to work again and to prepare, with the help of notes taken during the public reading of the confutation, the Apology of the Augsburg Confession, the defense of the Augsburg Confession. On September 22, 1530, the Apology was submitted to the diet in the name of the evangelical estates. The emperor refused to accept it. After Melanchthon had finally received a copy of the confutation, he wrote a revised and expanded version of the Apology that was published in April/May 1531. Together with the Augsburg Confession it was received* (i.e., accepted and affirmed) as an official confession in several church orders and at the meeting of the Smalcald League in 1537.

The Apology follows the structure of the twenty-eight articles of the Augsburg Confession and is an important commentary on it. It is much longer than the Augsburg Confession. In some of its articles the Roman Confutation is extensively refuted, while other articles remain short (or are even left out) where a consensus exists. The center of the Apology is the long (the longest text in the *Book of Concord*!) article 4 on justification as a witness to the basis and source of the Christian faith. Compared with the short formulations in other confessional texts, the Apology follows the style of a theological treatise and is therefore a different type of confession. Its Latin text is the original and the German version by Justus Jonas* (1493–1555) is a rather free rendering of the original.

5. The Smalcald Articles (SA, 1537)

In 1536 Pope Paul III called a general council to meet in 1537 at Mantua to deal with the religious divisions (the council actually opened in 1545 at Trent). The Lutheran side had often requested the calling of a free general council, and thus theologians welcomed its announcement. In preparation Elector John Frederick of Saxony* instructed Luther in December 1536 to write a theological position paper that could be submitted to the council. It should consist of (1) articles of faith in which agreement existed, (2) articles in which the Lutheran position had to be upheld, and (3) articles in which concessions might be made. Within a few days Luther's Smalcald Articles, as they were later (since 1553) called, were ready. A group of theologians in Wittenberg discussed the articles, proposed some changes, and then signed the text.

When the Smalcald League met in February 1537 at Smalcald, Luther's articles were proposed for acceptance. Luther was seriously ill and could not participate and present his articles in person. Because of his absence and of Melanchthon's fear that some of Luther's formulations might create doctrinal controversies among evangelical theologians, the convention did not accept Luther's articles. This decision was also influenced by the apparent unwillingness of the evangelical estates to participate in a future council. Many of the clergy present at Smalcald signed the future Smalcald Articles in their personal capacity, however, and Melanchthon added to his signature a note that is interesting because it allows for a superiority of the pope over the bishops according to human right. The Smalcald Articles were printed in 1538, and from the 1550s onward they were received into territorial church orders and, finally, into the Book of Concord.

The Smalcald Articles, whose German text is the original one, consist of three parts that, to a certain degree, correspond to the threefold mandate given to Luther even though the third part is not very conciliatory. The Smalcald Articles were written by Luther as his final theological witness and testament: "These are the articles on which I must stand and on which I will stand, God willing, until my death" (SA 3, 15.3; see also his preface). The basic criterion for his text is the "first and chief article" on justification for Christ's sake (2, 1).

6. Treatise on the Power and Primacy of the Pope (Tr., 1537)

In 1537 the Smalcald League decided that a confessional statement on the power and primacy of the pope and on the jurisdiction of bishops in matters of faith should be formulated as a supplement to the Augsburg Confession, not to the Smalcald Articles as some assume. Such a statement had been omitted from the Augsburg Confession in order not to endanger the negotiations at Augsburg in 1530. The theologians present at Smalcald were entrusted with preparing such a text and they asked their genial drafter, Melanchthon, to do the job again. His Treatise on the Power and Primacy of the Pope was immediately accepted in Smalcald as a confession of faith and signed by all the clergy present.

With the help of many biblical and historical references and in a highly critical manner, the Treatise presents the evangelical teaching on the power and primacy of the pope and on the power and jurisdiction of bishops. It can be divided into these two parts. Its original text is the Latin one, but a German translation was already made at Smalcald.

7. The Small and Large Catechisms (SC and LC, 1529)

The impulse to write his catechisms came from Luther's lively concern for the religious instruction of the laity and clergy within a church in the process of reform and in need of internal consolidation. During visits to congregations in 1528 and 1529, Luther was shocked by the deplorable ignorance of church members and by the inability of pastors to lead their congregations by preaching the gospel and renewing the church. Because of these depressing experiences he supported Melanchthon in writing the *Instruction for the Visitors of Parish Pastors in Electoral Saxony* (1528). In 1528, in order to instruct the people in the faith and liberate them from their ignorance, Luther himself preached three series of sermons on the Ten Commandments, the Apostles' Creed, the Lord's Prayer, Baptism, and the Lord's Supper. These sermons formed the basis of his catechisms. In December 1528 Luther began to write the Small Catechism while at the same time working on the third part of the Large Catechism.

His catechisms stand in the tradition of medieval four-part summaries (Commandments, Apostles' Creed, Lord's Prayer, and Ave Maria) of the Christian faith that were written for laypeople. Luther regarded the first three parts as sufficient for ordinary people and, accordingly, left out the Ave Maria. Nevertheless, in his catechisms he introduced five main parts—in line with his sermons of 1528 and 1529—by adding the two sacraments. More parts were added later.

The Enchiridion (handbook)—The Small Catechism of Dr. Martin Luther for Ordinary Pastors and Preachers—was first published in 1529 in the form of large posters or charts to be used in churches and schools. In May 1529 it was published in the form of an illustrated booklet in which the preface and Table of Duties were added to the existing parts: Commandments, Apostles' Creed, Lord's Prayer, Baptism, Confession and Absolution, Lord's Supper, Morning and Evening Prayers, and Grace at Table. Later additions were a Short Form of Marriage, a Short Form of Baptism, and the Litany. The Small Catechism was intended for ordinary people in their households but also for pastors. It soon garnered high esteem and became the most widely distributed text during the Reformation. It was included in several church orders and collections of confessional documents and became, finally, part of the *Book of Concord*. As a catechetical and pastoral text it represents a special type of confession. The German text is its original version.

The Large Catechism originally had the title "German Catechism"; "Large Catechism" first appeared as the title in 1541. A first edition was printed in 1529, and a revised edition with the additional Exhortation to Confession came out in the same year. A third edition with a second and longer preface was published in 1530. The Large Catechism is not an expanded version of the Small Catechism. They are different in style and orientation. The Large Catechism is addressed mainly to pastors to help them with the instruction of children and adults, and generally in their proclamation. It has preserved the structure of five main parts. The Large Catechism was included after 1570 in church orders and collections of confessions, and it was received into the *Book of Concord* in 1580. German is the official version.

8. The Formula of Concord (FC, 1577)

The middle of the sixteenth century marks a turning point in the history of the Reformation. Several events led to a crisis within the churches of the Augsburg Confession: Luther's death on February 18, 1546; the military defeat of the Smalcald League in 1547; the Augsburg Interim of 1548; and the Leipzig Interim (1548–1549), in which Melanchthon and some of his Wittenberg colleagues made concessions regarding the imposition of some formerly abolished rituals and practices that they called "adiaphora*" because they did not contradict Holy Scripture. As a result, Melanchthon was heavily criticized by Lutheran theologians who insisted on a rejection of the interim, and his role as a successor to Luther's leadership was seriously weakened. In addition, Protestant–Roman Catholic religious conversations came to an end with the interims and, finally, with the Colloquy of Worms in 1557, which revealed the internal discord among Lutheran theologians. This period saw also the end of attempts to preserve or to reestablish the unity of the entire Reformation movement.

Initiated and reinforced by these changes, an era of intra-Lutheran controversies lasted until the Formula of Concord in 1577. Differences among Lutheran theologians over the central issues of Reformation theology led to open and sometimes bitter theological battles. There were, on the one side, the strict (and occasionally overzealous) followers of Luther, the so-called Gnesio-Lutherans*, with Matthias Flacius* as their most important figure; and, on the other side, the followers of Melanchthon, the so-called Philippists*, who took a more moderate stance toward traditional Catholic* as well as certain Reformed or Calvinist teachings and among whom George Major* (1502–1574) played a leading role. These controversies are traditionally identified as the following:

Antinomian Controversy.* This controversy was concerned about the right relationship between law and gospel. It began in the 1520s and continued until after Luther's death (1546). Because of their strong emphasis on the gospel, some theologians denied that the law had any continuing authority for believers, even in the form of biblical admonitions (third use of the law). The opposite side emphasized the connection between law and gospel and a third use of the law. Melanchthon himself was against an antinomian position. See FC 5 and 6.

Adiaphoristic Controversy. This debate between 1548 and 1552 dealt with the role of adiaphora, that is, things that make no difference and are not essential. During the negotiations for the Leipzig Interim of 1548, when the new elector, Moritz of Saxony*, aimed at a milder form of the interim by the reinstatement of some rites and practices that had been abolished, Melanchthon and the Philippists declared such rites (liturgical ceremonies and ecclesiastical structures) to be adiaphora. Against this attitude Matthias Flacius insisted on making no concessions in times of persecution and coercion since adiaphora take on more importance when they are imposed as necessary parts of worship and piety. See FC 10.

Majoristic Controversy. This debate between 1551 and 1558 was about the significance of good works. According to Melanchthon's pupil George Major, good works were necessary for salvation by complementing faith. In the heat of discussion his opponents like Matthias Flacius and Nicholas von Amsdorf* went so far as to say that good works were detrimental to salvation. See FC 4.

Osiandrian Controversy. This debate between 1550 and 1566 centered on one aspect of the doctrine of justification. Andrew Osiander* taught that a real, transforming, inner justification is effected by the indwelling of the divine nature of Christ in the believer. Against this position both Gnesio-Lutherans and Philippists emphasized as the main elements of salvation the saving obedience of the *whole* person of Christ and the forensic application of Christ's righteousness grasped by faith. See FC 3.

Crypto-Calvinistic Controversy. In this debate, which lasted from 1558 to 1573, the Philippists were accused of moving toward a Calvinist interpretation of Christ's personal presence in the Lord's Supper together with its christological presuppositions (i.e., denying that the human nature of Christ participates in the omnipresence of his divine nature). Against this tendency the strict Lutheran side insisted on the words of institution and the sacramental union as confirming the real and substantial presence of the body and blood of Christ in the bread and wine. See FC 7 and 8.

Synergistic Controversy. Some interpreters of Melanchthon understood him to teach that the human will cooperated with grace in conversion and salvation. On the contrary, Flacius argued that through the fall original sin had become the substance of human nature and that therefore human beings could at the most only resist divine providence. This view was rejected as being too extreme, however, and FC 1 and 2 undertook to clarify the effects of the fall on the human will and its role in conversion and salvation.

After 1555 many efforts were undertaken to confront the crisis in Lutheranism. Their aim was to settle these controversies by an authentic and binding exposition of the unaltered Augsburg Confession of 1530 in order to preserve pure teaching, to overcome the disunity in the Lutheran territories, and to safeguard the confessional settlement of the Peace of Augsburg in 1555. For political reasons the evangelical princes and cities actively supported these efforts to reach an inner-Lutheran consensus. Three theologians played a leading role in this historical task: the Braunschweig superintendent Martin Chemnitz*, the Leipzig professor of theology Nicholas Selnecker*, and especially the Swabian theologian Jacob Andreae*. After a number of attempts at Lutheran theological and ecclesiastical unity were not successful, Andreae finally set in motion a process that led both to the Formula of Concord and to the *Book of Concord* (see pp. 29–32).

In 1573 Andreae preached *Six Sermons* on a true Lutheran understanding of (1) justification, (2) good works, (3) original sin and synergism*, (4) adiaphora, (5) law and gospel, and (6) the person of Christ. He was asked to recast these into theological articles that became the Swabian Concord of 1574. In north Germany Chemnitz and others revised the Swabian Concord into the Swabian-Saxon Concord of 1575. In 1576 another consensus was proposed in the Maulbronn Formula. Andreae liked this text, but suggested to Elector August of Saxony*, the main promoter of concord, that the Swabian-Saxon Concord be used as the basis of further work by theologians, who then met at Torgau in 1576 and produced the so-called Torgau Book. Andreae wrote a summary of this book that became part one of the Formula of Concord, the Epitome. Reactions to the Torgau Book were discussed at Bergen Abbey in 1577, and the product of these negotiations, known as the Bergen Book, became part two of the Formula of Concord, the Solid Declaration (SD). Reservations about the new Formula of Concord were dealt with in the preface to the Formula, which also became the preface to the whole *Book of Concord* and resulted from a longer drafting process, led by Andreae, between 1578 and 1580. During this period 86 territories and cities accepted the Formula of Concord (together with the *Book of Concord*) and 8,188 theologians, pastors, and teachers signed it.

The Formula of Concord, whose original text is German, consists of twelve articles on the major controversial issues and their resolution. It explicitly presents itself as a restatement and exposition of the Augsburg Confession, and it helped to preserve inner-Lutheran unity while marking at the same time the transition to Lutheran Orthodoxy*. It reflects many aspects of a lively, serious, biblically oriented theological struggle about the right understanding of the truth and is thus a prelude to the theological debate about the meaning and relevance of the gospel that still continues within Lutheranism.

Questions for Discussion and Further Study

1. How does the preface to the *Book of Concord* reflect the self-understanding of the Lutheran confessions? How is this self-understanding related to other authorities?

2. Why were secular authorities (princes of territories, city councils) so actively interested in the production and collection of the confessions? What was the political significance of such collections?

3. Is it correct to say that the first seventeen articles of the Augsburg Confession manifest a coherent and systematic theological order? Explain.

4. In what way are the Lutheran confessions an authoritative guide for confessing the faith today and where are their limitations? Give examples.

G. G.

CHAPTER FOUR

The Lutheran Confessions

The Structure
of the Faith

♦

The Norm: Scripture –
Tradition – Confession

1. Historical and Theological Background

In the first five centuries, Christianity was defined by a combination of Scripture and confessions of faith, especially the Apostles' and Nicene creeds. During the Middle Ages, the church in western Europe granted increasing authority to the decrees of the bishop of Rome, the pope. Councils of the church also issued rulings that required obedience and gradually became part of the church's body of law. A collection of these decrees was published around 1140 by the Italian scholar Gratian. His *Decretum*, widely used as a textbook, was supplemented by five other collections, and together they formed the body of church law, called canon law*, that was in use at the time of the Reformation. The late medieval church regarded this canon law as normative for the faith alongside Scripture, the creeds, and the teachings of early church theologians like Augustine* (354–430) in the west and John Chrysostom* (354–407) in the east.

This accumulation of authorities in the medieval church produced two problems. First, these authorities did not always agree. That disagreement showed itself in textbooks, in biblical commentaries, and in the different schools of medieval theology. Some decrees of popes and councils also conflicted with one another. Second, this disagreement raised the question: Who was the final authority? Who had the right to give the definitive meaning of a passage in canon law or in the Bible? Popes, bishops, and councils each claimed this right, and legal process in the church allowed people to appeal from one authority to the other. Thus Luther appealed his case from the papacy to a general council. When a pope disagreed with his predecessor, the dilemma was how to decide which pope was right. While some people wanted a general council to decide, another solution gradually gained strength—the notion of papal infallibility. One pope could not revoke the official rulings of an earlier pope and thus imply that the earlier pope had made a mistake. This doctrine was not officially promulgated until the First Vatican Council in 1870, but the idea was already present in 1500.

In setting forth their position and in resolving disagreements, the reformers of the sixteenth century appealed to Scripture alone. The motto *sola scriptura** needs to be carefully interpreted, however. It does not mean that the Reformation recognized Scripture as the only authority in the church but as the *chief* authority. Most reformers, Lutherans and others, used arguments from the creeds, early church theologians, the councils, and occasionally from canon law when they were proving a point about Christian faith or life. The decisive authority, however, was given to Scripture. The other sources were often called tradition (from the Latin *tradere*, to hand over or pass down). When they contradicted Scripture or one another, Scripture was the supreme authority. Luther made this point vividly in his declaration at Worms in 1521: "Unless I am convinced by the testimony of Scripture or by clear reason (for I do not trust either in the pope or in councils alone, since it is well-known that they have often erred and contradicted themselves), I am bound by the Scriptures I have quoted and my conscience is captive to the Word of God."[1]

Did this mean that all Christians were their own authorities, determining for themselves the true meaning of Scripture? In 1520 Luther did grant all Christians, by virtue of their baptism into the priesthood of believers, the "power to test and judge what is right and wrong in matters of faith."[2] He did not intend, however, for Christians to live by their individual interpretations of the Bible regardless of what the church taught. He meant instead that all Christians had the right to test what the church teaches by "our believing understanding of the Scriptures,"[3] just as he had tested the decrees of the pope. As Luther's case showed, the right to test the church presupposed the study of Scripture and of the church's tradition plus the willingness to debate one's views with others in community.

Furthermore, on the basis of their preaching and teaching, Luther and his colleagues in Wittenberg gradually developed their own criteria for interpreting Scripture. These criteria arose from their perception of what needed to be changed in Christianity as judged by their reading of Scripture and by their experience. First and foremost, they were convinced that people needed to hear the heart of Scripture, the gospel, which was the good news of God's promise made flesh in Jesus the Christ. This gospel was received by faith, that is, trust in the certain promise of God to forgive sin and save believers on account of Christ. Out of this emphasis on the gospel as the center of Scripture came the early confessional documents of Lutheranism that also became authorities for its faith and practice.

In this way, one might say, Lutherans and other Reformation churches developed their own tradition of normative interpretations of Scripture that were handed down from one generation to another and established their identity. These confessions were considered norms of the faith because they explained which teachings and practices supported and expressed the gospel at the heart of Scripture. The Reformation churches, therefore, have always considered the tradition contained in their confessions and in their worship to be subject to Scripture. The following distinction makes this point: Scripture was the standard that judged other standards (the *norma normans*), while the confessions were recognized as a secondary criterion for the faith and practice that had been shaped by Scripture (the *norma normata*).

Eventually, this unequal relationship between Scripture and the confessions marked an important difference between the Reformation churches and Roman Catholicism. At its Fourth Session in 1546, the Council of Trent* declared that Christian truth about faith and morals had been handed down by the apostles through both Scripture and oral traditions and that both forms of truth were to be treated with equal reverence by the church. It also maintained that, in matters of faith and morals, no one could hold an understanding of Scripture that contradicted the explanation of the church. The church alone determined the genuine sense of Scripture even if this interpretation went against the view of all the theologians of early Christianity.[4] Both the

Roman Catholic and the Reformation churches therefore appealed to Scripture and tradition in some form, but Lutherans placed their confessions under the authority of Scripture while Roman Catholics gave equal respect to extrascriptural tradition and the teaching office (*magisterium*) of bishops and the pope.

2. The Confessional Texts

No specific article is dedicated to the authority of Scripture by the confessional documents, but they appeal frequently to Scripture in support of their own teachings and in opposition to those that they find contrary to the gospel. An important example of this appeal is found in SA 2, 1. There Luther designates salvation through faith alone in Christ's saving work as the "first and chief article," on which "rests all that we teach and practice against the pope, the devil, and the world." This article is based on eight verses of Scripture, three of which come from Rom 3:23-28, a principal source of the Lutheran claim that justification by faith in Christ alone is the gospel, the heart of Scripture.

Supported by Scripture and by other authorities, this gospel is applied throughout the confessions as the chief criterion for acceptable teaching and practice. CA 15 is a prominent case of this usage. It approves traditional festivals and regulations that have arisen in the course of church history as long as they can be observed without sin and contribute to peace and order in the church. But those human traditions (i.e., observances with little or no basis in Scripture) that burden consciences "contrary to the gospel and the teaching about faith in Christ" (CA 15.3) are not permissible. For traditions to be kept "without sin" and without burdening consciences "contrary to the gospel" means that their observance cannot replace faith in Christ as the way to salvation. Examples of such harmful traditions are monastic vows and regulations about fasting and holy days that are dealt with in CA 26 and 27. In contrast, a tradition that has the direct command of Scripture is the distribution and reception* of both elements in the Eucharist. This command, conveyed in the words of institution, has to be obeyed as the direct ordinance of Christ (Ap. 22.15).

CA 26 provides a specific example of how the confessions argue their case. By requiring fasting, claimed Melanchthon*, the church taught people they were earning grace and making satisfaction for sin. This teaching explicitly contradicts "the grace of Christ and the teaching concerning faith" (26.2–4), that is, it contradicts the gospel, which insists that faith in Christ "is to be esteemed far above all works" (26.4). Such teaching about fasting, vestments, and holy days also contradicts the commands of God, that is, the Ten Commandments, because people thought it was more Christian and spiritual to observe religious regulations than to mind their everyday tasks according to the Commandments (26.8–11). To support the pastoral argument that such traditions have been a burden to consciences, Melanchthon appealed to two theologians who lived a thousand years apart: Jean Gerson* (1363–1429) and Augustine (354–430); and he condemned the medieval commentators on canon law for confusing people with their opinions (26.12–17). Melanchthon then cited several biblical passages, chief among them Matt 15:1–20, a text often employed by the reformers against human traditions (see, e.g., SA 3, 15). Finally, CA 26 invokes texts from the early church to support freedom in the use of ceremonies (26.42–45). To summarize: Melanchthon used a combination of authorities from Scripture and church history to bolster his argument. It was based not just on proof texts, however, but on the evangelical* principle that the observance of church regulations should not undermine the good news that salvation comes through faith in Christ alone.

Unlike the confessional documents of the Reformed tradition, Lutheran confessions did not contain separate articles on the authority of Scripture. Only the Formula of Concord, written after the Council of Trent, contains a specific treatment of biblical authority and how it relates to creeds and confessions. The prefaces of both the Epitome and the Solid Declaration make the same assertion. In opposition to Trent, the Comprehensive Summary, Rule, and Norm declares that no other writings, by either ancient or modern teachers, "should be put on a par with Holy Scripture." Instead, they should be subordinated to Scripture and received only as witnesses to it (FC-Ep 2). The Summary Formulation, Rule, and Norm also calls Scripture "the only true norm according to which all teachers and teachings are to be judged and evaluated" (FC-SD 3).

After Scripture, the creeds and confessional documents of the sixteenth century are described as authoritative statements of the faith especially appropriate for their time. Together one may speak of them as the tradition of Lutheran churches. The ancient creeds are "confessions of the orthodox and true church" that had refuted all the heresies that had arisen in the church "at that time" (FC-Ep 4; FC-SD 4). The Augsburg Confession and the other confessions preceding the Formula of Concord are the "unanimous consensus and exposition of our Christian faith" (FC-Ep 4). The Augsburg Confession is called the "symbol of our epoch, not because this confession was prepared by our theologians, but because it is taken from the Word of God and solidly and well grounded therein" (FC-SD 5). A mix of history and doctrine informs all these claims. Creeds and confessions have authority both because they are grounded in Scripture and because they state the Christian faith in a way both appropriate and necessary for their own time. The Summary Formulation even says that Lutherans appeal to the Augsburg Confession just as later synods and bishops appealed to the Nicene Creed (FC-SD 5).

Among the confessions, precedence is given to the Augsburg Confession and specifically to the unaltered version originally presented to Charles V in 1530 (see pp. 15–16). It is the basis for Lutheran theological unity. The other confessional documents are recognized as authoritative because they faithfully explain and transmit the heart of Scripture in accord with the Augsburg Confession (FC-SD 6–7). Even Luther's Catechisms are said to present the same theology, drawn from Scripture of course, in a form especially appropriate for laity (FC-Ep 5). Together these documents serve a catholic* function within Lutheranism; they are included in the *Book of Concord* because "they have always and everywhere been accepted as the common and universally accepted belief of our churches" (FC-SD 11).

Insofar as they appeal to the Augsburg Confession, the Lutheran confessions also make a broader claim to represent catholic Christian teaching throughout the ages. In this way the confessions fulfill a classic function of Christian tradition. In 1530 Melanchthon needed to prove to the emperor that Lutherans were not a new perversion of Christianity or a new version of an old heresy. Therefore he argued that Lutheran teaching and practice was genuinely catholic in the sense that it "agrees with the pure Word of God and Christian truth" and, further, that it is "grounded clearly on the Holy Scriptures and is not contrary or opposed to that of the universal Christian church" (*BC* 47.1). Melanchthon was hoping that the Roman theologians would recognize this claim and agree that the dispute was only about the

abuses in part two of the Augsburg Confession. Melanchthon's strategy failed because the abuses in part two specifically contradicted the
chief authorities invoked by the Lutherans for their catholicity and
orthodoxy: Scripture and the gospel.

This failure does not, however, invalidate the claim of the Augsburg
Confession that its teaching and practice are genuinely catholic.
Lutherans continue to make this claim by their adherence to the ecumenical creeds and by their respect for other writings and liturgical
traditions that do not contradict the gospel. Above all, they participate
gladly in the search for a common expression of this catholicity and for
genuine Christian unity.

3. Theological Summary

- Scripture is the primary authority for Lutheran churches. This primacy,
  however, does not exclude other authorities. The ecumenical creeds,
  early church theologians, and sixteenth-century confessions are also
  authorities for Christian faith and practice. These confessions understand themselves as grounded in Scripture and subject to its authority.
  They also understand themselves as public summaries and declarations
  of the faith that were necessary in order to restore and to preserve genuine catholic Christianity in their time.

- Lutheranism has its own tradition of interpreting Scripture. At the
  heart of Scripture it identifies the gospel as the criterion by which all
  teaching and practice should first be judged. This gospel is the message
  that salvation comes through faith in Christ alone and not through
  humanly instituted religious practices that undermine faith in Christ
  and are unsupported in Scripture. Since the primary aim of the confessional documents is to maintain this focus on the gospel at the heart of
  Scripture, the confessions are the principal form of tradition for Lutherans.

- Gospel and Scripture have a reciprocal relationship. Scripture is the
  source of the gospel and the gospel is the heart of Scripture. This reci-
  procity prevents Lutheranism from adopting a fundamentalist view of
  Scripture. The authority of Scripture does not rest mainly on claims
  made about its literal truth or the authenticity of its texts. Instead, the
  authority of Scripture rests on its witness to the truth of the gospel as
  well as on the role that the Bible has always played in defining Christianity.

- Proclaiming the gospel is also tradition in the best sense of the word,
  namely, handing on the central message of Scripture from generation to

generation. That is why preaching on the biblical text has been accorded such respect and authority in Lutheran churches. Hearing the gospel preached is to encounter God's Word just as truly as reading the Bible is to encounter God's Word. Although the Reformation helped to make the Bible available to everyone, its message spread mainly through preaching, and it intended for the Bible to be read and interpreted in the context of Christian community.

- The confessional documents are not just historical texts. They are also tradition, that is, vehicles for handing on the gospel as the central message of Scripture. Believers in every generation appropriate that tradition as they apply it to their own time and place, just as the authors of the confessions did. Subscription to the confessions, especially by public ministers of the church, means not just adherence to the words and their historical importance. Above all, it means making the authority of the gospel the center of their ministry and committing themselves to apply this tradition joyfully in their work today.

S. H.

◆

The Framework: Law and Gospel

1. Historical and Theological Background

The law weighed heavily on people in the late medieval church. Although God's grace was proclaimed in sermons and received* in the sacraments, people's lives were governed more by the law than by grace. In the form of the Ten Commandments law was used as the basis for hearing confession. Priests interrogated their parishioners by going through the Commandments one by one and asking if they had been broken. Penance was imposed on contrite parishioners according to manuals that matched the penalty to the severity of the sin. The Ten Commandments were also presented as a way to merit grace. By keeping the Commandments, with the aid of grace, people accumulated merit that qualified them to receive eternal life. No one asserted that keeping the Ten Commandments alone was enough, but their use as a basis for punishment and as a supplement to grace placed the law at the forefront of Christian life.

Freedom from the demands of the law was the most attractive message of the early Reformation. It stood at the center of evangelical preaching and echoed throughout the writings of Reformation theologians. Luther was responsible for this emphasis in two ways. First, he rediscovered that freedom for his own life. Luther had long puzzled over the phrase in Rom 1:17: through faith the righteousness of God is revealed in the gospel. As a student he had learned that the righteousness of God was the standard by which God judged and punished sinners. Since that standard was revealed through the law, Luther, like other Christians, tried as hard as possible to obey the law in order to become righteous in God's sight. If, however, righteousness was revealed in the gospel, as Luther now realized, then he became righteous through faith in Christ, not through the law. When the full force of this realization hit Luther, he felt as if he were born again.[5] He was freed from the oppressive sense of having to fulfill the law. He experienced the liberating reality of Paul's assertion that in Christ the righteousness of God had been revealed apart from the law (Rom 3:21–22). In Luther's own life the joy of the gospel began to outweigh the burden of the law.

Second, Luther declared the freedom of the gospel to a wide audience through his sermons, lectures, and pamphlets. He also explained how the law should be correctly used in relationship to the gospel. Luther had begun to clarify this relationship in his early lectures on Romans (1515–1516).[6] By the time the *Freedom of a Christian* was published (1520), the structure of law and gospel was in place. Its foundation is the division of Scripture into commandments and promises. Commandments express the law of God and lead to repentance because they show people where they have sinned and how much they need forgiveness. This forgiveness is declared through the promises of God, the other part of Scripture. They express the gospel because they bring remission of sin through faith in Christ and make the believer free.[7]

According to Luther, both law and gospel are part of Scripture, and both repentance and faith are necessary to the Christian life. This insight reappeared in the first formal summary of Reformation theology, the *Loci communes* (1521) of Luther's younger colleague, Melanchthon. He recalled Luther's words in a way that made them a principle of Lutheran theology: "Of the whole of Scripture," he wrote, "there are two parts: the law and the gospel. The law indicates the sickness, the gospel the remedy."[8] Melanchthon developed this principle in his *Instruction for Visitors* (1527: see pp. 16–18). According to

Luke 24:47, Melanchthon argued, "repentance and forgiveness of sins" in the name of Jesus are to be proclaimed to all nations. He concluded: "There neither is forgiveness of sins without repentance nor can forgiveness of sins be understood without repentance."[9] In Melanchthon's view, repentance comes from preaching the law prior to the gospel. Only after the law induces genuine sorrow for sin will the preaching of the gospel produce faith in the promise of forgiveness.

Law and gospel thus became an important feature of Lutheran theology and practice as it was defined during the 1520s. Not everyone agreed with Melanchthon, however. In 1527 he was challenged by a former colleague in Wittenberg, John Agricola*, now a preacher and teacher in Luther's birthplace of Eisleben. Agricola protested that preaching the law would not lead people to repentance but either to pride or to despair: to pride if they thought they could obey the law, or to despair if they feared they could not. Instead, argued Agricola, true repentance came from the gospel itself. Only after people heard God's promise and love for them in Jesus Christ would they be truly sorry for their sin and ready to receive forgiveness. For Agricola, who appealed to Luther's emphasis on justification apart from the law, it was dangerous and even unnecessary to preach the law. Melanchthon strongly disagreed. At a conference in 1527 Luther played the mediator, but the place of the law in the Christian life remained a persistent issue for Lutherans.[10]

2. The Confessional Texts

The earliest confessional documents, Luther's Catechisms, the Augsburg Confession, and the Apology, all manifest the principle of law and gospel in their theology. In the Small Catechism Luther concludes on the basis of Exod 20:5b-6 that the Ten Commandments contain both a divine threat and a divine promise. God threatens to punish all those who disobey the Commandments but promises grace and every blessing to those who keep them (SC 1.22). Returning to the same text in the Large Catechism, Luther says it contains "both a wrathful threat and a friendly promise" (LC 1.322). This friendly promise extends to the Apostles' Creed, which proclaims the remedy for human inability to obey the Commandments. Through the creed we come "to love and delight in all the commandments of God because we see that God gives himself completely to us, with all the gifts and his power, to help us keep the Ten Commandments: the Father gives us all creation, Christ all his works, the Holy Spirit all his gifts" (LC 2.69).

In the Augsburg Confession and the Apology, Melanchthon treats law and gospel in connection with the subject of repentance. Both CA 11 and 12, entitled "Confession" and "Repentance," respectively, contain the evangelical alternative to the medieval sacrament of penance*. Private confession and absolution are commended, but the interrogation that sought to elicit every sin and made confession so oppressive is rejected (CA 11.1–2).

Likewise, the notion of repentance is substantially revised. It embraces not only contrition but also faith "which is born of the gospel, or of absolution," and "believes that sins are forgiven for Christ's sake, comforts the conscience, and delivers it from terror" (CA 12.4–5, Latin). This two-part definition of "true repentance" (CA 12.3, German), contrition and faith, is based directly on the discussion of "true Christian penance" in Melanchthon's *Instruction for Visitors*.[11] In addition, the good news that forgiveness is available to Christians who sin and repent is distinguished from three contrary positions: the alleged perfectionist claims of some Anabaptists* who taught that, once baptized, Christians would not fall again into sin and therefore did not need to repent (CA 12.7–8); the rigorous position of third-century followers of Novatian*, who were deemed heretical because they denied absolution to Christians who did commit serious sins (CA 12.9); and the requirement of satisfaction (the third part of the medieval sacrament) that undermined the comfort of absolution by imposing additional demands on the penitent (CA 12.10).

Each of these contrary positions conflicted in some way with the Lutheran principle of law *and* gospel. The perfectionists denied there was any need for the law to make Christians aware of sin since they had no sin. The Novatians denied that after baptism Christians needed either law or gospel since, if they committed serious sin, repentance was unnecessary because they could not be forgiven anyhow. The requirement of satisfaction in the medieval sacrament undermined the comfort and certainty of forgiveness produced by the gospel in the form of absolution.

The distinctive feature of CA 12 is its emphasis on the forgiveness of sin through faith in Christ as the consoling outcome of repentance. Precisely this point was rejected by the Roman theologians in their

Confutation of the Augsburg Confession. Responding in frustration to their attack, Melanchthon exclaims: "this is the very voice of the gospel, that by faith we obtain the forgiveness of sins" (Ap. 12.2). This important issue involves "the chief doctrine of the gospel, the true knowledge of Christ, and the true worship of God" (Ap. 12.3).

Because it was so important, Melanchthon made Ap. 12 one of the longest articles in the Apology. The entire argument, however, hinges on the principle of law and gospel as the biblically based Lutheran alternative to the medieval sacrament of penance. In words reminiscent of his *Loci* from 1521, Melanchthon summarizes this structure at Ap. 12.53. There he identifies the two chief works of God in human beings as law and gospel. Law reveals, denounces, and condemns sin, while the gospel is the promise of grace granted in Christ.

Prior to this paragraph, Melanchthon explains why the medieval sacrament confused people about when or whether forgiveness actually took place (Ap. 12.4–27). Then he describes in more detail the two-part Lutheran definition of penitence (synonymous with repentance in the Augsburg Confession). He emphasizes the comfort and certainty of faith that is awakened and strengthened by absolution (Ap. 12.28–43). Referring to the traditional concept of the power of the keys* on which absolution was based, Melanchthon concedes that "absolution may properly be called a sacrament of penitence" because it forgives sins and nourishes faith (Ap.12.39–43). Finally, Melanchthon supplies passages from Scripture that support this definition of penitence as embracing both contrition and faith in Christ (Ap. 12.44–52).

The principle of law and gospel, therefore, governs the confessional theology of repentance and faith that form the rhythm of Christian life. A third part, the amendment of life in good works, follows as the fruit of repentance (CA 12.6). This principle also informs preaching and the sacraments. Pointing people to the law leads them to repentance and to sorrow for their sin. Hearing the gospel in a sermon, in absolution, or in the eucharistic words of institution awakens faith and effects the forgiveness of sin. This faith, in turn, brings forth a new life of good works produced by keeping the Commandments as taught by the catechisms.

As new pastors and congregations practiced this rhythm of law and gospel and as theologians reread the documents, confusion persisted over the exact meaning of certain terms. Did "repentance" have only the narrow sense of sorrow for sin or did it embrace both contrition and faith as it was used in CA 12 and Ap. 12? Did "gospel" mean the promise and declaration of forgiveness in the narrow sense of absolution, or did it also mean the entirety of teaching about Christ in the New Testament as implied by Melanchthon's phrase "the chief doctrine of the gospel"?

In the Smalcald Articles Luther offers his own explanation of these terms. In SA 3, 2–3 he distinctly prefers the narrow meanings of law and gospel, while he reserves the term "repentance" for the whole action of contrition and consolation through the gospel. The chief function of the law is to make sin manifest (SA 3, 2.4). The "beginning of true repentance" is the judgment of the law that makes sinners contrite (SA 3, 3.3). The gospel is the "consoling promise of grace" that is believed in faith and produces forgiveness (SA 3, 3.4). Luther also describes five ways in which the gospel "offers counsel and help against sin" (SA 3, 4): preaching, baptism, the sacrament of the altar, power of the keys (i.e., absolution), and the mutual conversation and consolation of Christians. Lutherans frequently call these ways the "means of grace," although they are better described as means of the gospel. The term "means" is used by CA 5, where it refers to the gospel and the sacraments as instruments through which the Holy Spirit produces faith.

This confusion over terms was complicated by continuing debates about the role of the law in the Christian life. Is contrition for sin a result of preaching the law or is it aroused by hearing the gospel? Can the law in the Ten Commandments both lead the Christian to repentance and serve as a guide to Christian living after repentance? These debates were called the antinomian* controversies and historians have identified up to three of them. After the first debate in 1527, another dispute erupted among Agricola, Melanchthon, and Luther in Wittenberg between 1537 and 1540. Agricola again questioned the wisdom of preaching the law to Christians, while Melanchthon upheld both preaching the law and teaching the Commandments. After several formal disputations, Luther publicly criticized Agricola in a treatise entitled *Against the Antinomians,* and Agricola left Wittenberg for good.

A third wave of controversies broke out among theologians after Luther's death. Some of these involved attacks by the Gnesio-Lutherans* on Melanchthon because he valued the law so highly and used the term "gospel" in the broad sense that embraced both repentance and faith. Article 5 of the Formula of Concord attempted to settle this issue. It concedes that the terms repentance and gospel have both narrow and broad meanings. Its main point, however, is that both law and gospel (in the strict sense of faith in Christ) must be preached in the church. Therefore it condemns the antinomians, "who cast the preaching of the law out of the churches and would have us criticize sin and teach contrition and sorrow not from the law but solely from the gospel" (FC-SD 5.15). Even though both are needed, however, law and gospel must remain quite distinct in the church's proclamation so that the gospel will not again be misunderstood as law. To this end, FC 5 commends the teaching of both Luther and Melanchthon, including CA 12 and Ap. 12; it thereby reinforces the distinction between law and gospel as a principle of Lutheran theology (FC 5.27).

FC 6 attempts to resolve one last dispute about the law that occupied theologians and pastors in the 1550s and 1560s. They disagreed over whether the law was a necessary guide for good works produced as the fruit of repentance and faith. This function of the law, which neither Luther nor Melanchthon ever questioned, is usually called the "third use of the law." The first function, called the civil use, designates the way in which every society utilizes a code of laws to enforce justice and to deter crime. The second function, called the theological or spiritual use, designates the way in which divine law reveals God's will and leads people to repentance. This second use is the meaning of law in the Lutheran principle of law and gospel. The three uses are summarized in FC 6.1.

The Lutheran pastors who protested against the third use (Andreas Poach in Erfurt and Anton Otto in Nordhausen) were afraid it would undermine Christian freedom and undo the principal benefit of the Reformation. If people were taught they had to obey the Commandments after they had been liberated by the gospel, they would fall once again under the oppressive burden of having to live by the law. As Luther had said many times, the genuine good works of Christians were the spontaneous fruits of faith that believers did with delight.

This position is described in FC 6.2. According to it, pastors like Poach and Otto did not need to teach the law. They had seen, probably in concrete pastoral circumstances, how quickly people would forget their Christian freedom once the law was again held over their heads.

Nevertheless, the authors of the Formula sided mainly with the opponents of Poach and Otto (FC 6.3–4). They could hardly do otherwise. The Ten Commandments were part of the catechisms, and both Luther and Melanchthon had urged teaching the law to Christians because they had seen the other extreme: once people had been told they were freed by the gospel, many of them showed no change of behavior at all, spontaneous or not. As the preface to the Small Catechism puts it, such people had "mastered the fine art of abusing liberty" (SC, Preface, 3).

Although it takes the other side, FC 6 does honor the viewpoint of Poach and Otto. Even though good works done by the liberated Christian conform to the law, they are not, strictly speaking, "works of the law but works and fruits of the Spirit" (FC 6.17). Still, believers should be taught the law. Why is that, if the Holy Spirit is automatically producing good works from their faith? Because Christians are not "fully renewed in this life" and are still subject to the conflict between spirit and flesh (FC 6.18). In other words, believers still sin. They are not perfect and can hinder or distort the Holy Spirit's work. They might revert to the illusion that they are perfect and that their holiness is the basis for pleasing God. Teaching them the law holds up a mirror (FC 6.4). It reminds them what the will of God is and what kind of works genuinely please God, even though such works remain imperfect because of sin and become acceptable to God for Christ's sake alone (FC 6.21–22).

The intent of FC 6, therefore, is not so much to define a third use of the law as to argue that both the second and third functions of the law apply to Christians. Because sin remains a reality in their life, Christians constantly need both law and gospel: law, to lead them to repentance *and* to guide their life in the Spirit; and gospel, to forgive their repeated failure to live perfectly according to God's will even with the Spirit at work in their life. For the confessions, law and gospel define the rhythm of Christian existence as well as the principle of theology and proclamation.

3. Theological Summary

- The phrase *law and gospel* is sometimes used as a slogan or formula for summarizing Lutheran theology. Law and gospel did develop as a way of condensing the Reformation message so that its uniqueness could be transmitted to a broad audience. The phrase is better defined, however, as a criterion or a principle rather than a summary. One finds elements of law and gospel in topics like the sacraments, two kingdoms, and sin and grace. But it does not cover all the theological points made in the confessions. The Lutheran reformers did not intend for all Christian theology to be reduced to this phrase.

- Law and gospel originated primarily as a way of interpreting Scripture that made the redeeming work of God in Jesus Christ the center of its story. To recover this center was the intent of the Reformation. Since preaching was the prominent channel of spreading this message, law and gospel also became a principle of Lutheran proclamation. It is not a substitute for regular exegesis or for the ongoing task of applying Scripture freshly and concretely to new situations. But this principle does remind preachers to balance God's joyful gift of faith in Christ (gospel) with God's earnest desire for repentance and justice (law).

- Law and gospel must be held together in Christian teaching and in Christian living. The reminder of the Reformation is that one without the other often leads to a distortion of Christianity. The confessions repeatedly warn against these distortions. To base Christian identity on the law alone teaches people they can please God by their goodness and therefore do not need Christ. To deny that the law has any place in Christianity can mislead people into thinking that the freedom of the gospel is the license to behave any way they wish or that God's will for humanity is not manifest in the commandments that define God's covenant with Israel.

- The principle of law and gospel requires believers to keep their balance in order to avoid these distortions. On the one hand, every generation faces new temptations to impose the law on believers as the essence of Christianity. The faith is always in danger of being reduced to a set of behaviors considered moral by a particular culture. On the other hand, Christian freedom can be so heady that it overlooks the persistence of sin or God's constant desire for justice. The faith is always in danger of being elevated to a spiritual level that neglects real human need and the human capacity for injustice. Keeping law and gospel in balance attempts to protect Christian faith from both legalism and antinomianism.

- In the last analysis, however, the gospel is the unique and joyful message of Christianity. God saves and forgives through faith in Jesus Christ. Any qualification of that message that makes obedience to the law a condition of salvation also distorts the confessional principle of law and gospel.

S. H.

◆

The Basis: God the Father, God the Son, God the Holy Spirit

1. Historical and Theological Background

The doctrine of God as expressed in the trinitarian and christological dogmas was not one of the major controversial issues that marked the Reformation conflict. The Lutheran confessions say as much. They have accepted and integrated the fundamental doctrinal decisions of the early church about the Trinity and Christology.

These decisions concerned, first, the Trinity of God, who is Father, Son, and Holy Spirit, one God in three divine "persons" (*hypostases*) of equal divinity and of one substance or essence (*homoousios*). This Trinity is confessed in the Niceno-Constantinopolitan Creed of 381, which is based on the Creed of the Council of Nicea* (325) affirming the unity of divine essence of Father and Son, to which the Council of Constantinople* (381) added the divine nature also of the Holy Spirit. This dogma was confessed later also in the Athanasian Creed: One God in three persons equal in glory and majesty, equally uncreated, unlimited, eternal, almighty, God and Lord, three persons in one Godhead and one God in three persons.

One important aspect in the development and interpretation of trinitarian doctrine is the distinction between an immanent Trinity and an economic Trinity. This distinction is also presupposed by the confessions. *Immanent Trinity* points to the interior relationship or communion (*koinonia*) of the three divine persons within the one Godhead. *Economic Trinity* refers to the three faces or manifestations of God's activity in relation to the world by means of God's creative and sustaining power, the saving mission of the Son, and the redemptive work of the Holy Spirit in believers and the church. But the insertion into the Nicene Creed (beginning with the sixth century) of the phrase that the Holy Spirit proceeds from the Father "and the Son" (*filioque**) has strengthened a tendency in the Western church to subordinate the Spirit to the Son or, in Protestantism, to the Word.

The doctrinal decisions of the early church concerned, second, christological dogma. The Councils of Nicea in 325 and Constantinople in 381 affirmed the equal divine substance of the Father and the Son and the saving mission of the Son in his incarnation, suffering, death, resurrection, and ascension. The decisions of the Council of Chalcedon* in 451 affirmed the presence and unity of the two natures, human and divine, in the one person (*hypostasis*) of Jesus Christ, the natures being united "unconfusedly, unchangeably, indivisibly, inseparably." This classical Christology, which confesses the unity and mutual participation of divine and human in the one and unique Christ, is the presupposition of the theology of revelation and salvation.

A conflict over Christology arose, however, between the Lutheran and Reformed, especially Zwinglian, wings of the Reformation that was then also reflected in the confessions (FC 8). This conflict was closely connected to and initially caused by the debate about the Lord's Supper. According to the Swiss Reformer Ulrich Zwingli*, the humanity taken up by Christ in his person was the pledge of human salvation. This humanity of Christ is preserved after the ascension in heaven and consequently cannot be present on earth in the Lord's Supper. Luther and his supporters rejected this interpretation and affirmed that because of his incarnation Christ is always present in the unity and mutual participation of the two natures in his person. On this basis the omnipresence or ubiquity* of the humanity of Christ, especially in the Lord's Supper, is to be affirmed.

The trinitarian and christological doctrines were accepted by the confessions and restated in their new Reformation context. The Lutheran reformers and their confessions were not interested, however, in the forms and methods used by late medieval theology to explain these doctrines. They did not share its high esteem of the power of reason and its frequent use of rational investigation and speculation in order to prove God's existence (e.g., by Anselm of Canterbury*, 1033–1109) and to explicate God's nature. But there were clear affinities of Reformation thought with tendencies in late scholasticism (and mysticism) represented by theologians like William of Ockham* (c. 1285–c. 1349), who pled for a stricter separation between reason and revelation and denied that reason alone could lead to knowledge of God.

2. The Confessional Texts

The Trinitarian God. The recognition of the trinitarian dogma by the Lutheran Reformation is attested by the inclusion of the three ecumenical creeds, and especially of the Athanasian Creed (3–25), in the *Book of Concord* (*BC* 19–21). This recognition is further confirmed in an exemplary manner by CA 1.1–4, which is introduced by an explicit reference to the Nicene Creed and implicit references to the Athanasian Creed. There is one undivided God in three distinct, divine, equal, infinite, and coeternal persons: God the Father, God the Son, God the Holy Spirit. The article offers an explication of the term "person" as a distinct entity (1.4) over against Modalism in the third century, which regarded the three persons as three modes or external manifestations of the one God acting as Father, or Son, or Holy Spirit. The article concludes by reaffirming the early church's rejections of antitrinitarian positions like the dualism of Manichaeism* (third century), the Gnostic Valentinians (second century), the Arians (the followers of Arius* in the fourth century), the Eunomians (the followers of Eunomius*, an extreme Arian of the late fourth century), the Samosatenes (followers of Paul of Samosata*, third century) and the New Samosatenes (referring to antitrinitarian spiritualists of the sixteenth century). It also adds the Mohammedans (Muslims), who were also regarded as antitrinitarian (5–6). The Formula of Concord also contains a rejection of the "Erroneous Articles of the New Anti-Trinitarians" (FC-Ep 12.29; FC-SD 12.37). CA 1 was accepted by the Roman Confutation* at Augsburg, and Ap. 1 only needs to repeat the affirmations of the Augsburg Confession.

Luther begins his confession in part 1 of the Smalcald Articles with the same theological perspective by testifying to the trinitarian nature of God and by indicating the inner relationship among the three persons of the Trinity (i.e., the immanent Trinity). Part 2 of the Large Catechism has a different focus. In the explication of the Apostles' Creed, Luther follows the trinitarian structure of its three articles. He includes longer sections on the trinitarian faith that emphasize the economic Trinity, that is, the outward revealing and saving actions of the persons of the Trinity in relation to the world, whereby the innermost being of God and the love, favor, and grace of the Father are revealed to believers by Christ and the Holy Spirit (LC 2.6–7 and 63–66).

Short references to the Trinity—"the greatest mystery in heaven and on earth" (FC-SD 8.33)—can also be found in FC-Ep 8.18; 12.28; and in FC-SD 8.6, 33; 11.66.

The Nature of God. In the first sentences of the Apostles' and Nicene Creeds, in the first section (7–17) of the Athanasian Creed, in CA 1.2–4, and in SA 1, God is confessed as Father, almighty, eternal, uncreated, Lord, unlimited, without end, of infinite power, wisdom, and goodness. The much longer statements in the Small and Large Catechisms speak in quite a different—personal and pastoral—way about God. In his interpretation of the First Commandment (LC 1.1–48) Luther begins with his famous definition of God as "that to which your heart clings and entrusts itself" (3), and then he describes the reality of God in the perspective of belief and unbelief. Again and again the faithful response to God's goodness, love, gifts, and blessings is confessed as absolute trust and confidence in that God in whom alone believers find consolation and from whom they receive everything (1–4, 13–16, 24–28, 39–48). But those who put their trust in worldly things and fix their heart on their own achievements, merits, and religious good works—against the criterion of justification—have a false God and are, in their pride, exposed to God's wrath (5–12, 17–23, 31–38). The contrast between God's wrath, which is God's alien work (*alienum opus*), and God's grace, which is God's own proper work (*proprium opus*), is made by the Apology in the framework of the dialectical relationship between God's law and God's gospel (Ap. 12.49–53).

God the Creator. The Apostles' and Nicene Creeds confess God as maker of heaven and earth and of all things visible and invisible. This confession is taken up in CA 1; yet here, as in SA 1, it is explicitly the triune God, three distinct persons in one divine essence, who is affirmed as the creator and preserver of all things visible and invisible.

Again, the much longer interpretation of the first article of the creed in the Small and Large Catechisms allows Luther to speak in a different mode about the creation and its creator. In a lively manner, both down-to-earth and full of wonder, God is confessed, interpreted, and praised as the creator and giver of the abundant wealth and diversity of earthly and eternal gifts, of all the necessities of personal and communal life. This comprehensive vision of creation is conceived as a manifestation and outreach of God's fatherly heart and love toward us. Creation, thus understood, is sustained and guarded by God against all danger, and all this without our merit—here again the criterion of justification is applied. The response of believers is thanksgiving, praise, and use of the divine gifts for God's service and glory (SC 2.2; LC 2.10–19 and 23–24). But Luther also has very critical words about all those, including Christians, who misuse the gifts and blessings of God for their own pride, greed, and enjoyment (LC 2.20–22). In his explication of the fourth petition of the Lord's Prayer in the Large Catechism (3.72–84) we find the same comprehensive and grateful vision of God's creation and care, the vision of a God who provides all things for all people. Where this is not acknowledged, public life is corrupted and the poor are exploited and oppressed.

God the Son. Like the doctrine of God, the christological dogma of the church as decided by the first four councils is received (i.e., accepted and affirmed) by the Lutheran confessions. This reception is confirmed by the inclusion of the creeds. The basic christological statement of the Apostles' Creed is expanded in the Nicene Creed with respect to Christ's eternal equality with the Father ("of one substance"), and in the Athanasian Creed (27–38) with respect to the divine and human natures of Christ. The christological dogma is affirmed in CA 1 and 3. In a way that is characteristic of the confessions, the emphasis of article 3 lies on the salvific and redeeming significance of Christ's death, resurrection, and ascension, on his sacrifice for original and actual sins, on his bestowal of life and grace on all who believe in him, and on the exercise of his eternal lordship and dominion. Article 3 of the Apology has only a few lines since the Roman Confutation had approved CA 3. Like CA 3, Ap. 3 puts special emphasis on the two natures of Christ in order to underline that only the divine-human Christ is able to reconcile sinners with God and to justify and sanctify them.

Part 1 of the Smalcald Articles reaffirms the christological dogma and sees no matter of dispute here. SA 2, 1 states the central significance of Christology for the Lutheran Reformation and its focus on the message of justification: It is *"the first and chief article"* on which "rests all that we teach and practice" (1 and 5), that Christ, our God and Lord, died for our sins and was raised for our justification so that those who have faith in him are justified by God. This basic conviction is also expressed in the Large Catechism: the "entire gospel that we preach depends on the proper understanding of this article. Upon it all our salvation and blessedness are based" (LC 2.33).

The explanation of the second article of the Apostles' Creed in the Small Catechism focuses on the redemptive work of Christ, truly human and truly divine (SC 2.4). The Large Catechism describes this work as a radical change of dominion: Christ liberates from the captivity to sin and evil, restores believers to the Father's favor, and becomes Lord in righteousness (LC 2.27–30). Redemption is grounded in and achieved by Christ's incarnation, suffering, death, and resurrection. In his ascension he has assumed dominion over all other powers (2.31).

The most elaborate treatment of christological dogma is found in FC 8. What appears at first sight to be highly abstract and speculative serves, in fact, to demonstrate the reality of Christ's saving work and of Christ's real presence in the Eucharist. This exposition is directed against "Calvinists (who have misled some other theologians)" (FC-Ep 8.1) or the "Zwinglians*," who taught "that the body of Christ could not be a true and genuine human body if it were present at the same time in heaven and in the Holy Supper on earth" (FC-SD 8.2). Zwingli is also described as teaching that "in Christ the divine and human natures are personally united in such a way that neither of the two *really* (that is, in deed and in truth) shares in the properties of the other but have in common only the name" (FC-Ep 8.3).[12]

Article 8 of the Formula of Concord describes the distinctiveness, mutual relation, and union of the divine and human natures in the person of Christ. This is developed in the tradition of the so-called Alexandrian Christology (fourth and fifth centuries) with many references to "ancient teachers of the church, both before and after the Council of Chalcedon" (FC-SD 8.18), and extensive quotes from Luther. The personal union and communion of the two natures, like soul and body, fire and iron, is neither a fusion nor a mere "coexistence" of the natures, but an exchange, a communication and mutual participation of their properties (the *communicatio idiomatum**) in the one person of Jesus Christ (FC-SD 8.6–35; FC-Ep 8.4–18). Martin

Chemnitz* had proposed three aspects of the communication of properties that the Solid Declaration takes up: (1) The properties or attributes of each of the two natures are ascribed to the whole person of Christ (FC-SD 8.36–45); this form of communication was termed in Lutheran Orthodoxy* the *genus idiomaticum*. (2) The person of Christ acts in, according to, with, and through both natures; consequently, each nature acts in communion with the other. Thus Christ is mediator and redeemer according to both natures (FC 8.46–47); this form was later termed the *genus apotelesmaticum*. (3) Because of the personal union, the human nature received in addition to its natural properties supernatural, heavenly prerogatives in power, glory, and majesty; this form was later called the *genus maiestaticum*. Such analysis made it possible to affirm Christ's human nature to be present also in the Lord's Supper (FC-SD 8.48–87). "Hence we consider it a pernicious error to deprive Christ according to his humanity of this majesty" (87). Both the Epitome and the Solid Declaration conclude with lists of rejected statements. The first four in FC-SD 8 (89–92) respond to the critique that the Sacramentarians* had made against the Lutherans, and the other three (93–95) are directed against Zwingli and his colleagues.

Because of the fundamental significance of Christology, many christological references are an integral part of other discussions in the confessional texts.

God the Holy Spirit. Only a few sections in the confessional texts deal thematically with the Holy Spirit. Yet these texts, together with many other pneumatological references in the confessions, clearly express the fundamental significance of the reality of the Holy Spirit for the theology of the Lutheran movement. This importance is underlined once more by the reception of the ecumenical creeds into the *Book of Concord*. In them we find a progression from the simple statement of belief in the Holy Spirit in the Apostles' Creed, to the affirmation of the equality of the Spirit as Lord and giver of life in the Nicene Creed, to the more developed confession of the equality of the Holy Spirit with the Father and the Son in the Athanasian Creed (3–26).

This traditional doctrine is affirmed in CA 1 (and repeated, because not disputed, in Ap. 1). Both confess the trinitarian equality of the Holy Spirit in divine essence, power, and eternity. CA 3 refers to the sanctifying work of the risen Christ through the Holy Spirit, while CA 5 articulates one of the crucial convictions of all confessional texts: The Holy Spirit, given by God through the gospel and the sacraments, "works" (Latin: "produces") faith when and where it pleases the Spirit (Latin: God) in those who hear the gospel. The Holy Spirit acts by means of Word and Sacrament and creates thereby faith (see also Ap. 24.70). The same article condemns the Anabaptists and others who teach that the Holy Spirit comes to us through our own efforts without the external Word of the gospel (CA 5.4). CA 7 also has to be understood in this perspective. If the church is the "assembly of all believers among whom the gospel is preached in its purity and the holy sacraments are administered according to the gospel" (CA 7.1), this implies: through these means of grace the Holy Spirit creates personal faith and at the same time gathers the assembly of all believers.

In the Apology the same understanding as in CA 5 is underlined in article 24: the Holy Spirit acts through Word and Sacrament (70). The Smalcald Articles (3, 3.40) refer to the sanctifying work of the Spirit, and stress like CA 5 that God gives the Spirit or grace only through or with the preceding external Word (SA 3, 8.3). This is stated against the claim of the enthusiasts* to have the Spirit without and before the Word.

In his explanation of the third article of the creed in the Small Catechism, Luther says everything essential about the Holy Spirit in a few lines: The Spirit leads individuals to faith, sanctifies them, and preserves them in the faith and—in a great leap from the individual to the worldwide perspective—calls, gathers, and sanctifies "the whole Christian Church on earth and preserves it in union with Christ in the one true faith." In this church the Spirit forgives sins and on the last day will raise the dead and grant eternal life to all who believe in Christ (SC 2.6). In its explanation of the third article of the creed the Large Catechism (LC 2.34–46, 57–70) emphasizes that the Holy Spirit is "sanctifier." The Spirit "brings us to the Lord Christ to receive this blessing [that is, of Christ's saving work] which we could not obtain by ourselves" (LC 2.39), and thus we are made holy. This sanctification is effected through the church, the forgiveness of sins, the resurrection of the body, and the life everlasting. The Spirit, always bound to God's proclaimed Word, causes, increases, and strengthens faith, and creates, calls, and gathers the church. Into this church the Spirit brings believers and forgives sins daily until on the last day the Spirit will raise the dead and grant eternal life (LC 2.35–45, 57–70).

The Formula of Concord states that the preaching and hearing of God's Word are the Spirit's instrument "in, with, and through which" the Spirit acts to convert people to God (FC-SD 2.52–53). Through the Word and the Holy Sacraments the Spirit initiates regeneration and renewal in us (66).

3. Theological Summary

The trinitarian and christological dogmas of the church were affirmed by the Lutheran Reformation and, consequently, occupy a fundamental place in the confessions. This reception was part of the new framework of the Reformation's programmatic intention of continuity and reform, that is, both to remain within the authentic tradition of the Christian faith and to restate this faith in response to a new historical situation. Thus the christological dogma with its soteriological significance "for us and for our salvation" (Nicene Creed) and its explication by the doctrine of justification form the central theological approach to the first and second articles of the creed and of the Christian faith as a whole.

- *Trinity.* That approach does not imply that the doctrine of the Trinity is secondary for the confessions because it has been completely overshadowed by their christological focus. Rather, the confession of the divine unity and communion of Father, Son, and Holy Spirit—the immanent Trinity—is presented as an indispensable basis and presupposition of the reality of the economic Trinity, which consists of:

   God's self-revelation: The only way for human beings to know and experience *God* lies in the encounter with "Immanuel," the God with us in *Jesus Christ,* and in the firm belief in this God enabled in us by the *Holy Spirit;*

   God's saving work: God's saving and transforming intention for humanity and creation is realized in the incarnation, death, and resurrection of *Jesus Christ,* both divine and human, and is received in the power of the *Holy Spirit* by faith alone;

   God's self-communication: Sinful and limited human beings can receive and appropriate God's self-revelation and saving work in *Jesus Christ* only by means of God's self-communication through the

Holy Spirit, who creates faith in human hearts and assembles the church.

• This trinitarian pattern with its close connection between the immanent and the economic Trinity is present throughout the confessions. They conceive of God's self-revelation, saving action, and self-communication in Christ through the Holy Spirit as a "condescending" movement from God toward human beings and not an "ascending" movement of scholastic* theology or, in our time, of spiritual or general religious effort toward God. In this movement of God's love and grace toward us, the confessions do not hide the other side of God, the righteous and judging God who confronts sinful human beings with judgment and the law and calls them to repentance, change, and a responsible life. But the emphasis of the confessions lies neither on a distant, wrathful God nor on the hidden God (*deus absconditus* according to Luther), but on the revealed God (the *deus revelatus*) who is near to us in Jesus Christ and active in us through the Holy Spirit.

• *Christology.* The reception of christological dogma by the confessions is placed into the context of God's movement toward us. Jesus Christ is confessed as the center of this movement because he is both human and divine, and thereby holds together and interrelates within himself both God and humanity. Consequently, the two natures of Christ receive prominent treatment. Their unity and communion (*communicatio idiomatum*) in the one and unique person of Jesus Christ grounds and explains the confession that in Christ God is suffering and dying in saving solidarity with humanity, and that in Christ humanity is carried through cross and resurrection to victory over the power of sin and death and to the promise of eternal life. This christological focus leads to an orientation of the confessions that is characteristic and decisive for them: the doctrine is "earthed," it is related to people by the joyous proclamation of its saving, transforming, and consoling content, which is the gospel, and of its comforting pastoral message for burdened, insecure, and questioning people in all ages (see also pp. 75–85 on justification).

• Two further elements of the trinitarian faith receive special attention in the confessions: the doctrine of *creation* and of the *Holy Spirit*. With regard to both doctrines Protestants in general and Lutherans in particular have been criticized that they have, at least until recently, (1) not sufficiently developed an adequate theology of creation and therefore have been coresponsible for an understanding of human domination over creation that has led to exploitation and destruction of the natural environment; (2) not given the reality of the Holy Spirit its proper place in theological reflection and Christian worship and life. However justified these criticisms may be, they certainly have no basis in the confessions. On the contrary!

• *Creation.* We encounter in them, first, an impressive and fascinating description, especially by Luther, of the richness, diversity, and goodness of God's creation. Not only the material necessities of human life together with nature and cosmos, plants, flowers, and animals, but also the social conditions of human life are included in a broad, comprehensive panorama of God's gracious and bountiful gifts and of God's sustaining love and care for them. The human response to God's creation is gratitude and praise of the creator, but also a responsible use of the gifts received. The misuse of the gifts of creation is an expression of the sinful condition of humanity. We find here a remarkable doxological and ecological vision of creation that can be a most helpful and inspiring contribution to a contemporary Lutheran theology of creation and its ethical implications.

• *Pneumatology.* We encounter in the confessions, second, a clear and consistent affirmation of the place and function of the Holy Spirit. Without the Holy Spirit there would be no Christians and no Christian church. Without the Holy Spirit we would not be able to grasp the mystery that people are led to believe in God and that the Christian church continues to exist in many lands despite persecution and discrimination from outside and failure and disobedience from within. According to the teaching of the confessions it is the Holy Spirit who creates faith and hope in each individual person, who leads to Christ and a right relation with God, who sanctifies and preserves the faithful in their faith, who inspires love toward God and neighbor, who brings together each individual Christian community, and who calls, gathers, enlivens, and enlightens the whole Christian church on earth. The church is thus the "product" of the Holy Spirit, it is the community in which the Spirit is at work, and it is the instrument with its proclamation, sacraments, and ministries through which the Spirit acts. This Spirit is not a free-floating Spirit that is present in all religions or in particular historical events, but it is the Spirit of God in Jesus Christ given through and together with the proclamation of God's Word and the celebration of God's sacraments. There is certainly much more room in Lutheran churches for the dynamic presence and activity of the Holy Spirit!

G. G.

◆

The Center: Justification of the Sinner

1. Historical and Theological Background

The message and doctrine of God's justification of the sinner for Christ's sake, by grace and by faith alone, was central to the Lutheran Reformation and received a decisive place in the Lutheran confessions. The historical and theological background of this doctrine is the biblical witness, especially the theology of Paul, and the development of the doctrine of grace in the Western tradition of the church from Augustine up to late medieval scholasticism at the time of the Reformation. The basic issue was, and has been throughout the centuries, the definition of the relationship between human nature and God's grace.

Augustine shaped and formulated the doctrine of grace in such a way that it was received by the church as its official teaching. It exerted a continuing influence despite later modifications and even distortions. Augustine clarified his teaching on grace in its later form in the controversy with Pelagius* (c. 350–c. 418) and his followers (Pelagians, Pelagianism). Pelagius rejected a doctrine of original sin and taught that human beings, because God created them good, possess a free will that enables them to fulfill God's commandments and thus earn their reward: salvation. Divine grace, which is external and facilitates what the will can do by itself, is given in proportion to merit. Augustine affirmed, on the contrary, that after the fall all human beings are under the impact of original sin, turned in on themselves in egoistic self-realization and turned away from God, so that their apparent freedom becomes in fact unfreedom to do what is essentially good. By their own efforts they cannot turn to God. Rather, from the outside God's grace in Jesus Christ effects a new orientation in believers, transforms their will, and enables them not only to do what is good but also to desire what is good. This grace is an unconditional free gift that makes people righteous before God so that they are justified by God. The absolute initiative in this process belongs to God, but human beings do, nevertheless, exercise their wills, whose freedom is constituted and determined by God's loving purpose. The willing human consent to salvation is thus also an effect of grace, and it is given only to those whom God has chosen by God's predestination. Augustine understood this grace in a "habitual" sense, that is, as a transforming force active within humans, an infusion of love through the Holy Spirit. This gratuitous gift of grace comes from Christ through the Holy Spirit and is communicated within the church by the external means of Word, Sacrament, and ministry. The Augustinian understanding of grace was received as the teaching of the church. Pelagianism was condemned by the North African Synod at Carthage in 418, and the Council of Ephesus in 431 condemned the Pelagians as heretics.

Between the twelfth and sixteenth centuries the different phases and schools of scholastic theology developed, restated, and sometimes also significantly changed the Augustinian doctrine of grace. The doctrine was explained with the help of technical terms and concepts that were built into more and more sophisticated systems of grace. Some of these terms reappeared a few hundred years later in the framework of Lutheran and Reformed Orthodoxy and then also in Methodism. Some of the most frequent terms for the different functions and roles of grace (*gratia*) were:

— *gratia gratis data* = God's free grace;

— *gratia praeveniens, gratia operans,* or *gratia concomitans* = prevenient or operating or accompanying grace, that is, the grace that comes before all human response to God and that is then active through the human will;

— *gratia infusa, gratia inhabitans, gratia inhaerens,* or *gratia iustificans* = infused, inhabiting, inhering, or justifying grace, that is, the indwelling justifying and sanctifying grace;

— *gratia gratum faciens* = the grace making gracious, that is, the habit of grace by which the sinner is justified or made righteous;

— *gratia subsequens* or *gratia cooperans* = the grace that follows the free will or cooperates with it, that is, the continuing grace that enables and supports a Christian life.

The connection between human effort and the efficacious intervention of God's grace was defined differently by the different scholastic schools. The so-called Franciscan school in high scholasticism of the thirteenth century held an ontological view of grace in which the way to salvation was a process of human actions combined with the effects of grace. In this process human nature, initiative, and goodwill contributed positively to the achievement of justification and salvation. Human participation in the process of justification and salvation and in preparation for God's grace or reward was described by the formula "to do what lies within you" or "to do your best" (*facere quod in se est**). The good works of such efforts would merit God's grace and justification because God was obliged to reward such efforts according to the mutual covenant established between God and humanity. Since such efforts were finite, imperfect acts of human beings, God promised to reward them with a proportionate merit. This proportionate merit or merit of congruity (*meritum de congruo**) was considered a sufficient ground for the infusion of justifying grace on the basis of God's generosity. By contrast, a full merit or merit of condignity (*meritum de condigno**) resulted from a work performed by the power of the Holy Spirit or in a state of grace and justly deserved salvation and justification.

In contrast to such synergistic* concepts, in which God and human beings work together for salvation, the most outstanding scholastic theologian, Thomas Aquinas* (c. 1224–1274), affirmed the absolute primacy of grace. He set forth an ontological concept of indwelling grace. Nature is oriented toward grace and human destiny finds its fulfillment in its communion with God. Without grace, human beings in their captivity to original sin are not capable of recognizing truth, doing something good, loving God, fulfilling the divine law, or gaining eternal life. Grace, then, is internal and understood as healing this corrupted nature and initiating (as *gratia operans*) goodwill and action, and it continues (as *gratia cooperans*) to strengthen and activate the will. Through the virtues infused by grace Christians are internally changed to such a degree that they spontaneously do what is good and thus freely fulfill the law of God. In this way justification is realized as effective change in persons and as participation in God. No claim to merit is placed before God as an expectation resulting from autonomous human efforts. But God graciously recognizes the cooperation of humans (along the lines of *meritum de congruo*).

In the so-called *via moderna** wing of scholastic theology of the fourteenth and fifteenth centuries, prominently represented by William of Ockham (c. 1285–c. 1349) and Gabriel Biel* (c. 1410–1495), one can notice a greater confidence in the natural possibilities of humans, that is, a stronger Pelagian orientation. Free human beings are able to act simply by nature in a God-pleasing way and are thereby justified by their good works, which are of little inherent value but accepted by God as if they were of much greater value. Contrary to this position, scholars of a more Augustinian persuasion, like Gregory of Rimini* (c. 1300–1358), undertook a reappropriation of Augustine's teaching. They taught that God alone could initiate and accomplish the justification of fallen and sinful human beings and that salvation was alone and fully God's work. Some scholars hold that the teaching of these theologians influenced the young Augustinian monk and professor Martin Luther.

The Reformation reacted against the more extreme scholastic positions on grace and justification with their emphasis on human cooperation in salvation and against the even more distorted popular expressions of late medieval theology in practical church life. The Reformation also rejected a related understanding of the church as the institution of salvation and mediatrix of grace through the sacraments. Reformation theology turned away from an ontological concept of grace, as an inherent quality, and highlighted instead a christologically based understanding of justification by faith and by grace alone. The main issue was no longer the question of how human nature could be transformed and healed by divine grace in a process of divine and human interaction. Rather, a radically new definition of humanity was given: humanity was completely captive to sin and therefore unable to cooperate with God for its salvation and was consequently utterly dependent on God's saving grace in the person of Jesus Christ.

While lecturing on the Bible between 1513 and 1516 Luther engaged in an existential and theological struggle to clarify his teaching on grace and justification. His insights were taken up by other reformers and found their place in the Lutheran confessions. Luther struggled with the destiny of the human person who is confronted with God's righteousness, and his breakthrough came when he recognized that God's righteousness was not a punishing righteousness but a passive righteousness, that is, a gift by which the merciful God justified sinners by grace and by faith alone. The core of this new insight was the saving event of Christ's cross and resurrection that he experienced with and for us. As a result, the righteous God imputed Christ's "alien righteousness" (*iustitia aliena*) to sinners and reconciled and justified them by this gracious and gratuitous judgment. God invited them to accept with confident faith this judgment, which had now become liberating gospel and was mediated to them by the Holy Spirit through Word and Sacrament.

The Roman Catholic response to the Reformation teaching on justification was given by the Council of Trent at its fifth session (1546) in the Decree on Original Sin, and at its sixth session (1547) in the Decree on Justification. The two decrees contain a series of condemnations (canons). Most of them aim, without naming the adversary, at Lutheran teaching on: the permanent nature of original sin, the sole initiative and action of God in justification, justification received by faith only, the assurance of salvation, and the inability of the will to contribute to salvation. Condemned are also the Lutheran rejection of human cooperation with prevenient and infused grace for justification and of the meritorious character of good works. Today Lutheran and also Catholic scholars hold that the Lutheran teaching on justification was not always represented in a correct way by the decrees of Trent.

2. The Confessional Texts

Augsburg Confession. The most concise definition of the doctrine and message of justification is found in CA 4. The salvation-historical sequence of the first seven articles is important: God's saving response to human sin in Jesus Christ leads to justification (1–4), which is communicated to believers by the Holy Spirit through the means of grace (5). This results in the new obedience of the justified and their community in the church (6 and 7). Article 4 refutes the possibility of obtaining forgiveness and righteousness by human effort alone. Its key expressions "by grace," "for Christ's sake," and "through faith" emphasize the free gift of justification, that is, forgiveness of sin, righteousness, and eternal life. This gift is presented both as *effective* and as *forensic* (juridical) justification, namely, (1) that we "become righteous before God," and (2) that "God will regard and reckon this faith as righteousness."

Apology. The Roman Confutation condemned the position of CA 4 because it denied that human works that are done with the assistance of grace are meritorious. In the first part (pars. 1–182) of article 4, the longest article in the *Book of Concord*, Melanchthon describes and refutes the scholastic background of his opponents and provides a first response based on the biblical witness and on Augustine (1–47). This is followed by a section entitled "What is Justifying Faith," which describes the nature of faith (48–60).

The next part, "Faith in Christ Justifies," contains a basic definition in par. 72: "To be justified means to make unrighteous [people] righteous or to regenerate them, as well as to be pronounced or accounted righteous. For Scripture speaks both ways" (i.e., with both an *effective* and a *forensic* understanding of justification). Love and good works must follow faith, but trust in them is excluded (61–74). Interpreters of the Apology have debated extensively about the precise relationship between these two formulations in par. 72. One issue concerns whether effective or forensic justification comes first. But there is general agreement that, according to the confessions, forensic and effective justification belong together in one action of God.

The section under the heading "We Obtain the Forgiveness of Sins Only by Faith in Christ" presents the christological foundation of justification. We are accounted righteous for Christ's sake (75–121). The section on "Love and the Keeping of the Law" (122–82) discusses the role of the law in the life of the justified and concludes that reconciliation or justification is received by faith alone, "though the keeping of the law follows with the gift of the Holy Spirit" (182).

The second part of article 4, entitled "Reply to the Opponents Arguments," employs extensive biblical and patristic* material in the form of a rebuttal. A more principled reflection (183–217) is followed by (1) a response to specific arguments of the other side (218–85) and (2) a more general disputation against scholastic teaching on issues like the understanding and role of reason, law, faith, love, merit, reward, penitence, works, and justification (286–385). In a concluding part (386–400) the main theme of the article is again presented: "We are justified before God, reconciled to him, and reborn by a faith that penitently grasps the promise of grace, truly enlivens the fearful mind, and is convinced that God is reconciled and propitious to us because of Christ" (386).

Smalcald Articles. In part 2 of the Smalcald Articles, article 1 opens with a famous designation of the reference to Christ and justification in Rom 4:25 as "the first and chief article" (1) and spells out the biblical basis of the message of justification. "Nothing in this article can be given up" and "on this article rests all that we teach and practice" (5).

In part 3, article 13 deals with the relation between justification and good works. The latter must follow faith, renewal, and forgiveness, otherwise "our faith is false and not true" (3). But the presupposition for considering good works is that *for the sake of Christ* the whole person and that person's works "shall be accounted and shall be righteous and holy" (2).

Formula of Concord. Article 3 responds to the inner-Lutheran controversy about whether Christ is our righteousness by dwelling in the elect only according to his divine nature, a position attributed to Andrew Osiander*, or only according to his human nature. The correct teaching in this case is that Christ is our righteousness according to both natures in their personal union (1–4). This controversy is taken up again at the end of FC 3. But first (FC 3.5–17) the Lutheran understanding of justification—"the chief article of the entire Christian doctrine" (quoted from Ap. 4. 2, German text)—is stated again by referring to Holy Scripture, the Apology, and texts of Luther (8–17): In justification the sinner is justified before God, absolved, declared free from all sins and from damnation, reconciled with God, receives the grace of God, adopted a child of God, and made an heir of eternal life. All this is received without merit or worthiness, by faith alone, solely through the merit of the total obedience, passion, death, and resurrection of Christ. His obedience is reckoned to all true believers as righteousness. These treasures are offered to us by the Holy Spirit in the promise of the gospel in Word and Sacrament. Faith is the only means whereby we can accept and appropriate these treasures to ourselves. In this way we are accounted righteous or declared righteous and holy by God. This *forensic* understanding of justification (*declared righteous*) is emphasized in the Formula of Concord.

The following section (FC 3.17–53) defines the relation of justification to contrition, regeneration, renewal, sanctification, love, virtues, and good works. These are necessary but must be clearly distinguished from justification and in no way regarded as means through which the grace of God is received. Accordingly, the right order is: After faith has been kindled and a person has been justified, the Holy Spirit renews and sanctifies believers and from this the fruits of good works will follow (41). All teachings that attribute the gift of justification to human activity, even in the form of renewal, sanctification, or virtues, are rejected. FC 3 then returns to the aforementioned controversy (pars. 1–4) and reaffirms the position of the theologians of the Augsburg Confession: Our righteousness does not rest on Christ's human nature alone, which by itself could not render satisfaction to God for the sins of the whole world; nor does righteousness rest on Christ's divine nature alone, which by itself could not mediate between God and us. Rather, our righteousness rests on the obedience of the person who is God and man at the same time (54–58). This conclusion is followed by another list of rejected errors (59–66). (See also pp. 163–74.)

Article 4 of the Formula deals with different interpretations among Lutherans about the role and place of good works in relation to justification (1–5). The article affirms that it is God's will, ordinance, and command that believers do good works, but only after they have been reconciled to God through faith and renewed through the Holy Spirit. Only works done as fruits of faith are pleasing and acceptable to God (6–13). More specifically, four points are made:

1. Rightly understood, good works are, indeed, necessary according to God's will. Faith without works is dead. Good works should not be done under compulsion, however, but willingly in obedience from the heart. Doing good works is not optional for believers (14–20).

2. Good works are necessary, but they must not be mingled with the article on justification and salvation, which rests solely on the grace of God and merit of Christ (21–29).

3. Good works are *not* necessary in order to preserve salvation, righteousness, and faith. Faith is the only means whereby these gifts are preserved by God (30–36).

4. When in false confidence people base their assurance of salvation on good works, then such works are, indeed, an impediment to salvation. But when good works are not done with this purpose in mind, they are an indication of salvation in believers. Christians are urged to do good works and are enabled by the Holy Spirit to do them. Accordingly, the position that such works are detrimental to salvation is rejected (37–40). (See also pp. 163–74.)

3. Theological Summary

- *Confessional center.* The message and doctrine of justification are at the center of Christian faith and the Lutheran confessions because: (1) in justification the relationship and communion between God and humanity and thus salvation are at stake; (2) justification is the central explication of the gospel and at the same time the decisive criterion for judging whether the teaching and structures of the church are under the gospel and serve it; (3) its focus on justification gives the Lutheran tradition one significant element of its specific profile and identity.

- *Structure of the texts on justification.* The statements in the confessions about justification are generally marked by the following three elements: (1) As elsewhere in the confessions, they affirm that no new teaching is presented. The teaching on justification is an exposition of Scripture and is in continuity and agreement with the teaching of the church throughout the centuries and the church catholic today. (2) There is the all-encompassing insistence on the sole saving initiative and activity of the triune God and the corresponding complete receptivity—but not passivity—of the human response by faith to God's gift. (3) All statements on justification have a personal and pastoral focus: the human heart, mind, and conscience are to receive peace and consolation because of the forgiveness of sins and the restored relationship with God.

- *The justifying, gracious God.* The right relationship and communion between God and human beings have been destroyed by original sin, which has corrupted human nature and the human will so deeply that humans are unable to come to God by their own efforts. The gracious God, who is also a judging and righteous God, justifies sinners unconditionally when they believe that Christ has reconciled them to God by his vicarious obedience. Communion with God is thus reestablished and its gracious benefits are given to believers by the Holy Spirit.

- *Christ—our righteousness.* Christ is the mediator. Through the vicarious and sacrificial obedience in his suffering, cross, and resurrection, Christ, who is both human and divine, has taken our sins upon himself so that they no longer separate us from God. His righteousness becomes our righteousness and we are reconciled to God.

- *The communication of justification.* Justification and forgiveness of sins come to us from outside. They are not produced or earned by our own efforts. The proclaimed Word and the sacraments celebrated in the midst of God's people are the outward means through which the Holy Spirit enables faith and through which God's justification is given and received by this faith. Through Word and Sacrament the triune God acts and effects what is promised.

- *The gift and response of faith.* The human response to justification and reconciliation is enabled solely by the Holy Spirit. This response takes the form of faith. Faith is primarily described as an attitude: trust in the promise of mercy in Christ; the firm acceptance and appropriation of God's offer of justification and forgiveness; the readiness that grasps the gift of grace and righteousness. Believers are justified by faith alone because justification is extended to us as a free gift of God, received by faith, a faith trusting that we are forgiven for Christ's sake. *By faith alone* means also that our own efforts, religious and other good works, cannot merit God's justification. Such faith and the glorious gift of grace it receives bring peace to the mind, consolation to the conscience, and new life to the heart.

- *Justification—forgiveness – reconciliation.* Justification *is* forgiveness of sins for Christ's sake and reconciliation with God through Christ. Justification happens when people, moved to faith by the Holy Spirit, are turned around and are brought back to a right relationship with God and to a life of sanctification and renewal. In this sense they are made just or righteous (i.e., effective or transformative justification) as well as accounted, reckoned, or pronounced just or righteous (i.e., forensic justification). Both belong together in one life-changing action of God.

- *Righteousness: unmerited communion with God.* Righteousness, God's gracious gift, follows from justification. It is primarily not a moral category but a relational one: to be received back into a right relationship with God. Spiritual righteousness (*iustitia spiritualis*) thus refers to the first table of the Decalogue, having fear, faith, and love toward God, trust in God, a surer knowledge of God. The reestablished communion with the triune God is enjoyed in righteousness before God.

- *Justification and sanctification.* Though justification includes forgiveness of sins and the promise of eternal life, the justified ones remain sinners. They are at the same time sinners and justified (*simul iustus et peccator*). Therefore they are in need of constant renewal and sanctification, which is the work of the Holy Spirit within them. Justification and sanctification have to be distinguished but not separated from one another. Sanctification follows justification and is concerned with living out the gifts of the Holy Spirit in spiritual and moral life.

- *Justification and good works.* Rightly understood, good works (in the sense of religious and ethical action) are necessarily related to justification. Faith without the fruit of good works is a dead faith. The new existence of the justified must include faith active in love. Again, the distinction has to be made: Good works are sinful and excluded when they are considered and undertaken as means to earn God's grace and justification. But they have their place and importance when they follow justification and are then signs of salvation. They should be done joy-fully and freely in the power of the Holy Spirit. They are pleasing to God.

- *The consequence: free and servant.* Being justified means to be liberated from the focus on oneself, one's good works, one's failures, one's bur-dened or guilty conscience, and being reoriented toward God. This implies: "A Christian is a perfectly free lord of all, subject to none." Being justified means also being reoriented in love and responsibility toward one's neighbors near and far. This implies: "A Christian is a per-fectly dutiful servant of all, subject to all."[13]

- *Overcoming the deep conflict about justification.* Official Lutheran–Roman Catholic theological dialogue in both international and national contexts since 1970 has led to the recognition "that a consensus in basic truths of the doctrine of justification exists between Lutherans and Catholics." This conclusion is stated in the *Joint Declaration on the Doc-trine of Justification,* which was prepared by representatives of the Lutheran World Federation and the Pontifical Council for Promoting Christian Unity (Geneva: LWF, 1997). This document does not claim a complete agreement on all aspects of the doctrine of justification and considers remaining differences of theological elaboration and emphasis to be acceptable. As a consequence of this agreement the condemnations by the Council of Trent (see p. 79) and by the Lutheran confessions are declared no longer applicable to the teaching of both churches as pre-sented in the *Joint Declaration.* If the Lutheran churches and the Roman Catholic Church accept the *Joint Declaration,* the major dividing conflict of the Reformation will have been overcome.

G. G.

Questions for Discussion and Further Study

1. What forms of tradition are referred to in the confessions, and how is tradition related both to Scripture and to the confessions?

2. Describe the different meanings of "law" in the confessions.

3. According to the confessions, why is the distinction between law and gospel of crucial significance for the structure of Lutheran the-ology and faith?

4. Identify the basic definitions of "gospel" in the confessions, reflect on them, and summarize the content and message of the gospel in your own words.

5. Why do the confessions emphasize the two natures of Christ?

6. The Holy Spirit has fundamental significance for Christian faith and the church. Explain this statement with reference to the confessions.

7. Describe the difference between the understanding of grace in the Lutheran confessions and the late medieval scholastic systems of grace.

8. Indicate (with examples) the way in which the doctrine of justification is applied in the confessions as the decisive criterion for evaluating Christian faith and practice.

9. In what way do the confessions support the claim that the message and doctrine of justification represent the most important explication of the gospel?

CHAPTER FIVE

The Lutheran Confessions

The Christian Community

◆

The Sacraments

1. Historical and Theological Background

One significant element of the Lutheran Reformation was its protest against certain sacramental teachings and excessive abuses in the sacramental practice of the late medieval church. This protest is reflected in the confessions, which were also clearly influenced by the development of sacramental thinking after Augustine.

Augustine* (354–430) was the first Christian thinker in the West to propose a terminology and theory of sacraments that became foundational for subsequent centuries. Central to his teaching—influenced by Neoplatonism*—is the concept of sign (*signum*): sacraments are visible signs of an invisible, divine reality. These "holy signs" (*signa sacra*) bear a likeness to those things that they signify (e.g., water washes the body and in baptism signifies a spiritual cleansing). Constitutive parts of a sacrament as sign are the *word* (which is a word of God or of Christ) and the *element*. The word defines the element and makes the sacramental action a sacrament of salvation. Hence Augustine's famous definition: "The word comes to the element and it becomes a sacrament (or: and the sacrament results), that is, a kind of visible word."[1] The Lutheran confessions positively adopt this definition by referring either to its first half (SA 3, 5; LC 4.18; 5.10) or to its second half (*verbum visibile*, Ap. 13.5). Augustine also introduced the term *res* (reality) in order to indicate the ultimate (inner) effect of the sacrament: grace

and salvation. In the sacrament an event, especially the passion of
Christ, is commemorated in such a way that what is signified is
received. Thus sacraments are effective because Christ and the Holy
Spirit act through them. Baptism and certain other sacraments have a
permanent effect on those who receive* them, later to be termed a
"sacramental character."

The debate about the sacraments between the eighth and eleventh
centuries was mainly about the relation between the sign and the signified reality. Accordingly, the nature and efficacy of sacraments were
understood either in a realistic-effective manner or in a symbolical-
spiritual sense. The church finally accepted the realistic interpretation.
In the twelfth and thirteenth centuries Augustine's two sacramental
aspects of word and element became "form" (forma), which refers to
the signifying words, and "essential matter" (materia), which refers to
the sensible things used in the celebration and whose meaning is determined by the form (the words). Peter Lombard* (c. 1100–1160) is the
next theologian who significantly shaped sacramental theory. He
clearly stood in the Augustinian tradition when he taught that every
sacrament is a sign and resembles the reality of which it is a sign. Lombard introduced the notion of cause and causality by saying that a
sacrament is the visible sign of an invisible grace of God and causes
what it signifies (efficit quod figurat). He determined that there are
seven sacraments and introduced the idea of intentio, that is, the intention of doing what the church does, of following the faith and practice
laid down by the church.

Thomas Aquinas* (c. 1224–1274), influenced by Augustine and
Lombard, clarified sacramental theory in a lasting manner. He taught
that a sacrament is a "sign of a sacred reality." Instituted as efficacious
signs and means of justifying grace and new life in Christ, sacraments
are necessary for faith and salvation. Their purpose is to initiate,
restore, and nurture the life of grace in believers, incorporate them
into the church, and confer on them the Holy Spirit. None of these
would be possible without the personal faith of the recipients. However, faith is not a major factor in scholastic* sacramental reflection.
Lutherans would later criticize this point. As signs, sacraments have
three functions: (1) commemorative of what was before, the passion of
Christ; (2) demonstrative of grace, which Christ's passion confers on us;
(3) prognostic of the future glory of eternal life. The sacramental sign

functions through sensible elements (*res sensibiles*) together with words (*verba*), which determine the meaning of the elements. To this distinction corresponds the distinction between form (*forma*) and matter (*materia*) (see above).

Thomas followed Lombard by teaching that sacraments cause what they signify (*efficiunt quod figurant*). But he went one step further by distinguishing between two kinds of effective causes: principal and instrumental causes. God in Christ is the principal cause, and the sacraments are the instrumental cause of the work of the principal cause, God. Thomas also elaborated the idea of sacramental character as participation in Christ's priesthood that is granted in baptism, confirmation, and ordination. He affirmed the number of seven sacraments and supported the concept of *ex opere operato**. What does this concept signify, and how has the number of seven sacraments emerged?

Beginning in the thirteenth century reflection on the sacraments included the concept that the grace of the sacraments was caused and conferred *ex opere operato*, "by the work performed." This means that the validity and efficacy of the sacrament depend on the grace-conferring power of the sacramental rite itself, understood as an action of Christ, and not on the merits of the recipient or the minister. This concept was a response to a problem that had existed since Augustine's defense of the efficacy and validity of Baptism and Eucharist against the Donatist* claim that unworthy ministers could not administer valid sacraments. The formula seeks to safeguard the objectivity of the sacramental action based on the belief that grace is a gift of God that is neither actuated nor obstructed by the human quality of the minister or the recipient. *Opus operatum* was often misinterpreted in popular piety and practice as a kind of spiritual automaton independent of God's action and the faith of the recipients. The Lutheran confessions reacted vehemently against such interpretations.

Up to the end of the twelfth century there was no fixed number of sacraments because there was no common definition of sacrament. It was Peter Lombard who determined that there are seven sacraments (in this order): Baptism, confirmation, Eucharist, penance, extreme unction, orders (ordination), and marriage. The Eastern (Orthodox) Church also accepted seven sacraments in the thirteenth century. The Council of Lyon in 1274 affirmed the seven sacraments, while the

Council of Florence* (1438–1445) in 1439 issued the first authoritative decree on the sacraments that (1) confirmed the number of seven sacraments, the first five given for spiritual perfection and the last two (orders and marriage) for governance and increase of the church; and (2) stated that the three essential characteristics of a sacrament were its *materia*, the elements, for example, of bread and wine; its *forma*, the words, like the words of institution; its *intentio*, the intention of the minister to do what the church does.

Within this sphere of sacramental theology and practice Luther arrived at his new Reformation insights. This process began with his inner search for the true meaning of the traditional sacrament of penance* during 1517–1519. He discovered that in the words of absolution God's promise (*promissio*) was fulfilled and that God's gracious righteousness and the unconditional gift of Christ's liberating grace were received by faith alone (*sola fide*). In 1520 he denounced the Babylonian captivity of the sacraments in medieval Catholicism (*The Babylonian Captivity of the Church*).[2] In this text he refused to consider four of the seven sacraments as sacraments, and he emphasized that the one true sacrament of God is Jesus Christ, while there are three sacramental signs—Baptism, Eucharist, and penitence. Later in the same text (as well as in the Large Catechism) Luther questioned whether penitence can be considered a sacrament because it has no instituted sign. In his longer texts of 1526 (*The Sacrament of the Body and Blood of Christ—Against the Fanatics*) and of 1528 (*Confession Concerning Christ's Supper*), which were part of his conflicts with Karlstadt* and Zwingli, Luther said little about a general concept of sacrament. He upheld Augustine's distinction between word and element, and he also used the analogous distinction between promise and the instituted visible sign. The decisive insight for him was the character of the sacraments as gospel, as gifts of God for believing people. The structure of his thinking was shaped by the relationship among promise, gift, and faith.

The reformers criticized a certain quasi-mechanical understanding of the sacraments in late medieval theology and practice in which explicit faith on the side of the recipients was not regarded as necessary as long as they put up no obstacle like a mortal sin. This understanding allowed the Eucharist to be celebrated even for the benefit of absent or deceased persons. Reformers also criticized the development by which the sacraments became a possession of the church, which distributed them like material things (especially in the case of indulgences). This led to an overemphasis on juridical aspects of sacramental life and to the neglect of God's word of promise that made a rite a sacrament. But there were also significant differences within the broader Reformation movement. Here the confessions rejected what they saw as a devaluation of sacraments by Zwingli and others who did not consider them to be means of grace. The abolition of sacraments in certain radical groups was even more strongly rejected.

2. The Confessional Texts

Augsburg Confession. Articles 5 and 7 affirm the fundamental significance of the proclaimed gospel and the distributed sacraments as means of grace through which the Holy Spirit creates faith and assembles and sustains the church (see also Ap. 24, 70). Article 8 states the traditional position that sacraments are efficacious even when administered by unworthy priests. They are efficacious because (Latin) of the institution and commandment of Christ and, according to Ap. 7/8 (28 and 47), because the priest administers the sacraments "in Christ's place and stead." Article 13 on "The Use of the Sacraments" follows the articles on the individual sacraments (9–12). It defines sacraments as *signs*, not only in an outward sense (implicitly against Zwingli), and testimonies of God's will for us with the purpose of awakening and strengthening faith; and for this reason sacraments require faith. According to Article 14 nobody should administer the sacraments without a regular call (also Ap. 14).

Apology. The Roman Confutation* accepts the above definition but requests that Lutherans agree that there are seven sacraments. Article 13 responds that the enumeration of the sacraments has varied and that their number is not an important issue (1–2, 17). The sacraments are then defined as "rites which have the command (institution) of God (*mandatum Dei*) and to which the promise of grace (*promissio gratiae*) has been added" (3; see also 6: "express command from God and a clear promise of grace"). Accordingly, the genuine sacraments are Baptism, the Lord's Supper, and absolution (the sacrament of penitence) (4). The word (of God) and the rite (sacrament) have the same effect. The word enters through the ears and the rite through the eyes to move the heart. The sacrament is thus a "visible word" or "a sort of picture of the word" (5). While confirmation and extreme unction do not have the command of God (6), ordination could be called a sacrament (10, 11), and other forms and actions might be called sacraments in a wider sense because they are not in the same way "testimonies of grace and the forgiveness of sins" (14–17). Over against the scholastic teaching of *ex opere operato* (see p. 89), which ignores personal faith (same criticism also in Ap. 12.12 and 24.12), the necessity of faith is underlined, because a promise is useless unless faith accepts it as a present reality and believes that the forgiveness of sins is actually offered (18–23). "Such use of the sacrament comforts devout and troubled minds" (22).

These reflections are taken up in Ap. 24, which defines the sacraments as "signs of grace" consisting of two parts: the sign (*signum*) and the word (*verbum*). The word is the added promise of grace, the promise of the forgiveness of sins. Yet without faith the ceremony is useless. Therefore the word was given to arouse faith, and the sacrament was "instituted to move the heart to believe through what it presents to the eyes. For the Holy Spirit works through the Word and the sacrament" (69, 70).

Large Catechism. Luther liked Augustine's formula: "The word comes to the element and the sacrament results" (see p. 87). He quotes it in LC 4.18, 5.10, and SA 3, 5 as stating the constitutive function of the word for the sacrament. In LC 4 we find a response to "the new spirits" (Anabaptists* and some Zwinglians*) who regarded external forms as less important or even superfluous. Luther stressed that faith must have something to believe, to which it may cling, and upon which it may stand. God has implanted his word in external ordinances and does everything in us through such external means in order that grace and salvation can be grasped by the senses and thus brought into the heart (28–31).

3. Theological Summary

- *An open concept.* The Lutheran confessions, like the early church, do not start and operate with a formally defined concept of sacrament that would then determine how many rites or actions should be considered and counted as sacraments. Rather, the confessions proceed from the main sacraments that they inherited, and by reflecting on them they arrive at the contours of a sacramental theology.

- *Continuing the tradition.* The confessions are obviously influenced by the tradition of the church since Augustine with respect to certain sacramental terms and concepts: the notion of sign, the connection between word (form) and element (matter), and the efficacy of the sacraments being independent of the moral quality of minister or recipient (the true meaning of *ex opere operato*).

- *An open number.* The absence of a fixed concept of sacrament also led to a certain openness concerning the number of sacraments. For the confessions sacraments in the strict sense are Baptism and the Lord's Supper and, according to Melanchthon*, possibly also absolution and ordination. Luther seems to prefer the two major sacraments only.

- *Means of grace.* Sacraments are constituted by two essential elements: a command (institution, mandate) of God, and a divine promise of grace. Both elements stress that sacraments are an action of God alone and not a human work. They are effective signs and pledges of God's grace and through them forgiveness of sins and communion with Christ are given.

- *Word and elements.* The reformers were not interested in the symbolical significance that the elements as such may have in their sacramental context. Rather, the meaning and impact of the outward elements are determined by the Word alone, that is, by God's word of promise, grace, and forgiveness. Only together with the Word do the elements become means of grace.

- *Effective signs.* Sacraments are not signs pointing toward a reality from which they are separated. They are, on the contrary, effective signs that participate in the reality to which they point. They communicate the reality signified; as signs of salvation they are saving signs as instruments of the saving work of the trinitarian God.

- *Sacraments and faith.* The greatest difference between the confessions and scholastic theology lies probably in the strong emphasis that the confessions place on faith. According to their institution sacraments are directed toward, and are received by, faith because their purpose is to strengthen faith, forgive sins, and comfort troubled consciences, and they require faith on the side of the recipients in order to fulfill this purpose. They have a clear personal and pastoral focus.

- *Proclamation and sacrament.* Proclamation of the Word and Sacrament are two equally efficacious means of God's saving action. Together they communicate the same undivided gift of salvation. But they do this in different ways, and in their diversity they represent the richness of God's grace, which is offered to the whole human person with all the senses. With the sacraments God has chosen elements of creation to communicate the gospel and thus addresses human beings differently from the spoken Word. Contemporary theological developments are helping to overcome a tendency in Roman Catholicism to overestimate the sacraments over against the Word and an opposite tradition in Protestantism to underestimate the sacraments over against the Word.

◆

Baptism

1. Historical and Theological Background

To uphold the tradition of the church and to regard the Sacrament of Baptism as indispensable and foundational for Christian life and ecclesial community—this was the clear intention of the Lutheran Reformation that is also reflected in its confessions. This intention included the acceptance of the practice of infant baptism. With the rapid expansion of the early church the practice of infant baptism, attested around the year 200, became gradually universal in the fourth and fifth centuries. Contributing to this general acceptance was Augustine's teaching about original sin against Pelagius*, who denied original sin and saw no need to baptize infants. Following Augustine, the Synod of Carthage in 418 decreed that infants must be baptized so that original sin would be remitted by this sacrament. In the sixteenth century infant baptism was rejected by some of the radical movements. This was the first time that infant baptism was programmatically rejected.

The general acceptance of infant baptism had implications for the structure of the rite of Christian initiation. This rite is most explicitly described in the Apostolic Tradition* (c. 215) of Hippolytus of Rome (c. 170–c. 236), which includes a long (up to three years!) period of catechetical instruction that was no longer possible when infant baptism became general practice. The baptismal rite consists of the renunciation of the devil and the acceptance of Christ, water baptism with the trinitarian confession and formula, a first anointing with chrism (blessed oil), presentation of the newly baptized to the congregation together with a second anointing and episcopal laying on of hands with prayer for the Holy Spirit, and finally the first participation in the Eucharist. Because bishops could no longer participate in every baptism in an expanding church, the part of the rite with episcopal anointing and laying on of hands had to be postponed to a later stage in the life of a young person. Beginning in the sixth century and generally from the twelfth century on, this new rite was called confirmation (*confirmatio*). The Council of Florence decreed in 1439 that confirmation was the second sacrament. In the Eastern (Orthodox) Church the unity of the initiation rite with its different elements has been preserved.

Augustine laid the foundations of a baptismal theology. Especially influential was his teaching that through baptism guilt and original sin are remitted and only a certain weakness, an evil desire (*mala concupiscentia*), remains. According to his basic sacramental formula (see p. 87), the sacrament comes into being when the word, that is, the baptismal formula, is added to the element, the water that outwardly signifies the inner effect of grace. Baptism by heretics is valid if administered in the correct form, yet the grace of baptism is received only within the Catholic Church. Consequently, baptism is not to be repeated when heretics reenter the church. This distinction between the sign and the reality signified became influential again. Against the Donatists the Council of Arles in 314 declared baptism by heretics valid, and this council as well as the Council of Nicea* in 325 rejected rebaptism. In scholasticism Augustine's teaching was upheld in many respects. The new (Aristotelian) terminology was used, according to which the form (*forma*) of baptism is the baptismal formula, and the matter (*materia*) is the water and the act of sprinkling or immersion. Thomas Aquinas applied his teaching on sacramental causality (see p. 89) to baptism and affirms that in baptism the trinitarian God is the principal cause and the baptismal water the instrumental cause. Through the infusion of a supernatural habitus the grace of baptism makes the baptized acceptable to God and provides the basis for all other sacraments.

Luther located baptism within the framework of promise (*promissio*) and faith (*fides*). In baptism the word of promise that forgives sins is to be received by faith. Baptism is not the work of simply performing the ritual action, but it is the free gift of drowning the old Adam and raising the regenerated person to a new life with Christ. Luther and the confessions continued to confirm infant baptism and much of the inherited baptismal theology but gave it new emphases. Both Luther and the confessions reacted vehemently against the theology and practice of baptism in radical movements. On the basis of their spiritualistic understanding of faith, the adherents of such movements rejected outward forms, including baptism, because they were not considered necessary for true and pure faith. The confessions also condemn the rejection of infant baptism by the Anabaptists, who saw no biblical justification for such baptism and required conscious faith in those to be baptized as a condition for baptism.

2. The Confessional Texts

Augsburg Confession. Article 9 on baptism states two basic convictions: (1) baptism is necessary for salvation and through it God's grace is offered; (2) children, too, should be baptized so that they are received into God's grace. The Anabaptists were condemned because they rejected the baptism of infants and children.

Apology. Article 9 underlines the necessity of infant baptism with these arguments: (1) It is certain that the promise of salvation also applies to (little) children according to Christ's command (Matt 28:19) because baptism is offered to all groups of people (1 and 2). (2) It is evident that God approves the baptism of children because God gives the Holy Spirit to those who were baptized as children. If such baptism were invalid the Holy Spirit would not be given to anybody; nobody would have been saved, and there would be no church. These arguments are made against the "ungodly and fanatical opinion of the Anabaptists" (3).

Smalcald Articles. Part 3, article 5, emphasizes that baptism is commanded by Christ's institution; Luther defines it as "the Word of God in water" and quotes Augustine's definition (see p. 87). He criticizes the teaching of scholastic theologians like Thomas, Duns Scotus*, and others for ignoring the fundamental significance of God's Word for the sacrament. He argues that children should be baptized because they too are included in Christ's promise of redemption.

Small Catechism. In part 4 Luther explicates baptism in four steps: (1) It is water used according to God's command and connected with God's Word (in Matt 28:19). (2) It effects forgiveness, delivers from death and the devil, and grants salvation to all who believe the word and promise of God. (3) This effect is realized by the Word of God connected with the water. With the Word the water becomes baptism, a gracious water of life and a washing of regeneration in the Holy

Spirit, so that, according to Paul, we might be justified and become heirs in hope of eternal life. (4) Baptism with water signifies that the old Adam in us, with all its sins, is drowned and a new human being comes forth daily to rise up and live forever in God's presence. *Large Catechism.* Part 4 contains the most detailed presentation of baptism in the confessions. After asserting that without the sacraments nobody can be a Christian and that by baptism we are first received into the Christian community, Luther treats baptism in three sections.

1. *Nature of baptism.* God commanded and ordained baptism (Matt 28:19; Mark 16:16); it is of divine origin, and its institution by God includes the commandment that we must be baptized in order to be saved. Over against radical reformers, who say that baptism as an external thing is useless, God's commandment and institution make baptism a precious and glorious gift and God's own work (2–13). Baptism is water comprehended in God's word and commandment; it is a divine, holy, blessed water when God's word is added to the element (Augustine's definition). Accordingly, the word and the water must by no means be separated from each other; only together are they Christ's baptism (14–22).

2. *Purpose and benefits of baptism.* The power, benefit, fruit, and purpose of baptism are to save, that is, to deliver one from sin, death, and the devil and to enter into the kingdom of Christ and live with him forever. Through God's word baptism receives the power to become the "washing of regeneration" (Titus 3:5; LC 4.23–27). "Thus faith clings to the water and believes it to be baptism in which there is sheer salvation and life." God has implanted God's Word in this external ordinance so that we may grasp the treasure it contains. Whoever rejects baptism rejects God's Word and Christ (28–31).

3. *Who receives baptism.* Faith alone makes a person worthy to receive the blessings of baptism because the words that accompany the water (and make it a sacrament) can be received only by faith. Without faith, baptism is of no use (LC 4.32–37). Since God's promise is bound to baptism, it becomes more glorious than anything else God has commanded, full of comfort and grace. It imparts the entire Christ and the Holy Spirit, and it is a priceless medicine for one's whole life. When troubled by sin or doubt the believer is comforted by the reminder "I am baptized." Through baptism body and soul shall obtain holiness and salvation (38–46).

Part 4 of the Large Catechism also deals with infant baptism. Against the Anabaptists, who reject infant baptism, it affirms, first, that the baptism of infants is pleasing to Christ because God has sanctified many who have been thus baptized and has given them the Holy Spirit. Otherwise, nobody would have become Christian and there would be no Christian church (47–51, same argument as Ap. 9). Second, baptism does not depend on the faith of the baptized but on the word and commandment of God. Even when faith is lacking, baptism is valid and there should be no rebaptism. Faith does not constitute baptism but receives it. Even if infants did not believe, which is not the case according to Luther, their baptism would still be valid. Since one should approach the sacraments trusting not in one's faith but alone in God's Word, children should also be brought to baptism with the purpose and hope that they may believe and that God may grant them faith. They should not be baptized on that account, however, but because God has commanded it (52–63).

The concluding section of LC 4 spells out that baptism, by which people are received into the church, has lifelong significance for Christians. Immersion into the water and rising out of it signify the slaying of the old Adam and the resurrection of the new human being that must continue throughout our life. "Thus a Christian life is nothing else than a daily baptism, once begun and ever continued." It is a lifelong struggle against sin and a lifelong growth in faith. Because of its significance for one's entire life, according to Luther baptism comprehends the third sacrament, formerly called penance, which is nothing else than walking in the new life received in baptism (LC 4.64–86; see also in this chapter, pp. 100–108).

3. Theological Summary

- *Necessity of baptism.* In discussing baptism but also when dealing with other topics, the confessions affirm the priority of God's action, the gracious movement from God to human beings in Christ Jesus through the Holy Spirit. Baptism has been commanded and instituted by God in Christ (Matt 28:19). It has God's promise and is necessary for salvation (Mark 16:16).

- *Baptism as God's action.* Though administered by humans (in the name of the Trinity), baptism is truly God's action: God uses human words and created elements as instruments.

- *Word and water in baptism.* The water (element) and the word of God (command and promise) are intimately connected in baptism and must not be separated. Together they form the sacrament. This corresponds to Augustine's definition of a sacrament (see p. 87). Water as such is not efficacious, but water comprehended by the word becomes a precious and holy water of life.

- *Effect of baptism.* Through God's action in baptism people are brought into the church and become children of God. Through this bath of regeneration they are led into a new life with Christ. God grants in baptism forgiveness of sins and eternal salvation, and those who are baptized receive comfort and strength, grace and consolation. Baptism delivers from death and the devil, and provides rich blessings. The baptized are led into the kingdom of Christ and receive the Holy Spirit and the gifts of the Spirit.

- *Baptism and faith.* Baptism and faith are interrelated. Faith is necessary for receiving the blessings of baptism. But the validity of baptism, when celebrated according to God's command and promise, does not depend on the faith of the baptized or of the one who baptizes.

- *Faith and outward elements.* The unity of the visible and tangible water and the audible word is an expression of God's way of communicating the divine grace through outward ordinances and forms. In this way God's Word appeals to all human senses, the mind and the heart, and believers are enabled to grasp the treasure contained in such outward forms. This is an aid to faith. We can be confident that everything that God does within us is accomplished through outward means.

- *Dying and rising in baptism.* Baptism symbolizes the drowning of the old Adam (by immersion into the water) and the rising of the baptized (by coming out of the water) to new life with Christ (Rom 6:4). The memory of this should always mark Christian life and make it a daily baptism.

- *Lifelong character of baptism.* The reality of baptism extends over the whole life of a baptized person. Baptism is not a temporary moment in the past but remains valid throughout one's lifetime. This lasting reality of baptism excludes rebaptism. Burdened by sin and distress, a Christian should remember: I am baptized, I have the sign of my consolation and salvation!

- *Infant baptism.* The confessions support infant baptism with these arguments:

    1. Infants and children are included in God's command to baptize and in the promise of salvation. This gift is offered to all people and children should not be excluded (Matt 19:14; Acts 2:39; Matt 28:19).

2. Baptism of infants and children is affirmed by God because they have received the Holy Spirit and have lived as Christians. The church could have endured only if their baptism is valid.

3. A valid baptism does not depend on the presence or absence of faith in the baptized, either in adults or in children. But infants and children are brought intentionally to baptism in the confidence that they will believe, and God is asked to grant them faith.

4. Through baptism adults as well as children are accepted into the Christian church.

- *Praise of baptism.* Christians are called to rejoice in God's gift of baptism and to honor and esteem the sacrament, for it is the most valuable and glorious treasure one can receive. It is a free and heavenly medicine, the most precious jewel for body and soul.

- *Conclusion for today.* The Sacrament of Holy Baptism is constitutive of Christian existence. It grounds life in a deeper and firmer foundation than human possibilities could ever provide: the incarnation, death, and resurrection of Jesus Christ. Through baptism, God effects a change of personal situation from hopeless self-centeredness to the glorious liberty and confidence of the children of God. The baptism of children symbolizes in a particular way God's unconditional and gratuitous acceptance and grace. Baptism remains a lifelong point of orientation and consolation and a lifelong challenge to repentance and renewal in a life of service to others. The sacrament incorporates the baptized into the worldwide communion of Christ's church and is a fundamental sign of the unity of this church. Baptism is already in this life a pledge and foretaste of eternal life.

◆

Repentance, Confession, and Absolution

1. Historical and Theological Background

During its first centuries the church recognized that Christians remained sinful after their baptism and that acts of forgiveness of sins and reconciliation with God and with the church were necessary. This recognition led to forms of repentance, confession, and absolution. One particular form was the public penance for grave sins; it followed specific regulations (therefore also called canonical penance), it was unrepeatable and entailed long and heavy penalties. A more pastoral and personal form of penance, which could be repeated, was introduced by Anglo-Irish monks and then exported to the European continent in the sixth century. In the Middle Ages this private confession, in place of public confession, became more and more the rule. In early scholasticism some theologians like Peter Abelard* (1079–1142) regarded priestly absolution merely as confirmation of the forgiveness already achieved by the sincere contrition of the penitent. Later, in high scholasticism, this understanding was contested, and theologians like Duns Scotus (1266–1308) emphasized priestly absolution itself as the operative element in the sacrament.

Over against the different positions Thomas Aquinas clarified the sacrament of penance by defining its matter (*materia*) as contrition, confession, and satisfaction of the penitent (*contritio, confessio,* and *satisfactio*) and its form (*forma*) as absolution (*absolutio*) by the priest. For Thomas the imperfect attrition (*attritio*) or sorrow produced by fear of divine punishment was sufficient preparation for the reception* of the sacrament, but in the course of confession attrition became perfect contrition (*contritio*), that is, sorrow for sin grounded in love of God. Later William of Ockham* (c. 1285–c. 1349) and Gabriel Biel* (c. 1410–1495) held that people can arrive at contrition by their natural efforts (*facere quod in se est**) and that God responds in absolution with the forgiveness of sins. After the Fourth Lateran Council* in 1215 penance became an obligatory sacrament (at least once a year), necessary for salvation, at which the enumeration of all sins was required. The teaching of Thomas was accepted by the Council of Florence in 1439 and then by the Council of Trent* (Session 14, 1551). Trent declared that penance was a sacrament instituted by Christ and consisted of three acts by the penitent—contrition, confession, and satisfaction—and the pronouncement of absolution by the priest.

The Lutheran Reformation agreed with the tradition of the church by teaching that continual repentance for sins after baptism and absolution were necessary and possible. Therefore, private confession was to be retained. Luther declared in the first of his Ninety-five Theses* (1517) that repentance must be a permanent feature of the Christian life. He and other reformers rejected the formalized system of penance that obscured the unmerited gift of God's forgiveness. In the everyday life of the church this system burdened the consciences of people by demanding harsh religious and material satisfactions; and it was mixed up with the horrible scheme of indulgences. For Luther the foundation of penance was not the human activity of contrition, confession, and satisfaction, but the authoritative declaration of the promise of God's forgiveness and grace received by faith. Since this promise was already an inherent part of the baptismal promise, Luther associated the sacrament of penance with the Sacrament of Baptism. Still, he continued to affirm the need and significance of private confession and absolution.

2. The Confessional Texts

Augsburg Confession. Article 11 on confession teaches that private confession and absolution should be retained but that a complete enumeration of sins (see Fourth Lateran Council above) is not necessary. Article 12 on repentance states that those who sin after baptism receive forgiveness of sin when they repent. True repentance consists of contrition and faith in the gospel and of absolution. It should be followed by good works (in the Latin text), which are the fruits of repentance. Condemned are (1) Anabaptists and others who deny that those who have been justified can lose the Holy Spirit (Latin text); (2) the third-century Novatians, who refused absolution to those who had sinned after baptism; (3) all those (i.e., Roman Catholic theologians) who teach that forgiveness is obtained (Latin text: merited) by human satisfaction.

Article 25 of the Augsburg Confession, also on confession, confirms that private confession and absolution are upheld by the evangelical* side and that this is also a prerequisite for receiving the Eucharist. People are taught to regard absolution highly because it is not simply a human word but the Word of God spoken in God's stead and by God's command. It is the power of the keys* necessary for comforting terrified consciences. Absolution requires faith because through such faith forgiveness is received. Forgiveness is granted without the burdensome demands of enumerating sins, of satisfactions, indulgences, and pilgrimages (1–6). The article repeats that people should not be compelled to present a detailed account of their sins because it is neither possible nor commanded by Holy Scripture. But confession is to be retained for the sake of absolution, "which is its chief and most important part" (7–13).

Apology. Article 11 responds to the Roman Confutation's approval of the continuation of confession and absolution in the churches of the Augsburg Confession and to the reassertion of the confutation that confession be made annually and that people should enumerate all their sins. The response invites believers to use the sacraments often, but a set time is not prescribed nor is an enumeration of sins necessary according to divine law (3–10). Ap. 11 highlights in its introduction the great consolation and encouragement that believers have received from evangelical teaching. It is, indeed, the command of God and the very voice of the gospel that the faithful should believe the absolution and that the forgiveness of sins is granted freely for Christ's sake (1 and 2).

Article 12 of the Apology continues the debate. It is the second longest article in the Apology and this indicates the importance of the theme. The Roman Confutation had accepted the first part of CA 12: those who have sinned after baptism can obtain the forgiveness of sin. The second part of CA 12, however, which confesses that repentance consists of two parts—contrition and faith—is strongly rejected. Melanchthon regards this rejection as a condemnation of the voice of the gospel and an insult to Christ's redemptive suffering for us (1–3).

After this prelude we can distinguish six parts of this article. The first part argues that the teaching of scholastic theologians on the sacrament of penance is full of error and obscures the blessings of Christ, the power of the keys, and the righteousness of faith. It is foreign to Holy Scripture and the church fathers (4–27). In part two (28–43) the position of the Augsburg Confession that penitence has two parts, to which a third part—fruits worthy of penitence—could be added, is repeated against the scholastics. The two parts, contrition and faith (*contritio et fides*), are related to the distinction between *law* (as judge leading to contrition) and *gospel*. Faith in the promise of the gospel obtains forgiveness of sins and justifies before God. The power of the keys administers and offers this gospel through absolution. "Therefore we must believe the voice of the one absolving no less than we would believe a voice coming from heaven" (40). According to Melanchthon, absolution "may properly be called a sacrament of penitence" (41).

The third part of Ap. 12 (44–58) goes on to show how the two parts of penitence and with them the distinction between law and gospel are related and grounded in Scripture. It concludes with the important statement that there are two chief works of God (*praecipua opera Dei*) to be found throughout Scripture: "One part is the law, which reveals, denounces, and condemns sin. The other part is the gospel, that is, the promise and grace granted in Christ" (53; see pp. 55–64 on law and gospel). These two parts are also found in the lives of the biblical saints (54–58). The fourth part (59–97) responds to the confutation's denial that people obtain forgiveness by faith: Forgiveness does not come *ex opere operato* because of contrition or because of our love and works. Rather, it comes through "special faith" (*fides specialis*), that is, not a general but a personal faith by which people believe that their sins are forgiven because of Christ. Thus there is a close relation, through faith, between the doctrine of penance and the doctrine of justification (see pp. 75–85).

The fifth part of Ap. 12 deals with the remaining aspects of the debate about penance: the enumeration of sins and satisfaction. After reaffirming the continuous practice and high esteem of private confession and absolution as the Word of God proclaimed through the power of the keys by divine authority (98–101), the text explains again (see CA 11 and 25.7–13) why an enumeration of sins in confession (102–12) and canonical satisfaction are not necessary by divine right for the forgiveness of sins and therefore are not a part of penitence (113–39). The death of Christ is the true and only satisfaction not just for guilt but also for eternal death. No works of supererogation (*opera supererogationis*) can render satisfaction to God's law and wrath. The genuine punishment for sins is the whole process of penitence, not works of satisfaction. Patristic* writings and conciliar decisions show that all those forms of satisfaction that used to be imposed were not necessary for the remission of guilt and its punishment. Even less does the gospel command that canonical satisfaction or nonobligatory works be performed as compensation for punishment (140–73). The long article ends with two additional and specific points: (1) a list of the spiritual and moral fruits of penitence; (2) a clarification of the tasks and limits of the power of keys exercised by the ministers of the gospel (174–77).

Smalcald Articles. Part 3, article 3 deals with repentance and elaborates the function of the law stated in article 2. The law, which reveals one's complete sinfulness, leads to passive contrition, true sorrow of the heart, and thereby to the beginning of repentance by recognizing the need for radical change. The consoling promise of grace in the gospel is immediately added to this office of the law. With the gospel comes consolation and forgiveness through the Word, the sacraments, and other means (SA 3, 3.1–9; see also 3, 4). A longer section on "the false repentance of the Papists" identifies the basic fault of scholastic teaching: its understanding of original sin. It allows that natural human powers like human will and reason have remained whole and uncorrupted. Accordingly, God will grant grace and forgiveness in response to repentance, confession, and satisfaction of a person understood in this way. People thus place confidence in their own works, while Christ and faith are not mentioned (10–14). The three parts of the Roman sacrament of penance—contrition, confession, and satisfaction—are criticized for their theological error and their pastorally devastating impact (15–29).

In contrast, SA 3, 3 affirms that the proper and straightforward understanding of repentance starts from the confession that we are wholly and altogether sinful. This understanding of repentance does not trust in anything that we are and do, no longer has its foundation in good works and the law, and is no longer rendered uncertain by its acts of satisfaction but relies completely on the suffering and blood of the innocent Lamb of God. Such repentance struggles throughout one's life with the sin that remains (30–41). A final section reacts against the position of radical reformers (with an implicit reference to the Peasants' War* of 1525), who claim that those who have received the Holy Spirit or the forgiveness of sins will persevere in faith and that sin will not harm them anymore (see CA 12.7). If people fall into open and persistent sin, Luther responds, then faith and the Spirit have indeed departed from them, because the Holy Spirit does not permit sin to rule and gain the upper hand (42–45).

Part 3, article 7 of the Smalcald Articles affirms the function and power of the keys given to the church by Christ to bind and loose sins (i.e., absolution). This is followed by article 8 on confession. Because absolution, instituted by Christ, is a consolation and help against sin, private confession and absolution should be continued and highly esteemed in the church (1 and 2). The remaining and much longer part of SA 3, 8 (3–13) declares that such absolution comes to us by the external, spoken word (which means that nobody can absolve herself or himself). On this basis the article rejects the position of "enthusiasts*" or "spiritualists," like the radical reformer Thomas Müntzer* (c. 1491–1525), who claim to have received the Holy Spirit either without or prior to the Word. Rather, "God will not deal with us except through his external Word and Sacrament" (10). Article 9 on excommunication—excluding manifest and impenitent sinners from the sacrament until they change their ways—complements the two preceding articles.

Small Catechism. Part 5 is an instruction of "plain people" about the meaning and practice of confession and absolution. On its meaning Luther says that confession has two parts: (1) to confess sins in both a general and a specific manner; and (2) to "receive absolution or forgiveness from the confessor as from God himself," firmly believing that our sins are forgiven (15–20). Luther then proposes a practical and pastoral form of confession (21–29).

Large Catechism. Part 4 on baptism contains the important conclusion that baptism, "both by its power and by its signification, comprehends also the third sacrament, formerly called Penance, which is really nothing else than Baptism" (74). This conclusion is based on Luther's emphasis on the lifelong relevance of baptism and its implication that repentance is a continuous return to baptism and its promise (75–86).

"A Brief Exhortation to Confession" was added to LC 5 on "The Sacrament of the Altar" in the 1529 revised edition of the catechism. The Exhortation begins by claiming that three abuses have been corrected: (1) coercing people to make confession; (2) the burdensome demand to enumerate all sins; and (3) the absence of any teaching about how comforting and useful confession is (1–4). The new freedom is, however, misused by some, who no longer see a need for confession and absolution and thereby exclude themselves from the church. But all others still need to be exhorted, encouraged, and instructed. Two kinds of common confession are expressed in the Lord's Prayer: confessing sins to God and to our neighbor (8–12). Besides this public, daily confession there is secret, private confession. Here God, through a human being, absolves from sin. This confession consists of two parts: first, the human act of lamenting my own sin and desiring comfort and restoration for my soul; second and decisive (!) is the work of God, which absolves me of my sins through a human word (13–15). The rest of the text (16–35) is mainly joyful and inviting praise of the surprisingly grand and noble thing that makes this confession and absolution so wonderful and comforting, a great and precious treasure to be accepted with gratitude. Absolution is something to which everybody should freely and gladly run more than a hundred miles. "Therefore, when I urge you to go to confession, I am simply urging you to be a Christian" (32).

3. Theological Summary

- *Pastoral application of law and gospel.* The theme of repentance, confession, and absolution occupies a remarkably broad space in the Lutheran confessions. This indicates the great significance that Luther, Melanchthon, and other reformers attributed to this theme. The center of Reformation teaching is at stake when it comes to the question of whether and how Christians prepare themselves for the forgiveness of sins and how they receive it. In other words, the teaching of the confessions on repentance, confession, and absolution is intimately bound up with the central Reformation doctrines of law and gospel and of justification by faith alone: it is the pastoral application of these two doctrines.

- *Luther and Melanchthon.* In the *Book of Concord* Luther and Melanchthon differ somewhat in their teaching on repentance. In CA 12 and Ap. 12 and within the series of sacraments described in CA 9–13, Melanchthon treats repentance, closely connected with the preceding article 11 on confession and absolution, as a separate sacramental act. Accordingly, Melanchthon can express the connection between repentance and confession and absolution by saying (in Ap. 12. 41) that "absolution may properly be called a sacrament of penitence" (using the traditional terminology). But Melanchthon also clearly emphasizes God's promise of the gospel as spoken through human words in the absolution. Here he agrees with Luther, who nevertheless loosens repentance from its close connection with confession and absolution and links it instead with baptism, which encompasses a lifelong penitential return to the baptismal promise and gift. Luther focuses on confession and absolution. He purifies the concept of confession from its late medieval condition of performing meritorious works of satisfaction and puts all the emphasis on absolution as the liberating and justifying Word of God, administered by the office of the keys.

- *Continuity and renewal of theological orientation.* The Lutheran confessions have not abolished the teaching of the church throughout the centuries concerning the need for repentance and public and private confession and absolution. They have, however, radically changed the ways in which repentance, confession, and absolution were understood and practiced in the late medieval church. They rejected the role of human efforts, possibilities, and good works, along with coercion, oppressive laws, and regulations. Central to the confessions are God's law, which leads to contrition, and God's gospel, which is the promise and declaration—in the words of absolution—of God's free gift of grace and forgiveness for the sake of Christ. The words of absolution not only declare but actually constitute a new reality within which repentance and active personal renewal are possible. This gift of reconciling sinners with God—justification—is communicated by the Holy Spirit to all who confidently believe that here, and here alone, is granted the life-renewing release from all that burdens and limits them. Such a transforming action of God in confession and absolution has, according to the confessions, sacramental character.

- *Significance for today.* This broad, joyful, and energetic emphasis on repentance, confession, and absolution in the confessions stands in sharp contrast to the marginal role that these important elements of Christian faith and life have played in many Lutheran churches. Still, efforts have been made in recent decades to recover the reality and practice of repentance, private and corporate confession, and absolution. This recovery could be significant for contemporary societies where many people suffer heavy psychic pressures, broken relationships, terrifying personal experiences, and hopeless life situations. In this context the Christian practice of confession and absolution can transcend all internal human efforts to overcome such problems. Coming from outside ourselves (*extra nos*), God's word of absolution and assurance reaches the deepest levels of human existence. This word, immensely more powerful than mere human words, leads to healing, reconciliation, and a new self-awareness of peace with oneself and responsible relations with others. Penance, confession, and absolution are also increasingly seen and called for as a social task. They can contribute to the resolution of conflicts, which often have religious elements, between social, ethnic, and religious groups. The Lutheran tradition with its resources in the confessions can render a healing service in addressing these personal and social situations.

◆

The Eucharist

1. Historical and Theological Background

The Lutheran Reformation and its confessions continued to affirm the teaching of the church about Christ's real presence in the Lord's Supper. But one dominant interpretation of this doctrine, transubstantiation, was rejected as an inappropriate attempt to explain something that is truly a mystery. In the early Middle Ages, when Aristotelian concepts replaced the patristic (and Platonic) understanding of symbol, which held together symbol (*figura*) and reality (*veritas*) or sign and signified reality (the sign participates in the signified reality), the relation between the eucharistic signs of bread and wine and the signified reality of Christ's body and blood became the subject of controversy. The extreme solutions that were proposed in this controversy from the ninth to the eleventh century sound like an anticipation of inner-Reformation conflicts five hundred years later: Paschasius Radbertus* (c. 790–860) taught a crudely physical presence of Christ's body and blood in the eucharistic elements, while Berengar of Tours* (c. 1010–1088) allegedly deemphasized the connection between the eucharistic gifts and Christ's body and blood, which remained in heaven. Berengar was, however, forced to affirm in 1059 and again in 1079 not only a eucharistic realism but also a change in the elements. Afterward there began to emerge a compromise between Paschasius's extreme physicalism and Berengar's symbolism.

From the thirteenth century on this solution was called "transubstantiation" and found, with the help of Aristotelian categories, its classical formulation in Thomas Aquinas: The substance or essence (*substantia* or *forma substantialis*) of bread and wine are transformed—transubstantiated—into the substances of Christ's body and blood, while the outward appearance (*accidens*) of bread and of wine remain. This interpretation of the sacramental presence of Christ in the Eucharist did not entail a physical presence (contact of quantity with quantity) but a metaphysical mode of presence (as the soul is present in the body). The validity of this sacrament was achieved *ex opere operato*, by the work performed (see p. 89). The Fourth Lateran Council in

1215 declared the doctrine of transubstantiation part of the faith of the church. During this period four other aspects of eucharistic theology and practice became prominent:

1. Already in early scholasticism, after the changes in the sacramental concept of sign and reality (see above), the eucharistic mystery was increasingly divided into the sacrament of the real presence of Christ (which became the dogma of transubstantiation), and the sacrament as sacrifice, which was understood as an image or allegory of Christ's passion and, accordingly, as a sacrificial action. In the late Middle Ages this sacrificial action was often understood as a bloodless repetition, a reenactment or complement of Christ's sacrifice on the cross, to be offered by the priest as a propitiatory sacrifice for the remission of sins and other needs not only of the living but also of the dead. This practice, which many scholastic theologians disowned, was rejected in the confessions as unbiblical and making the sacrament into a human work. The concept of the Eucharist as sacrifice was decreed as a dogma by the Council of Trent (Session 22, 1562) with less extreme formulations.

2. This belief that one could apply the benefits of the sacrifice of the Mass to absent people, alive or dead, led to a multiplication of private votive masses ordered and endowed for special purposes and celebrated by the priest alone. The confessions rejected such masses as contradicting Christ's institution of the sacrament for people who were present and received it.

3. The predominant focus on the humanity of Christ in both transubstantiation and the sacrifice of the Mass influenced also late medieval eucharistic piety. Since people could not understand Latin they were reduced to being silent spectators at the Mass. They seldom received Communion (during the thirteenth century perhaps only once a year). Some compensation was provided by paying devotion to the reserved sacrament (beginning in the eleventh century) and by displaying it in processions and using it later in benedictions. Again, these forms were rejected by the confessions as human and imposed inventions.

4. People received communion not only infrequently but also, from the thirteenth century on, only in one kind, the bread, while the priests were allowed to receive bread and wine. The danger of spilling the wine (Christ's blood) was given as the reason for this practice. Hussites* in Bohemia who challenged this tradition demanded distribution under both species (*sub utraque*). These Utraquists* were condemned by the Council of Constance in 1415; and the Council of Trent in Session 21,

1562, decreed that under each kind the whole Christ and thus the true sacrament was received (the doctrine of concomitance*). This doctrine and practice were firmly rejected by the confessions as contradicting Christ's institution of the Lord's Supper.

Modern historical research has shown that the confessions attacked, in fact, popular and extreme forms of late medieval theology and practice while regarding them as official Catholic teaching. Nevertheless, it is admitted that the protest of the confessions was justified and liberating for many people. Luther opposed the late medieval system at no other point so hotly as in the case of the Roman doctrine of the Mass. While unambiguously affirming the real presence, he radically restated eucharistic doctrine by emphasizing the unmerited character of the gift of this gracious gospel sacrament, the communal nature of the sacrament, the need to receive it frequently, the fundamental role of the words of institution (as Christ's institution, command, and promise), and the essential response of faith. Luther refused to explain the "how" of Christ's presence, emphasizing instead trust in Christ's promise of his saving presence, and the great and comforting benefits of receiving the sacrament.

Yet there was conflict about the Lord's Supper not only between Lutherans and the late medieval church. This sacrament was also at the center of Lutheran-Reformed relations. All efforts to preserve or restore the unity between different Reformation movements— Lutheran, south German cities, Zwinglian, and Calvinist—sought an agreement in faith. Such agreement depended decisively, particularly for Lutherans, on a consensus on the Lord's Supper and specifically on the real presence of Christ's body and blood. The division between Lutheran and Reformed churches that developed before the middle of the sixteenth century was to a large degree a consequence of their disagreement about the Eucharist (see FC 7 and 8).

The main stages of discussion about the Lord's Supper were:

1. Marburg Colloquy* (1529): Luther and Zwingli, together with other representatives of both sides, were able to reach agreement on fourteen articles of faith, but in the framework of the fifteenth article they could not overcome the difference "as to whether the true body and blood of Christ are in the bread and wine bodily." Zwingli could not accept Luther's insistence on a substantial and essential presence (*substantive et essentialiter*).

2. Wittenberg Concord* (1536): This concord, which owed a great deal to the persistence of Martin Bucer*, expressed an agreement between Lutherans and the churches in the major south German cities. It described the real presence as a sacramental union in which the body and blood of Christ are truly and substantially (vere et substantialiter) present, offered, and received with (cum) the bread and wine. Despite the efforts of Bucer, this concord was not accepted by the Swiss churches.

3. Consensus Tigurinus* (1549): In Zurich John Calvin* and Heinrich Bullinger* (1504–1575) reached a consensus on the Lord's Supper, which brought together the Genevan and Zurich reformations in Switzerland. It eliminated the chance that Lutherans and Calvinists (Calvin was theologically closer to Luther than was Zwingli) would come together.

4. The final division between Lutheran and Reformed churches, mainly on the basis of their differences over the Eucharist, was expressed by the Formula of Concord (1577), a document of inner-Lutheran consensus and rejection of Reformed teaching on the Eucharist, and by the Heidelberg Catechism (1563) and the Second Helvetic Confession* (1566), documents of inner-Reformed consensus.

2. The Confessional Texts

Augsburg Confession. Article 10 states in concise form Christ's real presence in the Lord's Supper: The *true* body and blood of Christ are really (*vere*) present *under the form of bread and wine* (similar to Catholic* formulations) and are distributed *and received* (i.e., the use of the sacrament is essential, not its reservation and veneration). The words in italics are not in the Latin version. Their addition in the German version most probably intended to stress similarity with traditional teaching on the real presence and to contrast the Lutheran position with that of the Sacramentarians*. Accordingly, the "contrary doctrine" (e.g., of Karlstadt, Schwenckfeld*, and Zwingli) was rejected. Article 22 justifies the reintroduction of both kinds* (elements) in the Lord's Supper to the laity by reference to Christ's command and to the tradition of the church (certainly up to the thirteenth century). The reference to "Cardinal Cusanus" (Nicholas of Cusa*, 1401–1464) is based on a letter in which Cusa claims that the Fourth Lateran Council (1215) authorized the distribution of only one kind (bread) to the laity. The reasons for this practice are discussed in Ap. 22.6–17. Processions with the sacrament are also abolished.

Article 24 on the Mass responds to Roman accusations of having abolished the Mass by emphasizing the great devotion, earnestness, and good preparation with which the Mass is observed in Lutheran churches. In the traditional liturgical forms only small changes have been made. (This is a reference to Luther's reforms of worship.) People are instructed about the great consolation to anxious consciences that they receive in this sacrament (1–9). Lutherans have abolished masses that were paid to be celebrated for individuals (i.e., private masses and votive masses for special purposes; 10–20). They also rejected the old error according to which Christ had by his death made satisfaction only for original sin. This error had led to the transformation of the Mass into a sacrifice for the (other) sins of the living and the dead, and it became a good work that was thought to obtain forgiveness (here the Augsburg Confession applies the criterion of justification; 21–23). Instead, CA 24 teaches (1) there is no sacrifice either for original sin or for other sins except the one death of Jesus Christ as satisfaction for all sin (24–27); (2) we obtain grace and are justified before God through faith, not through works (28–29); (3) the Mass has not been instituted as a sacrifice for sin but to awaken faith and comfort consciences by receiving grace and forgiveness (30–33). The Mass is a communion, a communal meal in which priest and people receive the Sacrament regularly. The Mass is now being observed communally in evangelical churches and hence "no novelty has been introduced which did not exist in the church from ancient times" (40; this is the thoroughgoing affirmation of continuity; 34–41).

Apology. Article 10 can be short since the Roman Confutation accepted the statement that the body and blood of Christ (which means the whole Christ) are truly and substantially (*vere et substantialiter,* again against Zwingli) present (but interpreted by the confutation in the sense of transubstantiation). Here, the article says, a basic agreement exists not only with the Roman Church but also with the Greek (Orthodox) Church. This assertion makes clear "that we defend the doctrine received in the whole church" (4) and that the Roman Church is not the only representative of tradition. It is the presence of the "living Christ" that is confessed (4). Article 22 defends the reintroduction of both kinds in the Lord's Supper on the authority of Christ's institution—"the entire sacrament was instituted for the whole church"—and with reference to this practice during the first centuries and in the Greek (Orthodox) Church (4 and 5). The claim of the

Roman Confutation that there has always been a distinction between lay communion under one kind and priestly communion under both kinds is rejected as a human, tyrannical device that elevates itself above Christ's order. Its sole purpose is to reinforce the distinction between laity and clergy (6–17).

Article 24 of the Apology repeats the statement of CA 24 about the high esteem in which the Mass is held in Lutheran churches and about the continued use of traditional liturgical forms (1). It defends (1) the use of German, together with Latin, against the critique of the Roman Confutation (2–5); (2) the reintroduction of the public or common mass alone in line with the early church and against the multiplication of daily and private masses (6–8); (3) the abolition of the Mass understood as sacrifice because the Eucharist does not, as sacrifice, grant grace *ex opere operato* and does not merit for others, whether living or dead, forgiveness of sins *ex opere operato*, that is, independently of their faithful participation in the Eucharist (9–13).

This last point leads to a longer discussion of sacrifice in article 24. It starts with the traditional distinction between sacrament (*sacramentum*), the act in which God offers us the content of the promise, and sacrifice (*sacrificium*), where two types are distinguished: (1) the *propitiatory sacrifice*, that is, the (human) work of satisfaction for sin that reconciles God or merits the forgiveness of sins for others; (2) the *eucharistic sacrifice*, which, by contrast, does not intend to merit forgiveness because there is only *one* propitiatory sacrifice: the death of Christ. Rather, in this sacrifice those who have been reconciled with God give thanks and express their gratitude for the forgiveness and blessings they have received (14–24). This eucharistic sacrifice, as "sacrifice of praise" or "spiritual sacrifice," is contrasted with the sacrifices offered to reconcile God *ex opere operato* for others. Such sacrifices are human works that contradict the biblical witness (25–32). This broader understanding of sacrifice is seen as fundamentally different from the Roman teaching, which limits sacrifice to the ceremony *ex opere operato* celebrated daily. Rather, the whole Mass comprehends the ceremony together with the proclamation of the gospel, faith, prayer, and thanksgiving. The commemoration of the death of Christ is the real daily sacrifice, the proclamation of the gospel and the faith which believes that by Christ's death God has been reconciled (33–43).

Against the critique of the Roman Confutation that the interior of evangelical church buildings is desolate, their real adornment is declared in Ap. 24 to be a more frequent and devout use of the sacraments by the people, the proclamation of the gospel with the proper use of the sacraments, practical and clear sermons, clear teaching, and ardent prayer (44–51). The biblical texts used by the confutation to prove that sacrifices merit *ex opere operato* reconciliation and forgiveness of sins, even for others, are shown to be falsely interpreted. Only the merit of Christ's sacrifice can be valid for the sins of others; he alone is our mediator (52–65).

Article 24 of the Apology concludes with four excursuses on specific issues. (1) "Patristic Teaching on Sacrifice" does not support the Roman teaching on the Mass, but refers to thanksgiving or Eucharist (66 and 67). (2) In "Sacrifice and the Use of the Sacrament" biblical and patristic references are used to define sacraments as signs of grace; they consist of the ceremony and the Word, and require faith (68–73). According to the fathers of the church, comfort for consciences belongs to the sacrament while thanksgiving and praise belong to the sacrifice. "From this the term 'eucharist' arose in the church" (76; 74–77). (3) In "The Term Mass" the article rebuts arguments in the Roman Confutation that seek to prove etymologically the Roman concept of the Mass (78–88). (4) This Roman concept is rejected in the final excursus on "Mass for the Dead" with extremely strong words like "contamination of the gospel," "corruption of the use of the sacraments," "a heresy that clearly conflicts with the prophets, apostles, and holy Fathers." The errors of the Mass "rob Christ's suffering of its glory and utterly destroy the doctrine of righteousness by faith" (89–99).

Smalcald Articles. The strong words of Melanchthon about the Mass find an even stronger echo in Luther's opening words in SA part 2, article 2: "The Mass in the papacy must be regarded as the greatest and most horrible abomination because it runs into direct and violent conflict with this fundamental article," that is, article 1 in part 2 on justification and redemption for Christ's sake, the decisive criterion (1). Luther believes that the Mass will be the decisive issue at the council for which, if Lutherans were to be invited, the Smalcald Articles were being written. For him the center of the faith is here at stake, and he would rather be burned than "allow a celebrant of the Mass and what he does to be considered equal or superior to my Savior, Jesus Christ.

Accordingly we remain eternally divided and opposed the one to the other" (10). Consequently, the Mass as a human work performed by the priest on behalf of others is to be abolished together with the awful abuses connected with it: private masses for one's own communion (8–9), purgatory (12–15), faked manifestations of the spirits of the departed (16–17), pilgrimages (18–20), fraternities committed to masses and good works for the benefit of the living and the dead (21), relics (22–23), and indulgences bought and granted for the living and the dead (24). The Mass and the other abuses are not commanded by Christ; they are unnecessary, useless, abortive, uncertain, and dangerous. They are—and this is the decisive argument—against the first article (SA 2, 1): "for the merits of Christ are obtained by grace, through faith, without our work or pennies" (24). This "fundamental article" asserts that it is not the celebrant of a mass and what he does but the Lamb of God and the Son of God who takes away our sin (7).

Part 3, article 6 on "The Sacrament of the Altar" confesses that the bread and wine are the true body and blood of Christ and are given to and received not only by godly but also by wicked Christians. Because it contradicts Christ's order and institution the article emphatically rejects the autocratically imposed practice of distributing the Sacrament in one form only, and the underlying teaching of the Council of Constance (2–4) that the body and blood are together contained and distributed even under one form (the doctrine of concomitance; see pp. 110–11). The "subtle sophistry" of transubstantiation (see pp. 109–10) is also dismissed.

Small Catechism. In part 6 on "The Sacrament of the Altar" Luther teaches that the sacrament, instituted by Christ himself, is the true body and blood of Christ "under the bread and wine." The essential and effective words in this sacrament are Christ's words "for you" and "for the forgiveness of sins." These words contain the life-giving and saving benefit of the Lord's Supper for all who believe them and who are, through their faith, truly worthy and well prepared.

Large Catechism. Part 5 on "The Sacrament of the Altar" emphasizes right from the beginning that the foundation for the doctrine of the Lord's Supper is found in Christ's words of institution (1–3). Luther then explains the Lord's Supper, which God has commanded and ordained, by taking up three questions: (1) What is the sacrament of the altar? It is the true body and blood of Christ "in and under" the bread and wine that Christians should eat and drink. The Word makes bread and wine a sacrament according to Augustine's definition (see p. 87). Even when the sacrament is received or administered by an unworthy person, it is the true sacrament because the Word that constitutes the sacrament is not rendered false through a person's unworthiness (4–19). (2) What is the benefit of the sacrament? It is a great treasure given to each person for the forgiveness of sins. It is a source of blessing and comfort, a sure pledge and gift against my sins, death, and all evil. It is daily food and sustenance for strengthening and refreshing faith (20–32). (3) Who receives the benefit of the sacrament? Those who believe and receive what the words say. This treasure is on everyone's table, and it is our responsibility to take it and confidently believe in it (faith has this active component; 33–38).

In a longer pastoral exhortation (39–87) Luther deals with the necessity and the joy of receiving the sacrament regularly and frequently because of Christ's command (45–63), the promise in the gracious words "given for you" (64–70), and the needs of people that should compel them to receive the sacrament (71–84). In this framework Luther affirms that all people are, indeed, included personally in the "for you," and they should not hesitate to use and regard the sacrament as a wholesome medicine that aids both soul and body because (here Luther anticipates modern psychosomatic insights) "where the soul is healed, the body has benefitted also" (68). Those who despise the sacrament and lead unchristian lives still receive the sacrament, but to their harm and damnation. Those who feel weak and unworthy should come anyhow because of God's commandment and the promise of Christ. They will "receive from Christ's lips the forgiveness of sins" (70), grace, the Holy Spirit, refreshment, comfort, and strength. This invitation and exhortation also apply to the education of young people so that they too can enjoy the fellowship of the sacrament (85–87).

Formula of Concord. Article 7 on "The Holy Supper" justifies the inclusion of this issue in the Formula (1): There are not only differences with the Sacramentarians about the Lord's Supper but also with theologians who claim adherence to the Augsburg Confession but think along the line of Sacramentarian interpretations. Accordingly, the article proceeds with explicit and implicit references to both groups, but especially to Zwingli. The consistent emphasis of article 7 lies on the fundamental significance of Christ's words of institution for the understanding of the Lord's Supper. On this basis the article intends to interpret the Augsburg Confession with the help of other confessions and of long excerpts from two main sacramental writings of Luther: his *Confession Concerning Christ's Supper* of 1528[3] (here called "Great Confession," 28–32 and 91–103), and his *Brief Confession Concerning the Holy Sacrament* of 1544[4] (here called "Last Confession," 33–34). Luther is presented as one "who understood the true intention of the Augsburg Confession better than anyone else" (33) and who is therefore the "chief teacher of the Augsburg Confession" (34). Article 7 can be divided into five parts:

1. *Affirmation of the real presence* (2–55). In contrast to descriptions of a spiritual presence of Christ in relation to the Lord's Supper by Zwingli and by several Philippist professors at Wittenberg and Leipzig (2–8), the teaching of the confessions and of Luther is restated as the right explication of the clear, literal sense of Christ's words of institution (9–55). It is the real presence of the body and blood of Christ in (but not locally enclosed in) the elements of bread and wine that alone brings the firm assurance of the forgiveness of sin and all other benefits of life with Christ. Among the texts quoted is (12–16) the Wittenberg Concord of 1536 (see p. 112), which is, however, immediately followed by Luther's statements in the Smalcald Articles (17–19) in order to prevent a Sacramentarian interpretation of the concord.

2. *Oral reception of the sacrament* (56–72). In order to underline the real presence, two forms of receiving the elements in the Supper are distinguished: a spiritual (i.e., by faith) and an oral or sacramental eating (*manducatio oralis**). The body of Christ is received orally also by unworthy communicants who are without true sorrow and faith and eat the sacrament for judgment (*manducatio impiorum* or *indignorum*); they do not receive it spiritually, however. Worthy communicants, who are perturbed Christians, terrified by their sins, for whom the sacrament was primarily instituted, receive the sacrament orally and spiritually (66–71).

3. *Consecration and use of the sacrament* (73–90). Christ's words of institution have consecratory character and power. Through them Christ himself effects also today what he has promised. Accordingly, these words are the most essential and indispensable part of the whole celebration, which is not a sacrament apart from its "use," that is, without all the actions instituted by Christ: consecration, distribution, and reception.

4. *Christ's bodily presence—possibility and modes* (91–106). Against Zwingli and others who deny that it is possible for Christ to be bodily present in the Supper (a position based on a different Christology), the reality and modes of Christ's bodily presence are supported by a long quotation from Luther's *Confession Concerning Christ's Supper* of 1528. Especially important is the explication of the spiritual, supernatural mode of Christ's presence in the Supper (100–106).

5. *List of rejected teachings* (107–28). This list begins with three "papistic" doctrines and abuses (108–10) and concludes with sixteen Sacramentarian opinions and doctrines (111–27). They are rejected as being erroneous and contrary to the doctrine grounded in the Word of God.

3. Theological Summary

• *Fundamental significance of the Lord's Supper.* The unceasing energy with which the Lutheran confessions hammer out basic eucharistic conceptions and reject understandings and practices that they consider erroneous is a clear witness to the fundamental significance that they attribute to this sacrament. Together with the proclamation of the gospel and the sacrament of baptism, the Lord's Supper is the principal means through which the triune God communicates to all people salvation, understood as justification and reconciliation, and all the blessings of a new life in Jesus Christ. Thus the Sacrament belongs to the existential center of Christian life and community, and this requires constant concern for its proper understanding and use.

• *Christ's institution and promise.* Christ's words of institution are constitutive. They contain the institution and command to celebrate this sacrament, they express its promise, and they indicate the way it should be understood. These words make clear that the Sacrament is a divine gift, embodying God's movement toward those who gather around this Supper in contrast to the futile efforts of the human spirit to ascend toward God. The promise of the Supper comes to expression in the words "given for you" and "for the forgiveness of sins." These words not only announce a promise; they also effectively convey what they promise. Filled by this promise the Sacrament becomes gospel, a message of comfort for body and soul, a defense against the terror of death and all evils, and a source that enables faith to persevere and renew itself.

• *Word and Sacrament.* The confessions follow Augustine by affirming the constitutive role of the Word for the reality of the Sacrament. Through Christ's words of institution and together with them the natural elements of bread and wine and the human rite become a sacrament, an effective instrument of the presence and action of the triune God in our midst. It is Christ himself who effects today what his words say. With them he makes himself and his gracious gifts present and available to all who follow his invitation to come and eat and drink. With and through him, in the power of the Holy Spirit, these words are words of consecration. They should be confidently believed in their direct, literal sense, not in a symbolical one. They must never be omitted from the celebration of the Lord's Supper.

• *Faith and the Sacrament.* The validity and efficacy of the Lord's Supper do not depend on the presence or absence of faith in those who celebrate or receive this sacrament. On this point, too, the confessions follow the tradition of the church. Nevertheless, faith as a gift of the Holy Spirit understood as trust and confidence is for them central and indispensable. Without the presence and active participation of believing people the sacramental action would lose its purpose and contradict its institution. The treasure is put on everyone's table, but it is only taken and appropriated when there is active faith.

• *The real presence of Christ and the elements.* The emphatic insistence of the Lutheran confessions on the real presence of Christ in the Lord's Supper was not motivated by a fascination with subtle theological speculation but exclusively by the concern for the certainty of salvation. The promise and grace of the Lord's Supper can be present, given, and received only if Christ himself is truly present and active among and for us in this sacramental action. This is expressed in a variety of formulations, but all of them emphasize that the body and blood of Christ—the *whole Christ*—are truly, really, essentially, substantially present. It is the bodily presence of the living Christ with all that he has done for us in his life, death, and resurrection—a presence for our salvation. This presence is always connected with the word, as the chief element, and the elements of bread and wine. Through the sacramental union between the material and divine, effected by Christ himself through his word, bread and wine are truly in a supernatural way the body and blood of Christ. This union and presence should not be visualized in a narrow localized manner (enclosed *in* the elements). It is a mystery, circumscribed with formulations like: under the bread and wine; in and under bread and wine; under the form of bread and wine; with bread and wine (the formula that bridged differences in the Wittenberg Concord of 1536 and the Leuenberg Concord of 1973). The usual Lutheran formulation, following FC-SD 7.35, has become "in, with, and under the bread and wine."

• *The use of the Sacrament.* For the confessions the "use" of the Sacrament consists of the whole visible rite and action: the consecration or words of institution, the distribution, and the reception. The gift of the Sacrament by itself is of no use if it is not distributed and received. The Sacrament is received not only spiritually but also orally. The oral eating and drinking is especially underlined in the controversy with Zwingli and his followers in order to support the real presence. An oral eating also means that unworthy communicants receive the Sacrament, but to their judgment. The proper *preparation* for receiving the sacrament is to believe the words of promise with the desire of the heart, inspired by the Holy Spirit, to receive this treasure; and those who are aware of their sin and unworthiness are invited to come. The Lord's Supper should be received *frequently* in obedience to Christ's invitation and command, and also by children.

• *The communal and sacrificial or eucharistic dimension.* Against forms of privatization of the Lord's Supper the confessions underline that the Supper is a communion, a communal meal. All who share Christ's presence in the Supper are together built up as Christ's body, his church. They are thereby bonded in a new community. The Lord's Supper, together with the proclamation of the gospel and the Sacrament of Baptism, is foundational for the existence, life, and mission of the church. In the Lord's Supper the church is strengthened and sustained; it is sent forth to share God's gifts with all people. This corporate celebration has *sacrificial* dimensions evangelically understood: the commemoration of Christ's unique and sufficient sacrifice for the sins of the world, and the response of the congregation to the rich gifts received in the form of its eucharistic sacrifice of praise and thanksgiving.

• *The ecumenical dimension.* In Europe the divisions between the Lutheran, United, and Reformed churches have been overcome by declaring full church fellowship between them on the basis of the Leuenberg Agreement of 1973.[5] This text also includes common statements about the Lord's Supper (2.15–16; 3.18–20). Despite remaining differences of interpretation in eucharistic doctrine, this agreement is further developed in *A Common Calling*, which served as the basis for the declaration of full communion in 1997 between the Evangelical Lutheran Church in America and The Presbyterian Church (USA), The Reformed Church in America, and the United Church of Christ.[6]

The other inherited deep difference from the time of the Reformation concerning eucharistic doctrine and practice between Lutherans and Roman Catholics has also largely been resolved. This is the conclusion of several dialogues, especially the official Lutheran–Roman Catholic dialogue in the United States (1966–1967),[7] and the official dialogue between the Lutheran World Federation and the Roman Catholic Church (1973–1978).[8]

◆

Ministry and Church Order

1. Historical and Theological Background

The statements on the ministry of Word and Sacrament in the Lutheran confessions have as their background the late medieval teaching, structure, and practice of the ministry. The confessions relate to this background in the form of rejection, restatement, and continuity. One of the more general expressions of this historical and theological context was the threefold pattern of ordained ministry: bishops, priests, and deacons. This pattern became the dominant structure in the church in the second and third centuries. In the Middle Ages these three ministries constituted the "major orders," and after the eleventh century they were divided into a "hierarchy of order" (bishops, priests, and deacons) and a "hierarchy of jurisdiction" (pope and bishops).

Closely connected with the emergence of this hierarchical structure was the concept of the apostolic succession of bishops that developed in the second century as a defense against heresies and as a safeguard of unity, continuity, and apostolicity. The requirement that only bishops are authorized to consecrate bishops and ordain priests was and is an essential ingredient of this concept of apostolic succession. From the first centuries onward the bishops were seen as constitutive of the church and superior to the other clergy. Yet, in the high Middle Ages (e.g., in the writings of Thomas Aquinas), they were not yet regarded as a ministerial order or grade that was sacramentally distinct from that of priests. At that time the power and privileges of bishops were massively enlarged, especially through the combination of spiritual and secular power in their hands (they were in many cases also territorial princes).

Augustine was one of the first theologians to consider ordination a sacrament and to regard baptism and ordination as two forms of consecration (imparting a permanent mark) that did not allow repetition. By the twelfth century holy orders were counted among the seven sacraments (Second Council of Lyons in 1274). In the struggle against

Donatism Augustine also prepared the way for the concept of a sacramental character, later called "indelible character*" (*character indelebilis*), imparted through ordination. Such a character consists, according to Thomas Aquinas, of a certain participation in Christ's priesthood present in his faithful people. This concept of character or spiritual sign was affirmed by the Council of Florence in 1439.

In the sixth century the priestly office became predominantly sacral and liturgical in nature, related primarily to the Eucharist through sacramental power to effect the change of the elements. The functions of proclamation, teaching, and pastoral care became marginal. Growing emphasis on the Eucharist as representing Christ's sacrifice on the cross gave more and more prominence to the power of the priest to offer this eucharistic sacrifice. The Council of Florence in 1439 confirmed this authority when it defined the "form" of the sacrament of order as the "power to offer the sacrifice in the church for the living and the dead."

Accordingly, priests and bishops came to be seen as mediators of salvation. Together with the special character received in ordination, this role widened the gap between clergy and laity and elevated the clergy to a state of superiority above the laity. In the collection of ecclesiastical regulations known as the *Decretum Gratiani* (c. 1140) clergy and laity were defined as two classes or orders. Consequently, the influence of the laity, even of their highest representatives, on church life and ecclesiastical affairs, already in decline since the eleventh century, was further reduced. The elevated status of clergy over laity was underlined by the requirement of clerical celibacy*. The first rules about celibacy in parts of the Western church date from the fourth century. In the Middle Ages many efforts were undertaken to enforce celibacy. It was generally prescribed by the First Lateran Council in 1123. The Second Lateran Council in 1139 went one step further and declared the marriage of priests unlawful and invalid. Despite this decision, clerical concubinage was still widespread in the late Middle Ages.

An important part of the historical and theological background of the confessions was the overarching reality of the papacy. The twelfth and thirteenth centuries, especially the years immediately before the outbreak of the Reformation (the Fifth Lateran Council* with its condemnation of the conciliar movement), witnessed an enormous increase of claims by the papacy to religious and secular supremacy.

The popes, as vicars of Christ, mediators between God and humanity, and invested with primatial (absolute and immediate jurisdictional) authority over the church, undergirded their claims by teaching that their office was of divine right (i.e., that it was grounded in God's will and institution revealed in Scripture).

Many people and movements in the late Middle Ages demanded reforms in the church. But it was the historical breakthrough of Luther and the Lutheran Reformation that revolutionized the late medieval system and practice of ordained ministry. It no longer focused on priests who offered sacrifices before God but on ministers of God's Word and Sacrament for God's people. This understanding of ministry (*ministerium*) that serves the gospel and the people by administering the means of grace had implications for other aspects of ministry. The qualitative distinction between clergy and laity was replaced by a new emphasis on the dignity and role of the priesthood of all baptized believers. Clearly rejected were the papal claim to primacy and power by divine right and the forms of its exercise, the combination of spiritual and secular power in the office of bishops, and the enforced celibacy of the clergy. Other aspects of ministry—like the essential place of ordained ministry in the church, the episcopal office, the distinction between ordinary (pastoral) and jurisdictional power, or the necessity of ordination—were not abolished but retained and renewed according to Reformation principles.

There was no open conflict with the emerging Reformed tradition about the understanding and forms of ministry. The ministry occupied a more important place in Reformed doctrine and church order because its structure was understood as biblically commanded. Over against radical movements the Lutheran churches insisted on the ordained ministry as an essential ministry of Word and Sacrament in the church.

2. The Confessional Texts

Augsburg Confession. Article 5 states that God instituted the office of the ministry (Latin: "the ministry of teaching the gospel and administering the sacraments") and entrusted it with the gospel and the sacraments. Through these means the Holy Spirit works faith in those who hear the gospel. Article 8 repeats the traditional teaching (defined by Augustine against the Donatists, who are condemned in this article) that the efficacy of the sacraments does not depend on the worthiness

of the ministers (Latin: because sacraments are instituted and commanded by Christ). This is further explained by article 7/8 of the Apology, which affirms that sacraments are efficacious despite unworthy
ministers because ministers do not represent their own persons but the
person of Christ, "because of the church's call" (28). The paragraph
continues: "When they offer the Word of Christ or the sacraments,
they do so in Christ's place and stead."

Article 14 of the Augsburg Confession decrees that nobody should
publicly teach or preach or administer the sacraments in the church
without a regular call. The Latin phrase used here, *rite vocatus*, refers
traditionally to ordination. Article 14 of the Apology also confirms
that CA 14 is referring to ordination. (But see below what this article
and Melanchthon's *Treatise* say about ordination by bishops.) The
interpretation according to which CA 5 refers to the common ministry
of all the baptized while CA 14 refers to the public, ordained ministry
has not found general agreement. Article 23 argues on the basis of the
biblical witness and experience that the obligation of celibacy for the
clergy is not God's will. History, patristic writings, and canons of the
church show that God commanded marriage and that many clergy
were married (until at least the eleventh century, when celibacy was
generally enforced by Pope Gregory VII). An appeal (CA 23.14–15) is
made to the emperor (because celibacy was part of imperial law) to
accept God's institution of marriage also for the clergy for the well-
being of the church and for the people who serve the gospel.

Article 28 deals explicitly with the office of bishops. The starting
point is the confusion of the spiritual power and authority of bishops
with their temporal power and authority. Both are to be respected as
gifts of God, but they also have to be distinguished and separated. The
power and office of bishops, according to divine law (i.e., commanded
by God), is to preach the gospel, to forgive and retain sins, to exclude
the ungodly from the community, to administer and distribute the
sacraments, to judge doctrine and condemn doctrine that is contrary to
the gospel. All this is to be done by God's Word alone. This spiritual
power of bishops should not interfere with the temporal power or government, which is concerned with the ordering of human life in the
world (1–21). Pastors and congregations should obey bishops. If they
teach or introduce something contrary to the gospel, however, it is
God's command not to obey them (22–28).

The power and jurisdiction of bishops in other matters like matrimonial cases or contributions to the church is by human right. But the bishops are not permitted to introduce—as happened so often—ceremonies or regulations in the church that are imposed in order to make satisfaction for sins and to obtain grace. This clearly contradicts the "chief article of the gospel," namely, "that we obtain the grace of God through faith in Christ without our merits" (29–52). Bishops or pastors may introduce regulations for the sake of good order in the church, and such regulations should be obeyed. But human regulations that contradict Holy Scripture and the tradition of the church should be changed because God is to be obeyed rather than human authority (53–78).

Apology. Article 13 on the sacraments contains the important statement that "the ministry of the Word has God's command and glorious promises.... The church has the command to appoint ministers ... for we know that God approves this ministry and is present in it." This affirmation is made against the "fanatics" (enthusiasts and Anabaptists), who wait for a direct illumination by the Holy Spirit without the ministry of the Word (11–12). Article 14 on "Ecclesiastical Order" contains the important statement that Lutheran reformers preferred to maintain the order of the church and the ranks of ministerial hierarchy although they had been created by human authority. Since the existing bishops were condemning evangelical doctrine and cruelly persecuting priests sympathetic to evangelical preaching, however, they were responsible for the abolition of the inherited structure of ministry (1–4). Yet Melanchthon again states emphatically that the Lutheran side is willing to keep the ecclesiastical and canonical order, provided that the bishops no longer fight against the emerging Lutheran churches (5). Article 23 is an extended rebuttal of the reasons in favor of sacerdotal celibacy brought forward by the Roman Confutation (1–5; 62–69). Enforced celibacy contradicts Holy Scripture, the tradition (theologians, councils, canons of the church), and experience, that is, it clashes with divine and natural law and is finally a matter of clerical domination (6–61). It is even more contrary to God's will and Word when the confutation asks the Reformation-minded princes to break up recent marriages of priests (70–71).

Article 28 of the Apology responds to the argument in the Roman Confutation that bishops have the power to establish forms and traditions that are allegedly necessary for eternal life. Against this the gospel testifies, says the article, that bishops have no authority to impose traditions on the church that would merit forgiveness of sins, or placate God as righteous acts of worship, or burden consciences so that it would be a sin to omit them (1–11). The old distinction between the power of order (*potestas ordinis*), that is, the pastoral ministry of Word and Sacrament, and the power of jurisdiction (*potestas jurisdictionis*), that is, the authority to excommunicate public sinners and to absolve them when they repent, is applied to the true office of bishop as pastor, not as tyrant or king. It is a legitimate task of bishops to institute traditions for the sake of good order and peace in the church, but not as necessary acts for the sake of meriting grace. The use of such ordinances should be left free and can be changed (12–19). When bishops create traditions contrary to the gospel, however, we are forbidden to obey the bishops (20–21). The article and the Apology end with the conviction that not the Reformers but those who have condemned and persecuted the clear truth are responsible for the schism in the church (22–27).

Smalcald Articles. Part 2, article 4 on the papacy rejects the claims and the exercise of this institution. The pope is not the head of all Christianity by divine right. He is only the bishop of Rome and of the churches that have agreed to be associated with him—as was the case in the early church. Since then the pope has usurped authority, and his diabolical deeds contribute to the destruction of the church; they contradict the "first, fundamental article" concerning redemption in Jesus Christ. The church existed for a long time without popes and several old (i.e., Orthodox) churches have never been under the pope. The papacy is a human invention; even if the pope would renounce his excessive claims, the papacy would remain unnecessary and useless (1–8). The church could be better governed by having all the bishops equal in office and joined in unity of doctrine, faith, sacraments, prayer, and works of love (9). The pope's claim that one has to be obedient to him in order to be saved has set the pope himself against Christ; he is the real Antichrist*. His teaching about masses, purgatory, monastic life, and human works contradicts God and cannot be accepted (10–14). According to the remark that Melanchthon adds to his signature under the Smalcald Articles, one could concede to the pope, if he would allow the gospel, for the sake of peace and unity

"that superiority over the bishops which he possesses by human right."
Obviously, Melanchthon wanted to modify Luther's severe judgment
on the papacy.

Part 3, article 9 on excommunication states that (ordained) ministers
of the church should not mingle civil punishment with Christian
excommunication and absolution. Article 10 on ordination expresses
the willingness—very much in line with Ap. 14—to accept existing
bishops, *if they were true bishops,* as those who ordain and confirm. But
they are *not* true bishops, and therefore Lutheran churches have the
right, following the early tradition of the church, to ordain for themselves suitable persons. Article 11 strongly denounces imposed celibacy
of the clergy, because marriage should be free as God has instituted it.

Treatise on the Power and Primacy of the Pope. This text focuses on
the office and ministry of the pope and of the bishops. Concerning the
power and primacy of the pope the text responds to *three claims:* (1)
that the pope is by divine right above all bishops and pastors; (2) that
the pope possesses by divine right "both swords, that is, the authority
to bestow and transfer kingdoms"; and (3) that it is necessary for salvation to believe these things. These claims are judged to be false, impi-
ous, tyrannical, and injurious to the church (1–6). The first claim is
refuted with arguments from Scripture (7–11) and the testimony of
early church history (12–21). Biblical references that were used to justify the particular power and primacy of the pope are shown to have a
broader significance than simply relating to popes (22–30). The second
claim is rejected because the mandate of Christ did not give the apostles power by divine right over kingdoms of the world. The exercise of
this power has had catastrophic consequences in history and contradicts the kingdom of Christ (31–37). Contrary to the third claim Scripture and the canons teach disobedience to heretical popes—and the
pope *is* heretical (38). Another section explains why the pope carries
the marks of the Antichrist or "adversary of Christ." The pope usurps
a threefold divine authority: the right to change the doctrine of Christ;
the jurisdiction over souls not only in this life but also after death; and
the exercise of power over the decisions of councils and the whole
church (39–51). Given the "enormous errors of the pope's kingdom
and his tyranny," a special appeal is made to the "chief members of the
church, the kings and the princes," to ensure that errors are removed,
consciences healed, and the unlimited power of the pontiffs restrained.

In conclusion: There are sufficient and compelling reasons for all the faithful not to obey the pope and "to resist him as Antichrist" (52–58). The second part of the Treatise deals with the power and jurisdiction of bishops. It begins with the basic statement that the tasks of preaching the gospel, administering the sacraments, and exercising jurisdiction—excommunication and absolution—belong by divine right to all who preside over the church: pastors as well as bishops. The distinction between bishop and pastor is not by divine right and, accordingly, an ordination administered by a pastor is also valid. Since the existing bishops, who have inherited the right of ordination, have become enemies of the gospel and are unwilling to ordain evangelical pastors (see Ap. 14 and SA 3, 10), the church, which alone possesses the priesthood, has the right to ordain ministers. This claim is supported by the testimony of Scripture and instances from early church history (60–73). The Treatise also rejects the exclusive right of bishops to exercise jurisdiction through the office of the keys as well as in ecclesiastical courts, especially in matrimonial cases, because excommunicating and absolving belong to all pastors and jurisdiction of the ecclesiastical courts should be taken over by secular courts (74–78). In conclusion: The evangelical churches should not recognize the existing bishops as bishops because of their heretical teachings and refusal to ordain evangelical pastors, the unjust and tyrannical exercise of jurisdiction that they have taken away from pastors, and their corruption (79–82).

3. Theological Summary

- *The basis.* The Lutheran confessions understand the ordained ministry of the church in relation to and shaped by the central emphasis of the Lutheran Reformation: the gospel message of the free gift of justifying grace, received by faith alone. This gift is communicated by the Holy Spirit through Word and Sacrament, and thus by the ministry serving these means of grace. Accordingly, the ordained ministry's only reason for existing is to be an instrument of the saving work of the triune God for all humanity.

- *The institution.* For this purpose God has instituted and commanded the office of the ministry. Through its service the Holy Spirit leads people to justifying faith. Thus the ordained ministry exists by divine right and is not just a practical arrangement created by the church in order to delegate to some individuals functions that are common to all. Rather, the church calls and ordains people into the ministry, which has been given by God.

- *The main functions.* The ministry is a necessary and integral part of the soteriological focus of the confessions: The movement of God in Christ through the Holy Spirit toward human beings by means of Word and Sacrament requires a ministry that serves these means of grace and through them the building up of the church (recall the sequence of CA 1 to 7; see p. 79). Thus the main function of the ministry is to preach the gospel and to administer the sacraments. This function is exercised in communion with all members of the church. It has kerygmatic, educational, liturgical, and pastoral components. It includes the office of the keys by exercising jurisdiction: excommunicating those who refuse to repent and absolving those who repent.

- *Ordination.* The confessions affirm that ordination is necessary for the exercise of public ministry. According to later Lutheran tradition, essential for ordination are a call, a blessing, and a mission (*vocatio, benedictio,* and *missio*) by God and the church. If ordination is related to the ministry of the Word, which has God's command and promise (the usual definition of a sacrament), Melanchthon is willing to call ordination a sacrament (Ap. 13, 11–12). Bishops can exercise the traditional function of ordaining. But when the bishops are not serving the gospel, the churches have the authority to call, elect, and ordain pastors. Not individuals but the church as a whole has God's mandate to appoint ministers.

- *Forms of the ministry.* The distinction between grades of the ministry like pastor and bishop exists by human right or authority and can therefore be retained. But there is only *one* public ministry in the church. The functions of proclamation, administering the sacraments, absolution, and jurisdiction belong by divine right to all who preside in the churches, pastors and bishops.

- *Bishops.* The confessions are open to the continuation of the office of bishop if bishops exercise their ministry as service of the gospel. The main functions of a bishop are the same as those of a pastor, and the responsibility of the special teaching office of bishops is to support right doctrine and to reject doctrine that is contrary to the gospel. Bishops, who are ready to serve the gospel and ordain evangelical pastors, could continue to ordain and even lead the church in a collegial manner. Pastors and churches should accept the authority of bishops, but where they teach or institute anything contrary to the gospel, God commands us not to obey them.

- *The nature of ministry.* The confessions describe the ministry in terms of service, not of elevated authority, hierarchy, or personal quality. This service (*ministerium*) is focused on Word and Sacrament and serves the general priesthood of all baptized believers. When pastors preach the Word of God and administer the sacraments, they do this service not on their own authority but by representing Christ, by serving in Christ's place and stead.

- *Church order.* The outward order and constitution of the church has its center in the mission of the church to proclaim and communicate the gospel though Word and Sacrament. All forms of ministry, mission, and life in the church should serve this central purpose. They exist by human right and can be changed and adapted when required by the tasks of the church in new situations.

- *Continuity in ministry.* The confessions affirm the readiness of the Lutheran Reformation to uphold the traditional structure of ministry, including the office of bishop in apostolic succession, understood as the succession of episcopal consecrations and ordinations. But since the bishops were unwilling to fulfill their task according to the gospel, the churches joining the Lutheran Reformation were forced to ordain their own pastors. They should not, therefore, be accused of breaking the continuity of ministry. The preference for upholding the traditional episcopal ministry in apostolic succession was realized at the time of the Reformation in Sweden (and Finland, which belonged to Sweden).

- *Ordained ministry today.* The Lutheran confessions help us today to appreciate the great freedom that Lutherans enjoy concerning forms and structures of ordained ministry as long as these serve the gospel. This freedom allows the continuation or reintroduction of the office of bishop in historical succession as an office of pastoral leadership, and it allows the creation of new forms of ministry in response to the needs of modern societies.

The confessions warn us against relegating the public, ordained ministry of the church to a practical arrangement for the fulfillment of religious and administrative functions. They encourage and challenge us to consider the ordained ministry as grounded in God's saving purpose. The ministry is part of God's intention to realize this saving purpose through outward means: human words, water, bread and wine, gestures of blessing, called and ordained women and men. The ministry is a service within and for the church in the midst of and together with the ministries and gifts of all the people of God.

The confessions remind us that the nonnegotiable priority of the ordained ministry is the responsible and diligent proclamation of the gospel and administration of the sacraments. It requires intensive and continuous theological study and an ordered spiritual life.

The confessions witness to us that fallible human beings, trusting in the power of the Holy Spirit promised in their ordination, become instruments of a precious calling: to declare in God's name to people that God offers them liberation from all that burdens them, that Jesus Christ comes in the common meal to them for their comfort and hope, that the Holy Spirit gathers them into a worldwide communion of Christians for the praise of God and service to God's world.

◆

The Nature of the Church

1. Historical and Theological Background

After final efforts to reconcile evangelical and Roman Catholic positions failed at Regensburg in 1541, and after the Council of Trent cemented the anti-Reformation stance of the Roman Church, it was obvious that the split within the Western church was becoming permanent. Already before the 1540s, however, a Lutheran understanding of the church was clearly expressed in the confessions. It was not formulated with the intention of justifying a separate ecclesial existence but of confessing the faith of the one, holy, catholic, and apostolic church. Lutherans developed this understanding in contrast to late medieval ecclesiastical reality and to radical Reformation thinking. It emerged alongside the ecclesiology of Calvin, with which it had important features in common.

A comprehensive and systematically developed theological reflection on the nature of the church was not yet part of medieval dogmatic systems (e.g., of Thomas Aquinas). It became, some interpreters maintain, a separate dogmatic locus only in the course of the Reformation. In late medieval thinking the reality of the church as an institutional, visible, hierarchical body dominated the understanding of the church as a spiritual, mystical body. In its tangible, hierarchical existence the church was seen as structured from above in line with the increasing importance assumed by the person and office of the pope. The schism between the Eastern and Western church that became definite in 1054 contributed to this rapid extension and exaltation of papal authority. Recognition of the pope became an essential sign of the church, of a pope-centered "perfect society." Pope Boniface VIII, in his bull *Unam Sanctam* of 1302, declared that submission to the pope was necessary for salvation. The church also claimed unlimited spiritual and considerable worldly power. It had the authority to administer and distribute grace. In practice this image of the church assumed extreme, corrupt, and immoral forms, so that within the late medieval church calls for reform became insistent.

There were, however, medieval theologians like Thomas Aquinas or Albertus Magnus (1193–1280) who maintained a distinction between the church as the mystical body of Christ, a spiritual, sacramental community, and the church as a visible, institutional, hierarchical society. Augustine was once more a precursor of Reformation thought. In the Donatist controversy of the early fifth century, he argued that the visible church had a mixed membership (*corpus permixtum*) of saints and sinners. This mixed body could not be sorted out by any ecclesiastical authority prior to God's final judgment (Matt 13:24–31), because the community of true and holy Christians was known to God alone.

Luther turned the late medieval understanding of the church upside down. For him the church is not primarily an institution but a living community of people in Christ, gathered by the Holy Spirit through Word and Sacrament; the structure of the church is not primarily a hierarchy but a common and equal priesthood of all baptized believers; the church is not a saving institution that distributes grace but a communion of faith, suffering, and love that lives by grace. The true church, according to Luther, is hidden in the visible church, where it exists with the false church. As a creature of the word (*creatura verbi*) the church can be understood and recognized with the help of marks like the holy Word of God; the Holy Sacrament of Baptism; the Holy Sacrament of the Altar; the office of the keys exercised publicly; the call and consecration of ministers (there must be pastors); prayer, praise, and thanksgiving to God; and the possession of the sacred cross: misfortune, persecution, and so on.[9]

For Calvin the Word of God and the sacraments were the essential marks of the church. In some Reformed confessions church discipline was added as a third mark. Calvin differed from the Lutheran understanding, however, by emphasizing the distinction between the invisible community of the living and departed elect (i.e., predestined) in

Christ and the visible church containing both true and false Christians, the true and false church. He also differed from Lutherans by insisting on a particular fourfold structure of ministry and form of ecclesiastical administration that he regarded as prescribed by the Bible. The followers of the radical Reformation rejected the existing church because they regarded it as totally corrupted through its close association with society and the state. In the Schleitheim Articles of 1527, the oldest confession of the Anabaptist movement, the idea of an identity of the Christian community with the civil community is denounced as an illusion. Consequently, separation from the world and radical discipleship of Christ are necessary. Anabaptists and spiritualists aimed at a pure church of true believers and morally impeccable Christians who, as a voluntary association of the faithful, separated themselves from a dangerous and degenerate world.

2. The Confessional Texts

Creeds. The statements of the Apostles' Creed on "the holy Christian (catholic) church, the communion of saints *(communio sanctorum),*" and of the Nicene Creed on "one holy, Christian (catholic), and apostolic church" are repeatedly taken up and interpreted in the confessions. They use these statements to argue that there is no intention to create a new church. Rather, their aim is to renew the church and to restate its understanding in continuity with the faith of the church through the centuries.

Augsburg Confession. Article 7 is foundational for a Lutheran understanding of the church. It is, however, not a comprehensive description of the church. It must be complemented by other statements in the confessions. The article presents three basic statements about the church: (1) it will be and remain forever; (2) it is an assembly of believers (Latin: *congregatio sanctorum,* assembly of saints) among whom the gospel is preached in its purity and the sacraments are administered according to the gospel (i.e., according to Christ's institution); the article implies that sharing in Word and Sacrament is both the causal foundation and the sustaining expression of the life of the church; (3) for its unity it is sufficient *(satis est)* that there be agreement on the gospel and the sacraments (a consequence of point two) while uniformity in humanly instituted traditions or rites and ceremonies (Latin text) is not necessary. The article is based on the twelfth Schwabach

Article (see p. 39), which in turn goes back to a formulation in Luther's Confession of 1528, an appendix to his *Confession Concerning Christ's Supper.* Article 8 complements article 7 by stating that in the church false and godly Christians are mingled together, though the sacraments remain efficacious even when administered by evil people (Latin: because of the institution and commandment of Christ). The position of the Donatists, who denied the efficacy of sacraments administered by priests who had been forced into apostasy, is rejected.

Apology. The Roman Confutation had refused to accept CA 7 if "assembly of saints" meant that false Christians were excluded from the church. In Ap. 7/8 Melanchthon responded that article 8 was added precisely to avoid the interpretation that false Christians were separated from the outward fellowship of the church and that sacraments administered by them were not efficacious (1–4). With reference to the Apostles' Creed the article affirms that the one, holy, catholic, and apostolic church is an assembly of saints who share the association of the same gospel and the same Holy Spirit active within them (7–9). Longer explications follow:

1. The church in the larger sense (*ecclesia large dicta*) includes both true Christians and wicked people, the latter being part of the true church only through participation in the outward marks or ceremonies. They are part of the church only in name, not in fact. This is distinguished from the church in the proper sense (*ecclesia proprie dicta*), which is the assembly of saints who truly believe the gospel and have the Holy Spirit and thus belong to the church not only in name but also in fact (Ap. 7/8.5, 6, 10–16, 22, 28, 29). The church as the kingdom of Christ is also distinguished from the kingdom of the devil, to which the wicked belong. But since the kingdom of Christ has not yet been revealed, the wicked can also belong to the church in its larger sense (16–19). A third distinction is made between the church as the assembly of saints and the church as an outward monarchy of the pope and his bishops (23–27).

2. The true church is not invisible, however; it is not a "Platonic republic," that is, a purely ideal body according to the Greek philosopher Plato, who saw in the realm of ideas the true reality that was only mirrored by the real world. The true church is recognizable in true believers throughout the world who have the Holy Spirit and in its marks: the pure teaching of the gospel and the sacraments. This church alone is the body of Christ and the pillar of truth (5, 20–21).

3. According to the creed the church is catholic: the church is made up of all the people throughout the world "who agree on the gospel and have the same Christ, the same Holy Spirit, and the same sacraments, whether they have the same human traditions or not" (10). Being "catholic" means being both universal and one in faith.

4. The statement of CA 7 that uniformity of traditions is not necessary for the unity of the church is again defended with the help of the criterion of justification. The righteousness of faith is not dependent on certain traditions, universal or particular. Moreover, church history shows that in the past a diversity of traditions did not prevent unity (30–46).

5. CA 8 had been accepted by the Roman Confutation, and the purpose of the article is restated (47–50).

Smalcald Articles. In the short article 12 of part 3 Luther writes against the "papists" the often quoted words that a seven-year-old child (the minimum age of discretion) knows what the church is: holy believers and sheep who hear the voice of their shepherd. Children know this because they confess in the creed the holy Christian church, whose holiness consists of the Word of God and true faith.

Small Catechism. Explicating the third article of the creed in part 2, Luther affirms that the Holy Spirit both gives faith to each person and at the same time calls, gathers, enlightens, and sanctifies "the whole Christian church (*Christenheit*) on earth." The Spirit preserves the church in union with Christ in the one true faith, forgives within it all our sins, and will grant us eternal life.

Large Catechism. Interpreting the third article of the creed in part 2, Luther again extols the outstanding significance of the Holy Spirit for the church. The Spirit leads people into the church and is active through the church for the sanctification of its members. As the community of the Holy Spirit the church is the *mother* that bears every Christian through the Word of God (37, 41–42).[10] Where Christ is not proclaimed there is no Holy Spirit to create and gather the church, and outside the church nobody can come to Christ (43–45, 56).[11]

Luther also discusses two formulations in the Apostles' Creed: "the holy Christian church" and "the communion of saints" (*communio sanctorum*). He considers this last expression to be a later addition to the creed (originally the phrase referred both to the community of the holy ones—*sancti*—and to the communion or participation in holy things or sacraments—*sancta*). Luther does not like the ambiguous word "church" (*Kirche*) because it could focus attention on the church building. (His derivation of the word *Kirche* from Greek *kyria* or *kyriake* is not correct, however; it comes from Celtic *kyrk*.) Luther prefers the designation "Christian congregation or assembly," "a holy Christian people" (47–48). Likewise the word *communio* should be understood as a community of saints, a holy community under Christ, its head, called together by the Holy Spirit in one faith, with a variety of spiritual gifts but united in love. The Spirit remains with the church until the last day; through it the Spirit gathers the people; by it the Spirit effects sanctification. In this Christian church we have forgiveness of sins daily, and toward this forgiveness everything in the church is directed so that consciences can be comforted and revived (49–55).

3. Theological Summary

Presupposition. The Lutheran reformers had no intention of creating a new church. Their aim was to reform and to renew the existing church. This is the framework of their conviction that the emerging evangelical churches were in continuity with Christ's church since the first Christian communities. Their ecclesiological reflection is governed by the center of Reformation thought: the church is the community of those who are graciously justified by God for Christ's sake and are assembled by the Holy Spirit through the gospel in Word and Sacrament.

- *The foundation of the church.* The church is not constituted by a gathering of like-minded people. Rather, its existence is grounded in the purpose and action of the triune God: *God the Father* justifies sinners on account of the saving work of *Jesus Christ,* and the *Holy Spirit* communicates this gift of grace through the gospel in Word and Sacrament served by the ordained ministry. Through these means of grace the Holy Spirit leads the justified into the church.

- *The nature of the church.* The church is the assembly, congregation, and community of believers and saints brought together and sustained by the Holy Spirit through the right and faithful preaching of the gospel and the administration of the sacraments in accordance with the gospel.

  The church is the people of God, the living body of Christ, and the kingdom of Christ. It is the creature of the Holy Spirit who creates, calls, and gathers it and remains the inner principle and power of its life. The Spirit works actively in and through the church.

The church is holy. It is a holy, Christian people, a holy community sanctified by God in Christ through the Holy Spirit. The church is catholic in a twofold sense: quantitatively through its universal, worldwide extension and qualitatively through holding fast to the one gospel, the same Christ, the same Spirit, and the same sacraments. The church is free with respect to its outward forms and traditions; these may be uniform or diverse.

In conclusion: The church is understood as a community of persons, as a spiritual reality, not as an outward, juridical, and hierarchical body. Its institutional elements of proclamation, sacraments, and ministry are means through which the triune God is actively present.

- *Salvation in the church.* Within the church there is forgiveness of sins and salvation through proclamation of God's grace, the sacraments, absolution, the comfort of the gospel, and also through mutual forgiveness and support of the faithful. Through the church the Holy Spirit sanctifies believers and leads people to Christ.

- *The church as a mixed company.* The church in the outward form and larger sense (*large dicta*) includes true believers as well as hypocrites. The church in the true, proper sense (*proprie dicta*) is the assembly of saints, justified sinners, who truly believe the gospel and have the Holy Spirit. The mixture of true believers and hypocrites (Augustine's *corpus permixtum*) cannot be resolved before the kingdom of Christ is revealed.

- *The marks of the church.* The true church is hidden under the church in its outward and larger sense. The confessions do not endorse, however, a distinction between a visible and an invisible church because, although the true church is hidden, it is not invisible or unreal. It can be recognized by marks (*notae ecclesiae*) that are also the constitutive elements of the church: the pure proclamation and teaching of the gospel and the celebration of the sacraments in accordance with the gospel. This church alone is the real body of Christ that is confessed in the Nicene Creed as one, holy, catholic, and apostolic.

- *The functions of the church.* The essential functions of the church are the proclamation of the gospel and the celebration of the sacraments, the declaration of forgiveness, catechesis, and the pastoral work of consoling troubled and uncertain hearts and minds.

- *The unity of the church.* The unity of the church requires agreement on the constitutive marks of the church: the right preaching and teaching of the gospel and the administration of the sacraments in faithfulness to the gospel. Uniformity of traditions or ceremonies is not necessary because they do not justify the sinner.

- *Ecumenical perspectives.* Different ecclesiologies are still a major barrier between churches. Nevertheless, ecumenical dialogues have led to common perspectives that can enrich our Lutheran tradition: As an integral part of God's saving history from creation to fulfillment, the church is a communion (*communio* or *koinonia*) that is created and sustained by the saving presence of the triune God. Through its communion with God it becomes a communion of people that is open to all and inclusive of all. Today the unity of the church is envisioned by many as a full communion of churches, a *koinonia* that includes the common confession of the apostolic faith, a shared sacramental life, a common life in which members and ministers are mutually recognized, a common mission, and conciliar relations of joint consultation and common action. The goal of full communion will have been realized when churches are able to recognize in one another the one, holy, catholic, and apostolic church.

- The church is to support reconciliation and to provide healing, to help overcome divisions within humanity, and to bring people into saving relationship with God. The church as communion is oriented toward God in praise and thanksgiving for all that God has done in creation and salvation. It is sent by God in Christ through the Holy Spirit to be the sign and instrument of God's saving and transforming purpose for all humanity and creation. In its failure to live up to its calling the church is constantly challenged to renew and reform its thinking, its life, and its structures. Where this happens by the Spirit's gracious guidance, the church becomes a foretaste of God's kingdom until God's reign reaches its fulfillment in a new heaven and a new earth.

Questions for Discussion and Further Study

1. Explain the continuity and the differences in the concept of sacrament in the confessions and in pre-Reformation theology.

2. Why do the confessions advocate the baptism of infants?

3. Repentance, confession, and absolution are emphasized in the confessions. What are the theological and pastoral reasons for this emphasis?

4. Indicate the christological presuppositions that led to the difference between the teaching (on the Eucharist) of the confessions and that of Zwingli.

5. What are some of the contemporary theological and ecumenical interpretations of the Eucharist that complement and broaden the teaching of the confessions?

6. In what sense do the confessions suggest that the ordained ministry is essential for the church?

7. In present ecumenical discussions the apostolic succession of bishops is one of the controversial issues. How can one argue this issue on the basis of the confessions?

8. The church is the "creature of the word" but also the "creature of the Holy Spirit." Explain.

9. In what sense is the church both the product and the instrument of redemption?

G. G.

CHAPTER SIX

The Lutheran Confessions

The Christian Life

◆

The Arena: Church and World—Two Reigns of God

1. Historical and Theological Background

The "two reigns of God" is an idea taken from Luther that usually appears in theological discussions as the "two kingdoms." Neither phrase is found in the *Book of Concord*, but it is useful to retain them in studying the confessions because they have become a traditional Lutheran concept.

Distinguishing two reigns of God is one way of answering a question that has occupied followers of Jesus since the beginning of Christianity: If the kingdom of God has already begun in Jesus, how should Christians live in the world until Jesus returns and the kingdom comes in its fullness? Long before the Reformation, Christian theologians used some notion of two kingdoms to describe how Christians should live in the world.

One such notion was the concept of two cities proposed by Augustine*. As the Roman Empire in the West foundered, Augustine proposed the concept of two cities as a way of assuring the faithful that Christianity was independent of Rome and would survive its decline. The church belongs to the city of God, said Augustine; it consists of true believers who love God above everything else. Rome belongs to the worldly city made up of pagans and hypocrites who do not have faith in the true God. Although these two cities are entwined with each other during the course of history, the city of God is preserved from the rise and fall of earthly empires and will culminate at the end of history in the glorious kingdom of God.

While Augustine made a sharp distinction between the Christian church and Roman society, Christians who lived in Europe during the late Middle Ages (1200–1500) viewed their entire society as Christian. They called it Christendom and deemed it to be ruled by two powers: a worldly power like kings, queens, and princes, and a spiritual power such as bishops, monks, and the pope. These powers were very much mixed up in each other's affairs. Bishops ruled territory and owned land while kings appointed clergy and supported churches.

Most leaders of the Reformation still thought of themselves as living in Christendom, but they had different ideas about the way in which Christians should relate to the world. Anabaptists were Christians who tried in most cases to separate themselves from the surrounding society. They refused to pay taxes or tithes to support the church; they often declined to swear an oath and were unwilling to hold public office. Civil and religious authorities (i.e., the secular and the spiritual powers) regarded them as heretical and seditious, but most of them were small cells of nonviolent men and women who posed no serious threat to public authority.

There were exceptions, however. Some radical leaders tried to create public Christian communities that they believed were the beginning of God's final reign on earth. Between 1522 and 1525, the radical preacher Thomas Müntzer* claimed that his followers in central Germany formed a League of the Elect in special covenant with God to bring in the kingdom and to annihilate the godless. Müntzer finally took over leadership of an army of peasants and led them against the princes in the battle of Frankenhausen (1525), where he and many of the peasants were killed. A similar thing occurred in 1534 at Münster in northwestern Germany. A group of Dutch Anabaptists* took over Münster and tried to inaugurate the kingdom of God in their city. After a long siege they were finally overthrown by an alliance of Catholic and Protestant* princes.

Müntzer and the Anabaptists at Münster identified their movements with true Christianity and with the kingdom of God. For them Christians were not to separate peacefully from the world but to take it over and wrest the kingdom from the godless. Some radicals also thought their kingdom was the thousand-year reign of Christ and the saints on earth that would precede the last judgment (Rev 20:4-6). This teaching, known as millennialism* or chiliasm* (from the Latin and Greek words, respectively, for "thousand"), was not uncommon during the Reformation. A form of this teaching inspired both Müntzer and the Münster Anabaptists. Lutherans dissociated themselves both theologically and politically from such radical notions. To do so they used the concept of the two reigns of God.

Luther publicized this concept in 1523 in the treatise *Temporal Authority* (LW 45:75–129). He was wrestling with how Christians could be good citizens and obedient followers of Jesus at the same time. To solve this potential conflict, Luther proposed that humanity is divided into the kingdom of God and the kingdom of the world. The kingdom of God encompasses "all true believers who are in Christ and under Christ," while "all who are not Christians" belong to the kingdom of the world (LW 45:88, 90). True Christians who live under Christ and the gospel in the kingdom of God are "always a minority in the midst of non-Christians" (LW 45:92), who live under the law in the worldly kingdom. Luther therefore spoke not only of two kingdoms but also of two governments: the government of Christ or the gospel, and temporal government or the law. God reigns through each government over both kingdoms.

Now the question facing Luther became: Since true Christians do not belong to the worldly kingdom, to what extent should they be subject to its government and its laws? Luther's answer was: in principle Christians have no need of civil authority or its sword (i.e., the power of coercion) since they are governed by Christ and live by the Sermon on the Mount. But "since true Christians live and labor on earth not for themselves alone but for their neighbors, they do by the very nature of their spirit even what they themselves do not need, but is needful and useful to their neighbors" (LW 45:94). For the benefit of others, therefore, the Christian "submits willingly to the rule of the sword" and fulfills the obligations of a citizen.

In 1525 Luther stressed the responsibility of Christians to obey civil authority. He believed that Müntzer and the peasants were wrong to claim that their grievances were specifically Christian and that they could realize the kingdom of God on earth. Later that year, after more violence erupted, Luther argued that in no case could Christians use force to accomplish worldly goals. Instead, Christians should work for justice through peaceful means even when civil authorities, whom he blamed outright for the plight of the peasants, were clearly in the wrong. Against Müntzer, Luther distinguished carefully between the two reigns of God, so that the spiritual kingdom would not be compromised by utopian attempts to perfect the kingdom of God on earth.

2. The Confessional Texts

In his catechisms Luther discusses spiritual and civil government in his explanation of the Fourth Commandment: "You shall honor your father and your mother." The terms actually appear at the beginning of his explanation of the Fifth Commandment (LC 1.180). Although he dwells on the duty of children to honor and obey their parents, Luther also believes that the Fourth Commandment covers obedience to civil government and to "spiritual parents . . . who govern and guide us by the Word of God" (LC 1.158); for "out of the authority of parents all other authority is derived and developed" (LC 1.141). Luther's language reflects the patriarchal society in which he lived, but he does not intend thereby to promote exclusively male authority or an attitude of submissiveness. Instead, he underscores the promise attached to this commandment (Exod 20:12: "that your days may be long in the land which the Lord your God gives you"). In a world that seemed to Luther to be "full of unfaithfulness, shame, misery, and murder" (LC 1.152), obedience to both temporal and spiritual authorities was the best guarantee of earthly "sustenance and peace and afterwards abundance and blessedness forever" (LC 1.164). The catechisms, published in 1529, reflect this need for order and reassurance in the confused circumstances that resulted from the religious and social upheaval of the 1520s.

In the Augsburg Confession and the Apology, the two reigns of God are discussed in a different framework. In his 404 Articles, John Eck* (1486–1543) associated Protestants with Anabaptists and accused them of shirking civic responsibilities by refusing to swear oaths and the like.[1] Consequently, in CA 16 Melanchthon* puts as much distance as possible between Lutherans and Anabaptists. First, he establishes that government and all civil rules and laws are good ordinances of God and "that Christians may without sin" occupy all civic offices and engage in secular pursuits (16.2). Furthermore, the gospel, that is, Christian life under the gospel, does not destroy civil authority, the state, and marriage, but intends (better translation of the German than "requires") for them to be preserved and respected as true orders of God (16.5). In addition, all Christians should "manifest Christian love and genuine works" in their stations of life.

Second, Melanchthon rejects any definition of Christian perfection that requires people to forsake their families or to forgo legitimate worldly activities. Melanchthon's targets include monks and nuns as well as Anabaptists. Protestant criticism of the Anabaptist movement had already compared it to monasticism, claiming that both required true Christians to withdraw from the world. Against the false teaching "that monks alone are in a state of perfection," CA 27 presents a different, positive definition:

> For this is Christian perfection: that we fear God honestly with our whole hearts, and yet have sincere confidence, faith, and trust that for Christ's sake we have a gracious, merciful God; that we may and should ask and pray God for those things of which we have need, and confidently expect help from God in every affliction connected with our particular calling and station in life; and that meanwhile we do good works for others and diligently attend to our calling (CA 16.49).

Unlike the Augsburg Confession, Ap. 16 explicitly names both Christ's kingdom and a political kingdom. "Christ's kingdom is spiritual; it is knowledge of God in the heart, the fear of God and faith, the beginning of righteousness and eternal life." It does not interfere in the political kingdom. Instead, "it let us make outward use of the legitimate political ordinances of the nation in which we live" (Ap. 16.2). Melanchthon's primary goal is to safeguard the integrity of Christ's kingdom and to prove it is no threat to contemporary governments. True, according to CA 16, there is a limit to Christian obedience. In cases where such obedience would require Christians to sin, they should obey God rather than human authorities (Acts 5:29). In principle, however, Melanchthon reaffirms that "our doctrine does not weaken but rather strengthens the authority of magistrates and the value of civil ordinances generally" (Ap. 16.13). That teaching, Melanchthon hoped, would allay any doubt that Emperor Charles might have about the loyalty of his evangelical subjects.

The rejection of monastic vows in CA 27 reflects this emphasis on the integrity of both kingdoms. CA 27 does not oppose the right of Christians to live in solitude or in a religious community, or to remain unmarried, or to devote themselves exclusively to a religious vocation. It opposes only the elevation of this kind of religious life above life in the worldly kingdom, in which a Christian works at a civil job or marries and raises children. Christian life in the world is just as good as withdrawing from the world. In fact, given their experience of monasticism in the late Middle Ages, the confessional authors think life in the world is better. In CA 27 Melanchthon summarizes the claims made for monastic vows and evangelical* arguments against them that, for the most part, Luther had made in his treatise of 1521.[2] Their objections are threefold: Monastic vows were not commanded by God; they undermine justification by faith and rob Christ of his honor because people think the monastic life earns God's grace; and monastic life is regarded as a state of perfection that contradicts true Christian perfection as defined above.

By no means did all monks, nuns, or Anabaptists think they were trying to earn salvation by their vows and or by their refusal to participate in civic life. In this sense, the charges of the Augsburg Confession did not apply to every individual. The response of the Roman Confutation*, however, indicates that CA 27 struck a central nerve of late medieval piety. The confutation offers a spirited defense of monastic vows and the monastic life, carefully disputing the Augsburg Confession's use of authorities like Augustine and Jean Gerson* (CA 27.34–35, 60). It also reproached the Augsburg Confession for claiming that young women who had been pressed to remain in convents were treated with special unfairness because they were the "weaker sex" (CA 27.7). The confutation rightly pointed out that nuns had often remained more constant in their vocation than monks and that they offered tough resistance to Protestants who threatened and cajoled them.[3]

In Ap. 27 Melanchthon rebuts the objections brought by the confutation. He reasserts his main argument from the Augsburg Confession: "It certainly is not a legitimate vow if the one making it supposes that by it the person merits the forgiveness of sins before God or makes satisfaction for sins before God" (Ap. 27.11). For living as a Christian, Melanchthon makes an important distinction in his discussion of when it is appropriate for Christians to "leave" spouse, children, and property. He disagrees with the confutation about the meaning of Matt 19:29: "And everyone who has left houses or brothers or sisters or father or mother or children or fields, for my name's sake, will received a hundredfold, and will inherit eternal life." According to Melanchthon, this text has nothing to do with "artificial religious" acts or with the monastic life. Instead, it is talking about leaving "which happens by a command of God, when a government or a tyranny forces us either to leave or to deny the gospel." This meaning is more clearly seen in the parallel passage, Mark 10:29, which adds the phrase "for the gospel." There it is clear that Jesus "is not talking about those who do injury to wife and children [by leaving them voluntarily], but about those who bear injury because of the confession of the gospel" (Ap. 27.41). Marriage and raising children and earning a living are valid callings for Christians in the world. "So it is perfection for each of us with true faith to obey our own calling" (Ap. 27.50).

3. Theological Summary

- The two kingdoms are so quickly identified with Lutheran theology that it is helpful to separate what Luther said about them outside the confessions from what is said in the confessional documents. Luther's early emphasis on the distance between the spiritual kingdom of true Christians and the worldly kingdom is tempered by Melanchthon's affirmation of full Christian participation in the life of the world. Still, both theologians knew when to stress the integrity of the spiritual kingdom (e.g., against political threats to the faith) and when to stress the integrity of the worldly kingdom (e.g., against false claims to religious perfection).

- The concept of two kingdoms defines the relationship between the church and the world in terms of the Christian life. It does not determine how church and government should relate to each other as legal structures or institutions. The confessions are interested in only one question: How do Christians who make up the church, the community of believers in Christ, live also in the world until the kingdom of God comes in fullness?

- In the confessions the term "world" is ambivalent. On the one hand, it is God's good creation, ordered and governed by laws and authorities that God has sanctioned. This world is the secular or political kingdom. Christians should affirm it, enjoy it, and cooperate with God in sustaining it through their secular callings. On the other hand, the world can also mean that part of God's creation that refuses to recognize God as creator (LC 2.21). Like the flesh and the devil, it is a source of temptation to Christians, assailing them and driving them to "anger and impatience" (LC 3.103). In this sense, the world is under the sway of the devil, who has usurped God's rule and established his own kingdom until it is finally overcome by God (LC 3.54, 115).

- The confessions stop short of saying that Christians *belong* to the temporal kingdom, but they affirm Christian life in the world in the strongest terms possible. This position is slightly different from a view that says that Christians belong equally to both kingdoms. According to the confessions, Christians are not torn between two allegiances; neither do they belong equally to two masters. Because God also rules the temporal kingdom, however, Christians may legitimately make use of (*uti* in Ap. 16.2, 12) civil ordinances and they are required to obey existing laws unless, of course, such obedience would cause them to sin (CA 16.7). They are also encouraged to serve their Creator and humanity through secular callings that enhance God's creation.

- The confessions distinguish sharply between the kingdoms because they are trying to counteract the mixture of spiritual and civil power in the Middle Ages. On the one hand, the church is itself a political power and constantly interfering in civil matters. The confessions therefore argue that the kingdom of Christ is spiritual and does not countenance such interference. CA 28.5–18 makes this argument forcefully against the misuse of temporal authority by medieval bishops. On the other hand, secular rulers make decisions about religious matters and exercise pressure on clergy at all levels. Although the confessions support the right of rulers to protect the gospel, they recognize the possible abuse of this right (hence the restriction on civil obedience in CA 16.7). The confessions affirm the equal dignity of spiritual and temporal authority (CA 28.18); nevertheless, for the confessions church interference in politics is the greater threat and most of their emphasis is on the integrity, if not the full autonomy, of the secular realm.

- This emphasis has led many observers to fault Lutheran theology for teaching that civil government and its laws are to be accepted uncritically except in those cases where government obviously prevents Christians from exercising their faith. Some phrases in the confessions can be read that way. For example, Melanchthon writes: "For the gospel does not destroy the state or family but rather approves them, and it commands us to obey them as divine ordinances not only from fear of punishment but also 'for the sake of conscience' (Rom 13:5)" (Ap. 16.5). The original Latin text does not mean to say that the gospel unconditionally approves of every particular government or household, but that the gospel, that is, Christian life under the gospel in the spiritual kingdom, does not destroy those structures through which God rules and nurtures the world. Note that the subject here, as in CA 16.5, is the gospel, not God. The point of the confessions is not that God endorses every government, but that Christian life under the gospel does not advocate the overthrow of civil government in general but rather calls Christians to obey government "in all that can be done without sin."

◆

The Conflict: Sin, Free Will, Election

1. Theological and Historical Background

The issues of sin and free will were at the heart of Luther's earliest challenges to late medieval theology. His first challenge, the *Disputation Against Scholastic Theology* (1517), was directed mainly against the theology of William of Ockham* and Gabriel Biel*, two theologians who belonged to a school of thought called Nominalism* in which Luther himself had been trained. According to the Nominalists, even before grace was received, the human will could choose to love God above anything else. Original sin was not strong enough to prevent people from obeying the substance of the commandments. In 1517 Luther strongly opposed this theology. Prior to grace, sin was so potent that it kept the will from choosing to love God. "It is false to state that human inclination is free to choose between either of two opposites. Indeed, the inclination is not free, but captive" (LW 31:9).

By attacking the Nominalists on this point, Luther thought he was contesting the Pelagian tendency of late medieval theology in the spirit of Augustine. The Pelagian heresy had taken its name from a serious Christian moralist who, in the early fifth century, challenged Augustine's doctrine of sin and grace. According to Pelagius*, if you deny that the will has power to reject sin and obey the commandments, you undermine the moral responsibility of believers. For Pelagius sin was like a bad habit, and Christians could overcome the habit of sinning by exerting themselves, with the aid of grace, to keep the law. Augustine, and Luther after him, argued instead that sin was not just the habitual trespass of commandments but active opposition to God contrary to the First Commandment. In his preface to Romans, Luther wrote: "The main and real sin is unfaith, despising God, which is what takes place when people do not fear, love, and trust in God as they certainly should" (LW 35:369). Believers could not simply reverse themselves and choose to love God above all things instead of despising God. The will first had to be redirected toward God by the Holy Spirit.

What then happened to the will after being released from its bondage to sin? Was it then free to love and trust God above all things? The power of the will after baptism depended on whether sin still remained in the believer. Lecturing on Romans in 1515 and 1516, Luther had maintained that sin did indeed remain in the baptized and that baptized believers remained sinners. In theses prepared for his debate with John Eck at Leipzig in 1519, Luther wrote: "To deny . . . that sin remains in the child after baptism is to trample down Paul and Christ" (LW 31:317). Luther's conviction challenged those theologians who believed that grace received in baptism had removed sin from the Christian. In their opinion, the believer was at worst plagued by an inclination to sin called concupiscence, which was no longer authentic sin.

Luther's most famous theological opponent on this issue was Erasmus of Rotterdam* (1467–1536), a Christian humanist who supported Luther at first but then surrendered to pressure to write against him on the subject of sin and the will. In his treatise *Free Choice* (*De libero arbitrio*, 1524), Erasmus adopted Nominalist views of the will's ability to choose God prior to baptism and to cooperate with grace after baptism. Luther's famous rebuttal, purposely entitled *Choice Bound* (*De servo arbitrio*, 1525; often translated as *Bondage of the Will*), held that the human will could not choose God either before or after baptism. Even after the power of grace had broken the bondage of the will to sin, that same will had to be held in faith and love toward God by the Holy Spirit.

To illustrate his position, Luther used an image that would influence later attempts to describe what the will does and does not do when it is converted from an unbelieving to a believing will. If the will cannot choose to believe of its own accord, then God has to change it. Does God therefore compel or force the will to believe? In 1522 Luther had already rejected that option: "One should not and cannot compel anybody to believe; one should and can only allow the gospel to draw freely whomever it draws" (LW 36:253). Accordingly, Luther adopted a position between compulsion and free choice. In 1525 he described it this way: "If God works in us, the will is changed, and being gently breathed upon by the Spirit of God, it again wills and acts . . . of its own accord and not from compulsion, so that it cannot be turned away by any opposition, nor be overcome or compelled by the gates of hell; but it goes on willing and delighting in and loving the good, just as before it willed and delighted in and loved evil" (LW 25:65). For Luther the will was drawn away from sin and held in faith by the Spirit of God.

The distinction between willing and choosing is essential to Luther's position. The will is always active, whether it is despising or loving God, but it cannot choose of its own accord to move from one stance to the other. Luther used the illustration of a horse and rider to make this point. The will is like a horse, always alive and active, but unguided unless a rider sets the direction. That rider, said Luther, is either God or Satan, guiding the will toward God or spurring the will away (LW 25:65–66).

If the human will is not free to choose God, how does God decide which people the Spirit will convert? Pushed by the Pelagians on this question, Augustine formulated his doctrine of predestination. Unlike the Pelagians, Augustine interpreted Rom 5:12 to mean that all human beings were born in sin and would suffer eternal death unless God chose some to be saved. God's election or predestination, not human choice, was therefore behind the conversion of some human wills to faith and salvation. "And those whom [God] predestined he also called; and those whom he called he also justified; and those whom he justified he also glorified" (Rom 8:30). To leave faith to human choice, argued Augustine, assumed wrongly that human beings were born into a state of neutrality and could in fact choose either faith or unbelief. Moreover, if they could choose to believe, salvation would then depend on their choice and not God's. Augustine rejected both points and argued that salvation was ultimately in God's hands even though God could be blamed for not choosing everyone. Augustine decided it was better to let God be blamed than to leave salvation up to human choice.

Luther agreed with Augustine's decision and held the doctrine of predestination throughout his life. He acknowledged its danger, however. Conceivably you could believe in Christ and still not be saved because you were not predestined. Luther admitted that such speculation had once almost driven him to despair. Fortunately, he had been consoled by his monastic superior and counselor, John von Staupitz*, who advised Luther: "Why do you torture yourself with these speculations? Look at the wounds of Christ and at the blood that was shed for you. In their light predestination will shine."[4] Luther learned from his own experience that predestination, which belonged to the hidden will of God, was secondary to faith in Christ, which was revealed in Scripture as the way to salvation. He then advised others to put the revealed Word of God ahead of speculation: "Accept the present promise [of Christ] and predestination, and do not inquire too curiously about the secret counsels of God. If you believe in the revealed God and accept his Word, he will gradually also reveal the hidden God. For 'he who sees me also sees the Father' (John 14:9)."[5]

2. The Confessional Texts

Sin. Even for baptized Christians, the confessions emphasize the presence of sin and stress the necessity of relying solely on Christ for salvation. In the Large Catechism Luther portrays the Christian life as a ceaseless conflict with sin and Satan (LC 3.86–87). Two things make this conflict so sharp. First, believers still live in the flesh, and that flesh does not trust or believe God. Luther gives very explicit descriptions of sin in his explanation of the sixth petition of the Lord's Prayer. Temptations come from the flesh, the world, and the devil (LC 3.101–4). They are more comprehensive than bad personal habits or moral misconduct; sin also encompasses various forms of violence, social injustice, and spiritual arrogance.

Second, the enemy of God, Satan or the devil, has not stopped challenging God for the souls of those same believers. Hence Luther constantly warns against false security and pride: "Although we have acquired forgiveness and a good conscience, and have been wholly absolved, yet such is life that one stands today and falls tomorrow" (LC 3.100). Christians must constantly be on guard, praying both for God's forgiveness and for God's protection. "In short, unless God constantly forgives, we are lost" (LC 3.91). "For if God did not support us, we should not be safe from [Satan] for a single hour" (LC 3.116).

The Augsburg Confession focuses on original sin because John Eck, in his 404 Articles, had attacked the reformers on this doctrine. Unlike Ulrich Zwingli*, therefore, who called original sin a disease that would not afflict children with eternal punishment,[6] Lutherans made clear that original sin was so serious that it would lead to damnation unless it was forgiven through baptism (CA 2.2, Latin). Melanchthon also wanted to define original sin in clear contrast to medieval views still operative in the church. First, original sin is not merely a defect or a tendency, but a virulent condition that Melanchthon describes in the Latin text as "concupiscent" and explains in the German text as "full of evil lusts and inclinations." Second, the disability imposed by original sin is much more serious than the absence of original righteousness as understood by medieval theologians. To be "unable by nature to have true fear of God and true faith in God" means that, on their own ("by nature"), human will and reason were prevented from knowing and trusting God. Some force had intervened, both inciting the will to evil and holding its natural powers in bondage. That force was sin.

The reaction of the Roman Confutation to CA 2 was ambivalent.[7] It approved the Lutheran assertion that original sin was truly sin, but it disagreed with both parts of Melanchthon's definition. For the most part, Melanchthon defended himself, and Luther, against the medieval notion that concupiscence which remains after baptism was not really sin. At the Heidelberg Disputation in 1518, Luther had declared that sin did remain after baptism, and this position, as the confutation pointed out, had been condemned by Pope Leo X in *Exsurge Domino*.

More is actually at stake here for Christian theology than the technical question of whether concupiscence is sin. The bigger issue is: In what sense are people different, if at all, after they receive* the Holy Spirit in baptism? If sin remains, then what point is there in being baptized and becoming Christian? Appealing to Luther in the Apology, Melanchthon argues forcefully that baptism is necessary not only because it forgives the guilt of original sin but because the sin that remains in the form of concupiscence* is so strong that it needs to be counteracted by the Holy Spirit, who mortifies the flesh and creates new impulses (Ap. 2.35).

Melanchthon tries to show that his opponents are the ones who take sin too lightly and thus minimize the necessity of baptism. First, he dismisses the notion of human neutrality as another error of scholastic theology. The gravity of original sin leaves human beings unable to choose God on their own (Ap. 2.42). This contention will have important consequences for the issue of free will. Second, Melanchthon reinforces an even more central point that he and Luther always want to make. If sin leaves human beings in bondage to the devil and actively despising God, then they cannot save themselves and "need the grace of Christ to be forgiven and the Holy Spirit to be mortified" (Ap. 2.45). If sin is taken as seriously as it should be, then Christ cannot be taken lightly. "Recognition of original sin is a necessity, nor can we know the magnitude of the grace of Christ unless we acknowledge our faults" (Ap. 2.33).

In the Smalcald Articles, minimizing original sin is for Luther a threat to Christianity itself. After listing seven errors of scholastic theology that result from underestimating sin, he declares: "if such teachings were true, Christ would have died in vain" (SA 3, I.11). Among the errors rejected are familiar formulas from Nominalist theology (SA 3, I.6–9) and the allegations of human neutrality already contested by Melanchthon (SA 3, I.4–5). For the first time in the confessions, Rom 5:12 is cited as the biblical basis of original sin (SA 3, I.1). The heart of original sin is not an obvious transgression like murder or adultery, but "ignorance or disregard of God" (SA 3, I.2), that is, disobedience to the First Commandment. We are blinded by original sin itself to how serious it really is (SA 3, I.3).

By the time the Formula of Concord was endorsed forty years later, original sin had become controversial among Lutherans themselves. FC 1 is the resolution of a dispute sometimes called the Flacian controversy, named after the ardent Gnesio-Lutheran* leader, Matthias Flacius Illyricus*. At a debate in Weimar in 1560, Flacius stated that sin is the substance of human beings. This statement was intended to capture the devastation wrought by original sin that both Luther and Melanchthon had taught. Flacius was also trying to refute the position of his opponent, Viktorin Strigel* (1524–1569), who wanted to preserve the integrity of the human will as part of the created essence of human beings that had not been destroyed by the fall. To Flacius, Strigel seemed to be minimizing the effect of original sin on the will, making sin an inessential part of humanity (a so-called accident in Aristotle's* terms) instead of an essential part (or substance). The opponents of Flacius feared that he was embedding original sin so deeply in the substance of human beings that he was guilty of denying that humans were created in the image of God. Flacius's theology evoked the Manichaean heresy, which had taught a materialistic notion of sin and evil.

The strategy of FC 1 is to reject the extremism of Flacius while portraying the effects of original sin as devastatingly as possible without equating sin with human substance. Paragraphs 5–15 describe original sin as a serious corruption of human nature and summarize Ap. 2 to this effect. Paragraphs 16–48 reject the Pelagian and Manichaean distortions of the doctrine. Paragraphs 49–62 discuss terminology, including how properly to use the Aristotelian language of substance and accidence to talk about original sin.

Several things are noteworthy about the text of FC 1. First, it reaffirms that original sin is not primarily an action but a condition that sets human beings against God. It is "a heart, sensation, and mind-set which, in its highest powers and the light of reason, is by nature diametrically opposed to God . . . and is actually enmity against God, especially in divine and spiritual matters" (FC 1.11).

Second, the Formula explores the origin of original sin. In order to preserve the goodness of creation, it denies that God is the "creator, author, or cause of sin" and blames Satan instead. On this point, FC 1 follows CA 19, which had located the cause of sin in the perverted will of the devil and of the ungodly. The point of this explanation is to exempt God from responsibility for sin (FC 1.40–41), while maintaining that all humans, in a derivative way, are born guilty of sin without claim to even a moment of innocence.

Third, the main problem facing the authors of FC 1 is to avoid saying that human nature is essentially evil once they have portrayed its corruption. Consequently, they devote more space to rejecting the Manichaean than the Pelagian threat (i.e., freedom of the will). Moreover, they take pains to explain how four chief articles of the Christian faith (creation, redemption, sanctification, and resurrection) all forbid the conclusion that original sin is the nature, essence, or substance of human beings (FC 1.34–48).

Do they succeed? Their discussion of language does reject the implication that human nature is sin. Nevertheless, the authors also say that original sin results in the loss of the image of God (FC 1.10), and they imply that human nature shares the evil of original sin that corrupts it (FC 1.29). The middle of the road they try to walk between the Manichaean and Pelagian extremes turns out to be a narrow path.

The Human Will. A corresponding middle road is taken by the confessions on the power of the human will. On the one hand, they argue that the will has no power whatever to overcome sin and make a person acceptable to God. On the other hand, they want to avoid a determinism that denies to the will any power to make choices.

CA 18 was probably formulated for the first time at Augsburg in response to Eck's charge of determinism. Against this charge CA 18 affirms that the human will can make choices in the civil realm where reason operates but not in the spiritual realm of our relationship to God. Using words that restate the definition of original sin in CA 2, the German text specifies how the will is unable to please, fear, and believe in God, or to expel lust from the heart (CA 18.2, German). Both German and Latin texts add that the will lacks this power "without the grace, help, and activity of the Holy Spirit" (CA 18.2), but they do not stipulate how much help the will needs. Does the Holy Spirit overcome sin without the will being active at all, or is the will, merely assisted by the Spirit, the main actor in regaining the right relationship with God? This ambiguity led to disagreement among Lutherans that would be resolved in FC 2.

Eck's charge of determinism was also the reason for drawing up CA 19 for the first time in Augsburg. According to Eck, Melanchthon had asserted that God was the cause of evil as well as good.[8] To prove his orthodoxy, Melanchthon used Augustine to support the position that the human will is responsible for its own sin.[9] The will is responsible, said Augustine, because, were God's grace "to withdraw itself," then human beings would fall again, cast down by their own free will. This is the meaning of the phrase in CA 19: "as soon as God withdraws support, the will turns away from God to evil." Melanchthon is not saying that God is unreliable and might withdraw help at any time. Instead, he is echoing Augustine's point that without God's *continuous* support, the human will chooses evil. The Latin text, "if not aided by God" (*non adiuvante Deo*), makes this point more clearly than the German, which reads "as soon as God removes the hand" and makes God sound arbitrary.

The Roman Confutation accepted both articles and even praised the affirmation of free will in CA 18. It believed that the Augsburg Confession had found the middle road between Pelagianism, which gives too much freedom to the will, and Manichaeism*, which takes it away.[10] In the Apology, however, Melanchthon was skeptical of this endorsement. He accused the Roman theologians of being themselves Pelagians, because they believed that human will and reason can love God, keep the commandments, and merit grace without the Holy Spirit (Ap. 18.2). The purpose of distinguishing between civil righteousness, where the will can choose, and spiritual righteousness, where it cannot, is to point out the need for the Holy Spirit (Ap. 18.9). While the confutation was worried more about denial of freedom to the will, Melanchthon was clearly more worried about attributing too much power to the will even in the civil realm. People still "obey their evil impulses more often than their sound judgment" and for that reason "even civil righteousness is rare" (Ap. 18.5).

The controversy dealt with by FC 2 was caused to some degree by Melanchthon himself. Trying to describe precisely how the will was involved in its own conversion from sin to faith, Melanchthon stated that the activity of the will was part of conversion. Beginning in 1535, he expressed this view in a formula that identified three elements in conversion: the Holy Spirit, the voice of the gospel, and the human will giving assent to the gospel. Melanchthon's main concern was to counteract the notion that persons being converted were lifeless blocks of wood or stone who could wait until they were "pulled by the hair to God."[11] Even though the will did not choose God from a state of neutrality, still it was active and could respond to the gospel once it had been moved by the Holy Spirit. At the Weimar Disputation (1560) Strigel appealed to this view of Melanchthon. Strigel argued that even the will under sin retained enough of its power to accept or reject the Spirit's initiative. As a result, Strigel and Melanchthon were accused of synergism*, the belief that the will cooperated with the Holy Spirit in conversion, and this controversy is called the synergistic controversy.

That label is simplistic. Neither Melanchthon nor Strigel believed that the human will cooperated with the Spirit as an independent, equal partner in the process of salvation. They did believe, however, that the corruption of original sin did not entirely prevent the will from responding positively to the gospel and to the prompting of the Spirit. Besides, the will that had been corrupted by sin was the same will that God had created; it did not have to be replaced by a new will, produced at conversion, as Flacius argued. Their position was nevertheless rejected by FC 2 because it sounded as if the will retained enough power to assent to the gospel of its own accord (FC 2.3).

One other matter is at stake: the external means through which the Spirit works. Melanchthon and others were afraid that an extreme view of the will's passivity encouraged people to dismiss the preaching of the Word. If the Holy Spirit did everything in conversion, then people could ignore the preaching of the Word on grounds that nothing they did would affect their possible conversion (FC 2.46). Against such people, whom it identifies with "ancient and modern enthusiasts*," FC 2 defends the necessity of preaching and of sacraments (FC 2.4).

The doctrine of the will adopted by FC 2 attempts to do justice to everyone's concerns, including Melanchthon's. It reestablishes as a base line the absolute captivity of the will to sin prior to its conversion. "Hence according to its perverse disposition and nature the natural free will is mighty and active only in the direction of that which is displeasing to God" (FC 2.7). The will under sin is so intractably hostile to God that it can be compared to a hard stone, a block, or a lump of clay (FC 2.17, 24). Nevertheless, to call the human being prior to conversion a stone or a block does not mean that the person is no longer a rational creature, or that the person can be converted without hearing the Word of God, or that in "external secular things" human reason and will cannot make decisions and take action (FC 2.19).

Since the will is captive to sin, not just conversion but the entire Christian life depends "altogether and alone" on "divine operation and the Holy Spirit" (FC 2.25). Christian life in the Spirit consists of "conversion, faith in Christ, regeneration, renewal, and everything that belongs to its real beginning and completion." These terms do not designate stages in a process, but are synonyms for the work of the Holy Spirit in the believer from baptism to death. To "be born anew, to receive inwardly a new heart, mind, and spirit, is solely the work of the Holy Spirit" (FC 2.26).

What then is precisely the role of preaching and the activity of the will in the Christian life? To answer this question, the authors of FC 2 place conversion under a magnifying glass in order to see all its parts in correct relationship to one another. First, conversion takes place only through the Word of God and the sacraments (FC 2.50). Second, to explain how the Holy Spirit converts through Word and Sacrament, FC 2 adopts language that had been used by both Luther and Melanchthon:[12] "The Lord God draws the person whom God wills to convert, and draws in such a way that darkened reason becomes enlightened reason and a resisting will becomes an obedient will" (FC 2.60). The image of drawing allows that the human will is alive and active in the process of moving from resistance to obedience. The will is enticed, not forced. By the same token, the active will does not initiate its conversion or contribute anything at the moment of conversion above and beyond the power of the Spirit.

Third, after the turning point is passed and the will is an obedient, renewed will, then the will does good and delights in the law (FC 2.63). One can even call this activity cooperation as long as one remembers that the will can only cooperate in great weakness and never as an independent partner in the way "two horses" cooperate "in drawing a wagon together" (FC 2.66).

But now a new question arises: Since Christians still live with sin, is there a significant difference between baptized and unbaptized or unconverted people? Their answer is a resounding yes. The converted will in a baptized and regenerate person is a liberated will even though "regeneration is not as yet perfect" and "the warfare of the flesh against the Spirit continues also in the elect and the truly reborn" (FC 2.67–68). The unregenerate person "resists God entirely and is completely the servant of sin," but the "regenerated person delights in the law of God according to the inmost self" (FC 2.85). In agreement with Luther the Christian life is portrayed as a ceaseless conflict with sin, but the conflict is felt more keenly in some Christians than in others, and even within the same Christian life it ebbs and flows (FC 2.68). The battle can occasionally be lost, at least temporarily, if believers "permit sin to rule in them and thus grieve the Holy Spirit within them and lose him." In that case, they have to be converted again, not through baptism but through the Word (FC 2.69).

A concluding segment summarizes this "thorough presentation of the entire doctrine of the free will" (FC 2.73). It also explains how some controversial language and formulas should rightly be understood, including Luther's use of passivity (FC 2.89) and Melanchthon's three causes of conversion (FC 2.90). All in all, FC 2 does remarkable justice to the concerns of both theologians.

Election. The position laid out in FC 11 on election corresponds to FC 2, although election as such had been the subject of controversy mainly between Lutherans and Calvinists. The objectives of the writers are to uphold the initiative of God alone in salvation while avoiding determinism; to maintain the necessity of external means; and to convince believers that God's election does not lead to "impenitence or despair" but to great consolation (FC 11.12).

To accomplish this, the authors have to make careful distinctions. Two of these are crucial to the argument. First, election is not the same as God's foreknowledge. Election pertains only to the children of God, who have "been elected and predestined to eternal life" (FC 11.5). Foreknowledge, however, pertains to everyone, both to those who will be saved and those who will not, and to everything, evil and good, that happens in the world. God knows all this ahead of time, but God is not the cause of evil or unbelief. Election is therefore not determinism.

Second, the authors plead for a careful distinction between what God has revealed in the Word and what God has not revealed. Although God knows who will ultimately be saved and who will not, that knowledge has not been revealed to anyone else. Christians are to rely on the way of salvation laid out in Scripture and summarized by FC 11.25–50. The thrust of that summary is that God saves the elect only through external means, that is, through the work of the Holy Spirit in Word and Sacrament in the church (FC 11.27). This affirmation provides reliable comfort to believers. The call of God is "not a deception" and God will continue to work through the Word to save those who are called (FC 11.29). There are no surprises. One cannot live a faithful Christian life and then be rejected by God while others, who were never converted, suddenly come out of nowhere to claim eternal life.

If all the elect are saved through Word and Sacrament in the church, of what use then is the doctrine of election? Primarily it backs up the doctrine of justification by faith alone and underscores the impotence of the human will (FC 11.43–44). Since God chose the elect to be saved long before they were born, justification and conversion proceed from God's initiative even before the call of the gospel goes out and the Holy Spirit begins to convert the will. Election also personalizes salvation and offers special support in times of trial and affliction, because it witnesses to the perseverance of the true church (FC 11.45–50).

Election is also presented as a christocentric doctrine. To say that God's eternal election should be considered "in Christ and not outside or apart from Christ" (FC 11.65) is to make the same point that Luther made about refraining from useless speculation. "Therefore, none who want to be saved should burden and torture themselves with thoughts concerning the secret counsel of God, if [i.e., whether or not] they have been elected and ordained to eternal life" (FC 11.70). Election must be a comforting doctrine that supports faith in Christ, and it must also challenge believers to take their Christian life seriously "so that the more they experience the power and might of the Spirit within themselves, the less they will doubt their election" (FC 11.73).

The authors are not arguing that Christians can prove they are elected by demonstrating great faith or virtue. They explicitly disclaim this position in pars. 75 and 88. Instead, they are trying to navigate between two perils that they had previously identified as "despair and impenitence" (FC 11.12). On the one hand, Christians should not despair at the thought of not being elected because their faith in Christ is the effect of that election. On the other hand, Christians cannot afford to be cocky because their election does not entitle them to take the Christian life lightly. They still sin and therefore must continually repent, receive forgiveness, and nourish their faith. The two dangers of "despondency or a riotous or dissolute life" are therefore best avoided by always seeking one's election in Christ (FC 11.89).

According to FC 11 the doctrine of election can serve the Christian life even without resolving the issues of God's justice or universal salvation. When used rightly, the authors believe that "this doctrine gives sorrowing and tempted people the permanently abiding comfort of knowing that their salvation does not rest in their own hands" (FC 11.90). Any presentation of the doctrine that does not have this pastoral effect is contrary to Scripture and to the intent of the Holy Spirit (FC 11.92). For the authors, this doctrine could not simply be replaced by a less offensive view like universal salvation, because God's election and God's judgment are found throughout the Bible and cannot be dismissed. Moreover, universal salvation would render the church and the Word just as useless as the false claim that a small number of elect would be saved regardless of faith in Christ. The possibility that God might not save everyone was for them no reason to reproach God, but all the more reason for the church to reach everyone with the Word so that all the elect might hear, believe in Christ, and finally be saved.

3. Theological Summary

The Lutheran confessions present a consistent picture of Christian life as a joyful and confident existence that is nevertheless exposed to hazards. Though their will has been liberated from sin and delights in the law, Christians remain at risk of yielding to sin and losing fear and trust in God that the Holy Spirit has created in them at baptism. Constant reliance on the Holy Spirit through prayer and adherence to the Word (SA 3, 4) is necessary to keep the devil at bay and the will directed toward God in faith. God's election is extra encouragement to those who make use of Word and Sacrament for constant forgiveness and the strengthening of their faith. Although the conflict with sin does not end in this life, God's final victory over sin and evil is certain to those who rely on the merits of Christ and not on their own goodness or ability. This picture is based on theological convictions that challenge some common religious assumptions.

- First, the scope of original sin is spatial as well as temporal. Original sin is better named universal sin, since it explains not so much where sin came from as why all human beings in all ages without exception are opposed to God and therefore need a Savior.

- Second, in the confessions sin is primarily a relational category. The assertion that all people are born in sin is not a denial of the fact that many people, Christian or not, are capable of avoiding private misconduct and can be defined by their society as good. Rather, to say that sin is universal means that the relationship between the world and God is disordered and that human arrogance leads to disordered relationships among human beings that go beyond private conduct to issues of justice and injustice between people. For example, stealing is sin not only because it results from an inordinate desire to possess but also because it exploits and deprives other people.[13] Everyone sins because no one, however moral their private conduct may appear, can avoid being implicated in the wider networks of injustice that cover the world.

- Third, the Lutheran picture of Christian existence depends on denying that human beings ever find themselves in a state of neutrality toward

God. The confessions therefore disallow the claim that anyone can choose God by themselves. This view contradicts the value placed on decision in contemporary Christianity. What feels like a human decision for God, the confessions would say, is actually the Holy Spirit turning the will from sin to God. The confessions do acknowledge conversion, but for them it is not a human decision but a feat of the Holy Spirit working through the Word of God and the sacraments. Because of this, the church must attempt to reach everyone with the Word. It cannot use God's election as an excuse for ignoring the call to mission. Even though people cannot choose God, God only chooses people through the Word.

- Finally, despite the hazards, this view of the Christian life is more positive than some Lutheran portrayals allow. For example, the confessions would not literally endorse the public confession made by many North American Lutherans: "We are in bondage to sin and cannot free ourselves."[14] According to FC 2.67, baptized Christians are not in bondage to sin but have "a liberated will." FC 2.67 identifies "a great difference between baptized people and unbaptized people" because the baptized have been born again "and now have a liberated will." Nevertheless, the baptized still sin (*simul iustus et peccator*) and constantly need strength and forgiveness so that they do not again become slaves to sin. The phrase "we are in bondage to sin" is valid if bondage to sin means that Christians constantly sin and are still subject to all sorts of misery "under the devil's kingdom" (LC 3.115). But if the liturgical phrase is taken to mean that Christian life after baptism is no different from life before baptism, then it is not endorsed by FC 2.67 and it fails to appreciate what Luther calls "the riches and glory of the Christian life . . . [which] is lord over sin, death and hell."[15]

◆

The Fruit: Good Works and Sanctification

1. Historical and Theological Background

The themes of sanctification and good works point to the change that repentance and baptism produce in the lives of Christians. As theologians in Western Christianity debated the nature of sanctification, they were again influenced by Augustine. He was convinced that faith would show itself in love, which he called charity (*caritas*) and which he regarded as the operation of the Holy Spirit in the believer. Charity became visible as Christians obeyed the commandments to love God and neighbor.

The terms used by medieval theologians to define sanctification, charity, good works, and obedience led to major debates during the Reformation. The crux of the medieval view lies in the relationship that was forged between faith and love. Since Paul praises love as the supreme virtue (1 Cor 13:13), scholastic theologians argued that the faith which justifies and ultimately saves the believer is faith that is perfected or "formed" by charity (*fides caritate formata*). Through the Holy Spirit God infuses this love or charity into the soul so that it becomes pleasing to God and begins to obey the commandments. God considers these acts of love and obedience worthy of eternal life, and they can properly be called meritorious good works. No medieval theologian believed that ordinary Christians became perfectly holy or righteous prior to dying; but, if they did good works and made use of the sacraments, they had within them a basis for claiming they deserved eternal life.

As soon as Luther began to teach justification by faith alone, his opponents recognized he was challenging this picture of the Christian life. Luther understood Paul to mean that justification by faith "apart from works prescribed by the law" (Rom 3:28) excludes good works and merit from the righteousness that we have through faith in Christ. Luther never intended to say, however, that good works and obeying the law are excluded from the Christian life as a whole. Consequently, he had to define the relationship of faith to good works and the nature of good works themselves. Furthermore, he had to explain how obeying the commandments fit into the Christian life and how one could speak of Christians as righteous and holy without contradicting the teaching that justification and salvation depended alone on faith in Christ. In order to accomplish all this, Luther had to make three important distinctions.

First, Luther distinguished between two kinds of righteousness in a sermon of the same name preached in late 1518 or early 1519.[16] The first kind is the righteousness of Christ that is given to people when they are baptized or truly repent of their sins and believe. Since this kind is "the righteousness of another, instilled from without," Luther calls it an alien righteousness. Only this righteousness justifies, and it is received only by faith. The second kind is "our proper righteousness," which is generated in part by us and consists of self-discipline, love of neighbor, and reverence toward God. "This righteousness," says Luther, "goes on to complete the first for it ever strives to do away with the old Adam and to destroy the body of sin." It is not the righteousness by which believers are justified, but it is certainly part of their Christian life.

The second distinction is between the right and wrong kind of good works. In his *Treatise on Good Works*,[17] Luther says he very much wants "to teach the real good works that spring from faith." These works correspond to God's commandments since no genuine good works exist apart from what God has commanded. In their desire to be holy, however, people think that truly good works are religious activities such as praying, fasting, and almsgiving. Instead, says Luther, the tasks and pleasures of daily life are just as good as long as they are done with confidence in God.

The third distinction made by Luther is between faith and love.[18] He knew the medieval concept of faith formed by love, but he rejected it. If love is added to faith, then justification by faith "apart from works prescribed by the law" has been compromised and salvation is attributed to something other than faith in Christ. This separation is a radical reversal of medieval theology. Instead of love perfecting faith, Luther argues that faith perfects love: "Love is true and genuine where there is true and genuine faith."[19] Moreover, genuine faith is "a living, busy, active, and mighty thing which does good works without ceasing"; and it is a "vital, considered confidence in God's grace, so certain that it would die a thousand times for it."[20] This faith alone establishes the saving relationship with Christ and frees love to express itself fully and genuinely in good works done for others.

Luther's distinctions are related to the fundamental issue already discussed in the sections on sin and the human will. FC 2 expresses this issue as the question: How different are baptized believers from the unbaptized? We can also ask it this way: How new and different is the Christian life?

2. The Confessional Texts

The catechisms were designed to support the Christian life at every turn. Departing from the order of most medieval catechisms, Luther set the Ten Commandments before the Apostles' Creed, the Lord's

Prayer, and the sacraments. To account for this order, Luther once used the following analogy:[21] The Ten Commandments are like the diagnosis; they disclose the sickness of sin because believers are forced to realize they can never perfectly obey them. The Apostles' Creed identifies the remedy; this early summary of Christian faith grounds the healing of sin in the redemption of God's world in Jesus Christ. The Lord's Prayer and the sacraments provide the treatment; prayer, absolution, baptism, and the Lord's Supper are means through which the Holy Spirit applies the remedy of redemption to us.

The Ten Commandments, however, not only effect repentance but also act as a guide to genuine good works. The form of Luther's explanation in the Small Catechism makes this dual function obvious. Every explanation contains both a prohibition and a positive exhortation. In fact, his explanation of the Sixth Commandment ("You shall not commit adultery") is entirely positive: "We should fear and love God, and so we should lead a chaste and pure life in word and deed, each one loving and honoring his wife or her husband" (SC 1.12).

The Ten Commandments, therefore, offer a resource for faith amid the hazards of the Christian life. This resource functions in three ways. First, when they act as a mirror, the Commandments enable Christians to see themselves as they really are, still subject to the spirit of revenge and anger. Before anger gets the best of them, the Commandments remind Christians "to be attentive to God's will and with hearty confidence and prayer to commit to God whatever wrong [they] suffer" (LC 1.187). Second, God has placed the Fifth and all other Commandments "as a boundary between good and evil" (LC 1.183). For example, the Fifth Commandment ("You shall not kill") constructs a wall around people so that no harm will come to them from the anger and violence of others (LC 1.185). It also reminds Christians to treat both their friends and their enemies with kindness and to protect them from injustice and suffering (LC 1.189, 195). Third, the Commandments are a guide to the kind of good works that God truly desires. They are "a summary of divine teaching on what to do to make one's life pleasing to God. They are the true fountain from which all good works must spring, the true channel through which all good works must flow" (LC 1.311).

The relationship between faith and works dominates the treatment of sanctification and good works in the Augsburg Confession. Despite all that Luther had written by 1530 about good works and the Ten Commandments, Eck's 404 Articles accused Luther and Melanchthon of rejecting them. [22] For that reason, CA 6 insists that justifying faith "should produce good fruits and good works and that we must do all such good works as God has commanded" (CA 6.1, German).[23] The remainder of CA 6 underscores the point that even though good works are necessary, they do not merit the forgiveness of sins, that is, they do not justify as faith does. In support of this position, both Scripture and a theologian from the early church are cited: Luke 17:10 (also cited by Melanchthon in Ap. 4.334), and the Ambrosiaster*.

Since evangelical theologians had repeatedly been accused of forbidding good works, however, an elaboration of CA 6 was proposed in Augsburg and finally included as article 20. Lutheran theologians felt the relationship between faith and works was so important and so easily misunderstood that evangelical teaching on this subject deserved a longer treatment. (CA 20 is by far the longest article in the first part of the confession.) The rationale for article 20 distinguishes between "true Christian estates and works" and "childish and useless works" (CA 20.2–3). The latter, it claims, are no longer so highly praised by the Roman theologians; instead of asserting that works alone justify, they now make the claim that faith *and* works justify (CA 20.4–7). Because this claim is no more comforting than the former, however, the authors of article 20 decided to explain in detail why only faith justifies and how the right kind of good works can proceed from this faith.

Four things about CA 20 are noteworthy. First, to defend justification by faith, Melanchthon reaffirmed that Christ alone "is the mediator who reconciles the Father" and that seeking to merit grace or to reconcile God by works is to despise Christ and to seek one's own way to God (CA 20.9–10). Second, Melanchthon argued that only justification by faith can have a comforting and salutary pastoral effect. In the Latin text (CA 20.15–18) Melanchthon made the audacious claim that justification by faith can be understood and appreciated only by people who really need it, that is, by people who have experienced a terrified conscience (CA 20.17). When Melanchthon denied that "inexperienced and profane" people can understand this, he was not thinking of the young and the naive but of people of any age who have never been in despair and forced to look beyond themselves for help. (A better translation of the Latin *imperiti* would be "untried" or "untested" instead of "inexperienced.")

Third, Melanchthon defined justifying faith as much more than the historical faith of medieval theology. Even though it is not perfected or formed by charity, justifying faith "is not merely a knowledge of historical events but is a confidence in God and in the fulfillment of God's promises" (CA 20.25).

Fourth, he attempted to explain how faith can spontaneously produce the works that must be done by Christians without having them rely on those works to earn grace. This explanation recalls the way in which Melanchthon and FC 2 describe the conversion of the human will. The will is converted when the Holy Spirit comes and produces faith. At the same time, says Melanchthon, the "heart is moved to do good works" that it was too weak to do when it was under the power of the devil before the Holy Spirit came (CA 20.29–31).[24] In conclusion (CA 20.35–39), Melanchthon enumerated the "great and genuine good works" that can be done only with the help of Christ,[25] in contrast to the "childish and useless works" already identified at the beginning of the article (20.3). The place of good works fits perfectly into the picture of the Christian life presented in discussions of perfection (CA 16) and of sin and the human will (CA 2, 18, 19).

When the Roman Confutation rejected this presentation of faith and good works, Melanchthon was incensed. Ap. 20 therefore recalls the principal argument against justification by works made repeatedly in Ap. 4 and in CA 20.9–10: justification by works eliminates the need for Christ. The confutation does not ignore Christ, however. It says human works receive meritorious power from the meritorious suffering of Christ. Furthermore, like a good shepherd, Christ set an example for the sheep to follow in doing good works and in taking up the cross.[26] To Melanchthon this reasoning probably made little difference, since he had already dismissed justification by a combination of faith and works as pastorally ineffective (CA 20.7). He repeated, therefore, the pastoral argument from CA 20: "Pious consciences will have no sure foundation where sin and death terrify them and the devil tempts them to despair unless they know that they must believe in the forgiveness of sins freely given for Christ's sake. This faith gives support and life to the heart in its hardest struggle against despair" (Ap. 20.8).

In Ap. 4.218–85 Melanchthon had already discussed many passages of Scripture cited in the confutation against justification by faith; but now he selected a new one cited against CA 20, namely, 2 Pet 1:10: "Therefore, brothers and sisters, be all the more eager to confirm your call and election, for if you do this, you will never stumble." Melanchthon conceded that the text is talking about good works, presumably the kind of behavior in support of faith advocated in 2 Pet 1:5-7. He would not concede, however, that these works cause believers to be elected and called in the first place; instead, such works confirm the call because they keep believers alert and prevent them from losing the call by sinning again without repentance (2 Pet 1:9).

It was especially difficult for evangelical Protestants to explain how good works could be necessary to the Christian life without meriting either grace or salvation. The introduction to article 4 of the Formula of Concord summarizes the problems. Since good works must follow faith that justifies and saves, can one say that good works are necessary to salvation? Since faith alone in Christ saves and good works cannot merit God's favor, is it better to say they are detrimental to salvation so that people will not put their trust in works? Or should one stress that works are spontaneous in order to avoid the impression that believers are forced to do them against their will (FC 4.1–5)?

All these questions played a role in the controversy that made FC 4 necessary. It is called the Majoristic controversy for the Wittenberg professor Georg Major (1502–1574), who alleged that "good works are necessary to salvation" in the early 1550s. Major did not think that good works merited salvation. Indeed, he defended justification by faith alone when Nicholas von Amsdorf*, his former colleague, attacked its absence in the Leipzig Interim (see pp. 25–26). Major had served on the consistory of electoral Saxony that exercised oversight over the pastors and parishes of the territory. Like Luther and Melanchthon in the 1520s, Major was alarmed at the laxity that he observed. For him it was essential to inculcate the necessity of good works against an attitude described in FC 4 as "a complacent Epicurean* delusion, since many people dream up for themselves a dead faith or superstition, without repentance and without good works, as if there could simultaneously be in a single heart both a right faith and a wicked intention to continue and abide in sin, which is impossible" (FC 4.15). For Major, good works had to be present if a person was to be saved, because the faith that saved would produce them.

Nicholas von Amsdorf (1483–1565) demanded that Major's statement be repudiated. To make his point in a most dramatic and logical way, von Amsdorf asserted that "good works are harmful to salvation." Von Amsdorf could rightly appeal to Luther for such a formulation,[27] but FC 4, like Luther, approved this statement only when people considered their works meritorious and relied on them for salvation (FC 4.37). Otherwise, the Formula rejected Amsdorf's statement because it "might weaken discipline and decency, and might introduce and confirm a wicked, wild, complacent, and Epicurean way of life" (FC 4.39). In other words, FC 4 agreed that believers should be encouraged to do good works.

As for Major's statement that good works "are necessary for salvation," FC 4 rejects it, because it contradicts justification and salvation by faith alone and undermines the comfort which that doctrine brings to "tempted and troubled consciences" (FC 4.22–23). Since the Augsburg Confession and the Apology say in various ways that good works are necessary, however, FC 4 has to examine the correct meaning of "necessary." To say good works are necessary is to say they are the inevitable result of faith and are done "from a spontaneous spirit by those whom the Son of God has set free" (4.18). Consequently, believers are neither compelled to do good works nor do they have a choice about whether to produce good works.

If works are inevitable, however, then it is tempting to look for them as proof that one has faith and will be saved. FC 4 also discusses this issue in the following form: "Whether good works preserve salvation or are necessary to preserve faith, righteousness, and salvation" (FC 4.30). This issue was exacerbated by the Council of Trent* (1545–1563), which condemned both of the following positions: that righteousness already received is not preserved or increased by good works, or that works are *only* the fruit and sign of righteousness already acquired and not the cause of its increase."[28]

In the Apology Melanchthon had argued that the "exceedingly great promise" of the forgiveness of sin needs external signs. In addition to baptism and the Lord's Supper, "this same promise is written and pictured in good works, which thus urge us to believe more strongly." FC 4 supports Melanchthon in a twofold way. On the one hand, it agrees that the presence of good works in a Christian's life is an indication that faith in the promise is alive and well and that the person is justified and saved. On the other hand, it does not mean "that faith accepts righteousness and salvation only at the beginning and then delegates this function to works, as if works should henceforth preserve faith, the righteousness that has been received and salvation" (FC 4.34). The Christian life cannot be divided into stages, such that in the beginning faith in the promise makes one righteous and then in the middle and at the end good works make one righteous. Despite their necessary presence in the Christian life and their usefulness as an indicator to believers, good works in no way deserve any credit for salvation. Because the formulation of the Council of Trent implies that they do, the Formula rejects it (FC 4.35).

While FC 4 clarifies one of the difficult issues about the Christian life, FC 3 attempts to untangle another disputed question: In relation to believers, where is the righteousness of Christ that justifies and saves? This question was raised by the Lutheran reformer Andrew Osiander*. For him, the righteousness of Christ that justifies is equivalent to the divine nature of Christ and is infused into those who have faith. Osiander felt that this view was close to Luther's teaching and that it was richer than a forensic view of justification, which attributes the righteousness of Christ to the faithful from without. Osiander believed that the divine nature of Christ was more important than the human nature and that union with this divine nature agreed with comments by Luther that Christ dwells in us and gives us his righteousness.

Osiander's critics feared that his theology would undercut justification by faith alone. It sounded to them as if Osiander ultimately made justification dependent on something in the believer, even though that something was called faith, or the righteousness of Christ, or even his divine nature. Regardless of what it was called, believers would be encouraged to look inward and start wondering if they had enough of Christ or divinity in themselves to be saved. They might start believing they could be saved only if they became more and more Christlike and divine. If so, the consolation of faith in Christ alone would be lost.

Although Osiander died in 1552, so many theologians had weighed in on the matter that the framers of the Formula thought it necessary to settle the question once and for all. In so doing, FC 3 makes several important contributions to the Lutheran view of the Christian life.

First, it refuses to play off one nature of Christ against the other. FC 3 asserts that "our righteousness rests neither upon his divine nature nor upon his human nature but upon the entire person of Christ, who as God and man in his sole, total, and perfect obedience is our righteousness" (FC 3.55). Second, FC 3 makes clear that faith justifies because it lays hold of the merit of Christ, not because "it is so good a work and so God-pleasing a virtue" (FC 3.13). This answers the objection that justifying faith itself seems to be a work. Third, FC 3 clarifies the term "regenerate," which Melanchthon had left unclear in Ap. 4.72. FC 3 concedes that regeneration can be taken as the renewal that follows justification as long as one remembers that such renewal remains incomplete and imperfect in this life (FC 3.23). But the authors clearly prefer a position in which regeneration means the same as justification. Regeneration is not an addition to justification that is necessary to salvation.

In this connection, FC 3 sets up an informal order of salvation (*ordo salutis*), a technical term for the stages of Christian life that lead to salvation. It is forced to do this in order to clarify logically what belongs to justification and what does not: "If the article [i.e., doctrine] of justification is to remain pure, we must give especially diligent heed that we do not mingle or insert that which precedes faith or follows faith into the article of justification" (FC 3.24). It offers two versions of the order. The first is: contrition, justification by faith, good works (FC 3.27). Although both contrition and good works are necessary to Christian life, neither is part of justification. The paragraphs that follow (28–39) elaborate this point before another form is offered in par. 41: justification by faith, renewal and sanctification, fruits of good works. The Formula does not intend, however, for Christian life to be conceived in linear stages that move the Christian along a progressively holier path. Whether at the beginning, the middle, or the end, the righteousness that saves comes only from the "total obedience of Christ's total person" (FC 3.56).

3. Theological Summary

- According to the confessions, the Christian life is a delicate balance of faith and good works and of justification and sanctification. It is a fertile garden in which good works sprout from faith at the same time that sin keeps pushing its head above ground. Repentance is constantly needed in order to check cockiness and prompt the faithful to rely on God's promise alone. It is a realistic picture of Christian living in a world still haunted by sin, death, and the devil, but it is not easy to preach. This difficulty was obvious from the beginning. As soon as evangelical pastors stepped into the pulpit, they began to complain that people misunderstood justification by faith to mean they no longer had to repent, obey the Commandments, or do good works. To prevent this misunderstanding is a main goal of the confessions, and this goal influences to a large extent how they speak about the Christian life. The same misunderstanding is still a challenge to Christian preaching and theology. How does one proclaim the promise of forgiveness in a way that inspires people to acts of justice and mercy but does not encourage them to rely on the same acts for salvation?

• This picture of the Christian life refutes some stereotypes of Lutheranism. The opinion that Lutherans do "not have to do anything" to be saved is true in the sense that good works do not merit salvation. The documents in this section, however, argue that all Christians, including Lutherans, have to obey the Commandments and produce genuine good works and that they will do so if the Holy Spirit has converted their wills from sin to faith. Consequently, Lutherans can regard good works as signs of their faith, although this is typically said of Calvinists.

• Another misrepresentation of Lutheranism maintains that its emphasis on Christians as saints and sinners prevents Lutherans from being more active in their pursuit of justice. The documents in this section, however, urge Christians to seek justice on behalf of their neighbors. Not one time is it said that because Christians remain sinners they should be content with the status quo. The view of the confessions is not that sin stymies good works and makes the Christian life static, but that sin requires constant repentance in order to keep faith vital and producing fruit. "We say that after penitence . . . must come good fruits and good works in every phase of life" (Ap. 12.131).

• The Christian life is dynamic in another sense as well. Salvation is not automatic and baptism does not guarantee it regardless of how the Christian lives. Along with God's promise baptism gives Christians access to the means whereby the Holy Spirit continually fights their sin, forgives it, strengthens their faith, produces good works, and preserves them unto eternal life. These means are prayer, preaching, and the sacraments, and they are available in the Christian community. The confessions would never condone the statement: "I am baptized and read the Bible; I do not have to go to church." The means provided by

God need to be used or else Christians run the risk of having sin overcome their faith to the point that they stop repenting and are lost. The certainty that believers have is not that God will save them no matter what they do, but that God will save them as they repent and use the means offered to keep their faith alive. That happens in the church, where the Holy Spirit "daily and abundantly forgives all my sins, and the sins of all believers, and on the last day will raise me and all the dead and will grant eternal life to me and to all who believe in Christ. This is most certainly true" (SC 2.6).

• Finally, the confessions demonstrate that Luther and Melanchthon fundamentally agreed on the nature of the Christian life. This is true not only for the Formula of Concord, which tries to do justice to both of them, but also for the rest of the confessions written by the two theologians themselves. Lutheran scholarship has made many attempts to discover differences between the two, and there were some. No two theologies are exactly alike. Ever since the late 1520s, one or another controversy tried to set Luther and Melanchthon at odds, with Melanchthon usually coming out second best. Both theologians agree, however, on the elements of the Christian life: the Commandments have to be obeyed; good works are the inevitable fruits of faith; Christians belong to the spiritual kingdom but can participate fully in civil life; Christian life is a conflict between real sin that remains after baptism and the Holy Spirit; the converted will is held in faith by the Holy Spirit but can fall again under the power of sin if it does not make use of the means in church; God's election is a useful way of confirming faith if believers do not try to figure out who is and who is not elect; believers who do make use of the means can be certain that the Holy Spirit will keep their faith strong and productive and will lead them into eternal life. Both also agree that it is up to pastors, teachers, and parents to instill this pattern of Christian living and its resources in every generation.

◆

The Goal: Eternal Life

1. Historical and Theological Background

From the beginning Christians have expected Jesus to return in glory, the dead to be raised, and the kingdom of God to come in fullness. In the late Middle Ages people expected the end of the world to come at any time. Christ would then preside at a final judgment that would determine, on the basis of their earthly behavior, whether they deserved the reward of eternal life.

Much of late medieval theology and piety was designed to prepare Christians for this judgment. In theology the reward of eternal life was promised to those who merited it. The basis of this merit was the cooperation of the human will with grace to produce works that fulfilled the Ten Commandments. Since so many people failed to produce these meritorious works, several remedies were available. First, the sacrament of penance* offered the opportunity of working off the penalty of one's sin both in this life and in purgatory. Second, the mass could be said privately (i.e., by a priest alone) for the souls of people who had died and were working off the last of their sin in purgatory. Third, one could invoke the aid of Mary and the saints by praying to them or by endowing altars in their honor. They were more popular advocates than Christ, who often appeared in the role of judge.

The reformers concluded that this system was based on fear and uncertainty. Christ was the judge and the verdict was in doubt. Even though people made use of all the saints and sacraments provided by the church to produce the required merits, they could still not be certain they had done enough to earn eternal life. In place of this fear and uncertainty, the reformers taught people to place their trust in Christ alone. They also believed that Christ might return at any time to judge the living and the dead. For them, however, those who had placed their trust in Christ alone for salvation had nothing to fear. The focus of the Lutheran confessions, therefore, is not on the future but on the present life of the Christian. They are not interested in details of the end of the world or the afterlife. They try to teach Christians to live in joy and confidence here and now.

2. The Confessional Texts

The confessions affirm the resurrection of the dead, a final judgment, and eternal life. CA 17 asserts this teaching against views now commonly called universal salvation and millennialism or chiliasm. In 1530 such views were held by various radical theologians, some of whom had been in Augsburg (see pp. 142–43). The notion that neither the devil nor the ungodly will suffer eternal punishment is ascribed to Hans Denck* (c. 1500–1527), an Anabaptist with spiritualist views who stayed off and on in Augsburg and was challenged by the Lutheran preacher there, Urbanus Rhegius* (1489–1541).[29] The authors of the Formula of Concord testify that they will give an account of their teaching "with intrepid hearts before the judgment seat of Jesus Christ" (FC-SD 12.40).

Luther's explanation of the second petition of the Lord's Prayer indicates how the reformers focused on the present life of Christians. When we bid "Thy kingdom come," says Luther, we pray that all which Christ and the Holy Spirit have done for us "be realized in us and that God's name may be praised through his holy Word and our Christian lives" (LC 3.52). This kingdom is not limited to the present, however. Its beginning in the lives of Christians will bring others through the Holy Spirit into the "kingdom of grace," so that everyone may live eternally in the same kingdom. There are not two kingdoms of God, but one kingdom in two forms. After it comes here first in Word and faith, it then comes in eternity through the final revelation (LC 3.53). Now it overthrows the devil's kingdom through the Word and the Holy Spirit, "until finally the devil's kingdom shall be utterly destroyed" (LC 3.54). Consequently, says Luther, when Christians pray this petition, they are not praying for something perishable, "but for an eternal, priceless treasure and everything that God possesses" (LC 3.55).

Since the kingdom of God is entered by Word and faith, the reformers removed the parts of medieval piety designed to help people either earn eternal life or influence the verdict of Christ the judge. The confessions therefore reject the invocation of saints, purgatory, satisfactions for sin, and special masses for the dead. One can see this clearly in Luther's rejection of purgatory in SA 2, 2. This rejection is part of a revolution: redirecting the mass from its use "almost exclusively for the dead" to a celebration for the living alone "for whom Christ instituted the sacrament" (SA 2, 2.12). Luther had already argued that the Mass as then understood and celebrated ran into "direct and violent conflict" with the fundamental article of justification by faith in Christ alone (SA 2, 2.1). Applying this criticism specifically to the dead, Luther then rejects for the same reason purgatory, the invocation of saints, and a host of other practices. In one way or another, all of them add requirements to faith in Christ alone as the way to eternal life. Christ is no longer the only mediator between believers and God. Angels and saints exist, Luther believes, and they may even pray for Christians "as Christ himself also does." But it is idolatry to pray to them and do all sorts of religious activities to invoke their aid (SA 2, 2.26).

Even when one trusts in Christ alone for salvation, however, Luther still believes that God's commandments must be obeyed and that one can even speak of rewards in that connection. In LC 1 Luther takes seriously the threat and promise contained in the Ten Commandments (Exod 20:5-6; LC 1.320). God will punish those who disobey them and bless those who keep them. Obeying the Commandments, however, is a consequence of true faith in God rather than an extra performance that earns God's favor over and above faith. Rewards do follow from obedience, but these rewards are not earned by the obedience as if one were adding merits to faith. Instead, they are the consequences of "a spontaneous impulse and desire gladly to do God's will" (LC 1.330). Rewards are God's fulfillment of God's own promise attached to the Commandments.

In the Apology Melanchthon goes to great pains to make this point: "We grant that eternal life is a reward because it is something that is owed—not because of our merits but because of the promise" (Ap. 4.362). In other words, God is obligated to keep the divine promise and give eternal life to those who have trusted in that promise. This view is not unprecedented in medieval theology. Nominalists taught that the divine covenant made God a debtor to believers, but Nominalists also believed that the covenant obligated believers to produce works befitting eternal life ("merited by the merit of *condignity* through good works"; Ap. 4.356). On the basis of Scripture and a famous statement by Augustine,[30] Melanchthon insists that eternal life is a gift (Ap. 4.356–57). He believes that rewards and punishments can usefully be preached as the consequence of belief and unbelief (Ap. 4.365); and he holds the common medieval view about heaven that "there will be distinctions in the glory of the saints" (Ap. 4.355; usually based on 2 Cor 3:18). In the last analysis, however, eternal life is not awarded on the basis of how good one's Christian life has been. Always "the crown is owed to the justified because of the promise" (Ap. 4.363).

3. Theological Summary

- The acceptance of a last judgment fits the view of Christian life presented in all the confessional documents. On the one side, they assume that not everyone is elected to salvation, nor that everyone will be converted, produce the fruits of faith, and enjoy eternal life. There is an ultimate difference between believers and unbelievers. Believers have something to look forward to. The consummation of Christian life is eternal life. On the other side, the confessions deny that eternal life is a reward merited by the good works of believers in this life.

- By taking obedience to the Commandments seriously and by recognizing what they call the "devil's kingdom," the confessions give the power of evil and injustice its due and call Christians to do battle against that power. Christians are engaged in God's struggle to overthrow evil; the Commandments provide guidance for that struggle and obedience to them has consequences for that struggle. The outcome, however, is not based on our performance but on the absolute trustworthiness of God's promise of victory.

- At the center of that promise stands Jesus Christ. The Christian life, present and future, is centered on faith in Christ alone. In the present, that faith brings joy and confidence to people who are troubled by sin and disheartened in their struggle with evil. In the future, that faith will be transformed into sight and eternal life in the kingdom of God.

Questions for Discussion and Further Study

1. What is meant in the confessions—and *not* meant—by the "two reigns of God"?

2. In what sense can Lutherans speak about a free will, and what are its limits?

3. Indicate the difference between the Lutheran and Roman Catholic understandings of sin as argued by the confessions.

4. According to the confessions, how could one define "sanctification," and how is sanctification related to justification?

5. What conclusions can one draw from the confessions about the relationship between church and state in religiously neutral societies?

6. What theological stance might one take toward a new millennium in light of what the confessions say about eternal life and the kingdom of God?

S. H.

CHAPTER SEVEN

The Confessions in the Worldwide Lutheran Communion

The Confessions: Essential Elements of Lutheran Identity

The Lutheran Church has regarded itself always as a confessional church, as a church that emphasizes its primary calling to confess and proclaim the gospel of Jesus Christ. It is committed to confessional writings that clarify, safeguard, and communicate in a binding manner the content of this gospel as the foundation and norm of its faith, life, and mission. In this way the church as a communion of believers has a common basis and bond of unity and is marked by an *identity* understood as its shape and profile, its "face," with clear, discernible contours. This is the ideal, but not always the Lutheran reality.

The Lutheran claim to be a confessional church has often met with critical reactions from other churches that understand this term to indicate a narrow, inward-looking stance (from which Lutheran churches, like other churches, are not always free). The contemporary ecumenical commitment and active involvement of most Lutheran churches no longer evoke such reactions. On the contrary, other churches too are increasingly concerned about developing a clearer Christian and confessional identity. This need is seen especially in the context of ecumenical dialogue, where only an encounter between partners with a clear profile can be fruitful and mutually enriching. Churches—Lutherans included—see this need for clearer profiles also as a condition for being identifiable and committed Christian communities amid much Christian vagueness and confusion and amid growing religious pluralism.

The confessional writings of the Lutheran *Book of Concord* are thus essential elements and criteria of Lutheran identity. All Lutheran churches in the world have accepted the *Book of Concord* or some of its texts, including in every case the Augsburg Confession and Luther's Small Catechism. In their church constitutions, under the norm of Holy Scripture and together with the ecumenical creeds, the Lutheran confessions are described as true witnesses to the gospel, as pure expositions of the Word of God, or in similar terms. They are generally described as authoritative guides for the proclamation, teaching, and life of the Lutheran churches. At their ordination future pastors commit themselves to the confessions. Yet Lutheran identity is a lived, dynamic reality that cannot simply be equated with this collection of texts. This identity is shaped and sustained by fundamental theological and pastoral convictions, which are based in the confessional texts but which are also shaped and nourished by the tradition and living faith of the Lutheran Church.

The following basic theological and pastoral convictions are essential components of Lutheran identity:

1. Confession of the primary, prevenient, and exclusive initiative of God. Lutherans confess that the triune God—Father, Son, and Holy Spirit—comes to us lost human beings. God condescends to us in the incarnation and continues to come to us through human words and elements of creation in the proclamation of the Word and the celebration of the sacraments. We are not able to come to God, but God comes to us, suffers for us, is present with us: this is the only way to salvation and eternal life.

2. Witness to the justifying and liberating action of God in the death and resurrection of Jesus Christ. Since the Reformation this action has been confessed as the center of the message of salvation, the gospel, as the criterion of the church's proclamation and life, and as the foundation of Christian existence. Believers are accounted and made righteous by God on account of Christ's redeeming work for us. By being justified they are reconciled with God and receive forgiveness of sins and renewal of life. This gift is freely granted through the Holy Spirit by grace and faith alone.

3. Distinction (not separation) between God's Word as gospel and God's Word as law. This is an important criterion in order to protect and pre-

serve the gratuitous character of the message and gift of salvation and
to exclude the illusion of meritorious human efforts before God.

4. Emphasis on the proclamation of the Word and administration of the
   sacraments as outward means of God's action that are necessary for salvation. Lutherans highlight these two means of grace. Through them
   the Holy Spirit creates faith, and Christ, through the Holy Spirit, is
   truly present with his salvation and new life for each believer and for
   his whole church.

5. Understanding the church as a community of believers and saints who
   are brought together and sustained by the Holy Spirit through Word
   and Sacrament served by an ordained ministry. One consequence of
   this basic conviction is the teaching that the primary visible marks of
   the one, holy, catholic*, and apostolic church are the right proclamation
   of the Word and the administration of the sacraments in accordance
   with the gospel.

6. Emphasis on the ordained ministry as well as on the priesthood of all
   baptized believers. Lutherans affirm that there must be an ordained
   ministry, instituted by God, of publicly proclaiming the Word and
   administering the sacraments and the office of the keys. But just as
   important is the general priesthood, which all believers receive in their
   baptism. This priesthood expresses the equality of all Christians before
   God and their apostolic obligation to witness in their particular contexts in word and life to the gospel. Both forms of ministry belong
   together and should serve together.

7. Affirmation of the world, despite its ambivalence and finite character,
   as God's good creation. This does not imply that Lutherans should
   accept the world as it is. But just as God is present and active in the
   church for salvation, so God is present and active in the world in order
   to create and sustain life and to consummate it at the end of time in a
   new creation.

8. Definition of the secular responsibility of Christians as faithful participation in God's sustaining and transforming activity in the world.
   Lutherans see this participation not as a gradual realization of the kingdom of God or as the means of one's own justification before God, but
   as serving God's purpose of justice and peace for all humanity and creation.

9. Use of Holy Scripture as the norm of the church's proclamation and
   teaching. Most Lutherans distinguish between the gospel and Scripture
   as a collection of texts. The gospel, as the center of Scripture, constitutes

the foundation of the authority of Scripture and provides the criterion and orientation for its interpretation.

10. Appreciation for the theological and spiritual tradition of the church. The Lutheran Church did not start ex nihilo in the sixteenth century but considers itself part of the tradition of the church, renewed in the Reformation, since the time of the apostles. This tradition and its continually new interpretation and application are expressions of and means of the continuity and unity of the church.

11. Commitment to the church's confession: the ecumenical creeds and the Lutheran confessions. The most obvious element of Lutheran identity in church constitutions is this commitment; it serves as an authoritative guide for the faith and life of the church and as a hermeneutical means for focusing on the center of Scripture. This commitment provides a criterion for distinguishing between true and false proclamation and doctrine and is a means to express and to preserve ecclesial communion in each Lutheran church and among the Lutheran churches worldwide.

12. The practice of intensive theological reflection and study. The reason for the emphasis on theological study and training in the Lutheran tradition has not been fascination with scholarly inquiry for its own sake, but the concern to clarify and interpret the truth that is to be proclaimed here and now. This theological work is undertaken by listening to the biblical witness, to the church's confessions, and to the tradition of the church, but also by engaging in a critical encounter with the intellectual and social challenges of the time.

These fundamental convictions are complemented by other expressions of Christian life and thinking that are also part of the identity and profile of Lutheran churches. Some of these expressions are:

— a tradition of interpreting social, ethical, and religious issues from a theological standpoint that has influenced the social, intellectual, and cultural life of many societies;

— an emphasis on the need for Christian education in order to help all members of the church understand and appropriate the faith;

— the continued use and renewal of liturgical forms of worship that are shared with other Christian churches;

— a highly developed and widely appreciated tradition of church music;

— a rich tradition of hymns, many of which contain sung explications and confessions of faith;

— an awareness of the fundamental theological and pastoral significance of the sacraments;

— an openness for diverse forms of church ministry and church structures with a preference for episcopal structures where appropriate;

— a recognition of the relative independence and integrity of forms and institutions of secular life that, though being part of God's creation, should be free from ecclesiastical domination;

— a clear ecumenical commitment in our time that aims at closer relations or full communion with other Christian traditions.

Several of the basic convictions and expressions of Lutheran identity are shared by other Christian traditions. Taken together in their interrelatedness, however, these convictions and expressions shape the faith and life of the Lutheran community of Christians and thereby constitute the components and contours of a specific Lutheran identity. This identity does not aim at isolation or separation but seeks to express our common Christian identity.

◆

The Confessions and the Establishment of Lutheran Churches Worldwide

The Lutheran Reformation began in small German territories and towns about 480 years ago. Since that time Lutheranism has come to every continent and a worldwide communion of Lutheran churches has become a reality today. In the movement of this church from its centers of origin to near and distant lands the Lutheran confessions played important roles. They helped to preserve the fundamental doctrinal and pastoral convictions of the Lutheran Reformation; they were indispensable for the establishment of Lutheran churches in new countries; and they served the coming together of Lutheran groups and churches into larger ecclesiastical bodies. These roles of the confessions can be seen in the following survey of the worldwide expansion of Lutheranism.

1. Expansion of Lutheranism
during the Reformation

The movement of Lutheranism beyond its German homeland began already during the first decades of the Reformation. The pressure and the longing for ecclesiastical reform was so strong in other parts of Europe that the liberating gospel of God's unconditional and saving grace was welcomed in many places. As a result, Lutheran churches arose in many European countries. Their official, legal establishment was prepared and accomplished everywhere through virtually the same processes of reform. These included evangelical* preaching, Bible translations, reforms of worship, new hymns, the study in Wittenberg by many future Lutheran leaders, pamphlets, and in some cases the formulation of confessional documents.

In the course of such processes all the churches in northern Europe became Lutheran national churches in the sixteenth century. In 1536 and 1537 the Reformation was officially introduced into Denmark, to which Norway and Iceland also belonged, but the first law referring to Holy Scripture and the Augsburg Confession as a basis of faith appeared in 1665. Then, in 1683, a final decision on confessional commitment in the law of the country named Holy Scripture, the three Ecumenical Creeds, the Unaltered Augsburg Confession, and Luther's Small Catechism. The process of settling confessional status also took a long time in Sweden to which at that time Finland belonged. There the Lutheran movement had been growing for decades, but it was only in 1593 that a great church council at Uppsala decided that the three Ecumenical Creeds and the Augsburg Confession constituted the doctrinal standard of the country. Nearly one hundred years later the Royal Law of 1686 broadened the doctrinal basis by including the whole *Book of Concord*. In the Baltic region, today Estonia and Latvia, the Lutheran church was introduced about the same time by way of Germany and Sweden. As of 1997, the Church of Sweden with more than 7.5 million members is the largest Lutheran church in the world. The Lutheran churches of Denmark and Finland have more than 4.5 million members each, while the Church of Norway has 3.8 million and the Church of Iceland 244,000 members. In all these countries more than 85 percent of the population is Lutheran. The Lutheran churches in Estonia and Latvia, which are rebuilding their church life after the Soviet period, have together fewer than

400,000 members, and the minority church in Lithuania has 29,000 members.

In eastern and southeastern Europe the Lutheran Reformation was accepted in the sixteenth century by large sections of the population in what is today Austria, Croatia, the Czech Republic, Hungary, Poland, Slovakia, Slovenia, and Yugoslavia. One interesting example of confessional development took place in Hungary, which then included Slovakia in the framework of the Habsburg Empire. In 1549 a synod of pastors signed the Augsburg Confession, and a confession of five free cities—*Confessio Pentapolitana*—was also drawn up. In 1610 and 1614, however, the official confessional position was settled for the first time by a commitment to the whole *Book of Concord*. Several other churches in this region accepted the *Book of Concord*, others the Augsburg Confession and the Small Catechism only. The strong Lutheran presence in this part of Europe was reduced to minority churches in Catholic lands by the persecution and discrimination of the Counter-Reformation. Today the membership of the Lutheran churches in this region is: Hungary 430,000; Austria 337,000; Slovakia 329,000; Poland 80,000; and in the other countries together about 170,000. Most Lutheran churches in this region refer to their confessional commitment in their name, for example, the Evangelical Church of the Augsburg Confession in the Slovak Republic.

Lutheran churches also emerged at the time of the Reformation in western Europe: In France in the regions of Montbeliard and Alsace-Lorraine (today 250,000 members) and in the Netherlands (today 17,000 members). The country with the largest Lutheran population in the world is still Germany. Nearly 14 million people belong to the ten regional Lutheran churches (*Landeskirchen*), eight of which form the United Evangelical Lutheran Church of Germany, which was founded after World War II on the basis of their common confessional commitment. But there are also many Lutheran congregations and Lutherans in the other regional United Churches (Lutheran and Reformed). The confessional commitment of the German Lutheran churches in their constitutions reflects the diversity of Lutheran churches worldwide: the constitutions refer to the *Book of Concord*, to "the Lutheran confessions" or "the Lutheran confession," or to the Lutheran confessions with special reference to the Augsburg Confession and Small Catechism.

2. Expansion of Lutheranism through Emigration

From the seventeenth century until the middle of the twentieth century, and predominantly in the nineteenth century, Lutheran emigrants took their faith and church from Europe to other continents. In North America in the second half of the eighteenth century Lutheran congregations came together in a *ministerium* (Pennsylvania and New York) and then in many synods on a regional and ethnic basis. During this early development the confessions did not play a major role. While the Ministerium of Pennsylvania had no word about the confessions in its new constitution of 1792, they became increasingly relevant in the nineteenth century as part of a growing confessional awareness that reacted to Anglo-Saxon liberal Protestantism and was influenced by the Lutheran revival in Germany. In particular, the early movements toward Lutheran cooperation awakened the need to clarify the basis of Lutheran unity and identity. By the middle of the nineteenth century a confessional commitment of synods and of larger ecclesial units became the rule, though in different forms and with different interpretations. In 1864 the General Synod, to which several synods had belonged since 1820, finally had to insert a doctrinal basis into its constitution: the Word of God in Holy Scripture and the Augsburg Confession. In 1895 this basis referred specifically to the Unaltered Augsburg Confession because, in addition to Melanchthon's* *Variata* of 1540, there was now in North America an Augsburg Confession that some Lutherans had considerably modified in 1855. The other and more conservative body of synods, the General Council, referred in its Fundamental Principles of 1867 to the Unaltered Augsburg Confession and to the other parts of the *Book of Concord* as guarding and interpreting the Augsburg Confession.

The individual church bodies that were formed in nineteenth-century North America reflected in their confessional subscription their mother churches in Europe. Those of Finnish and Swedish background adopted the whole *Book of Concord*, those of Danish and Norwegian background the creeds, the Augsburg Confession, and the Small Catechism. The constitution (1846) of the Lutheran Church-Missouri Synod drew on its strong confessional background in Germany and included from the beginning a confessional statement that required unconditional acceptance of Holy Scripture and all the symbolical books of the *Book of Concord*. In 1934 the United Lutheran Church in America declared that the basis for union in one single Lutheran church in America was the common commitment to the Lutheran confessions. This expression of one century's experience helped to bring about the formation of the Evangelical Lutheran Church in America (ELCA) in 1988. Its differentiated confessional basis includes the acceptance of Holy Scripture, the creeds, the Unaltered Augsburg Confession, and the other writings in the *Book of Concord*. The more recent development of Lutheranism in Canada was closely connected to the two founding churches of the ELCA, the Lutheran Church in America and the American Lutheran Church, and to the Missouri Synod. As of 1997 in the United States there are 5.1 million members in the ELCA and 2.6 million members in the Lutheran Church-Missouri Synod, along with 480,000 Lutherans in smaller churches. The Evangelical Lutheran Church in Canada has 198,000 members, and there are 90,000 Lutherans in other churches.

In Latin America the first Lutheran congregations were founded in 1741 and 1743 by Lutherans from Amsterdam in (Dutch) Surinam and Guyana (northern part of South America). Immigration from Europe, especially from Germany in the nineteenth century, and a further wave of immigrants after World War II, led to the formation of the present Evangelical Church of the Lutheran Confession in Brazil (note the name!), which now has over one million members and subscribes to Holy Scripture, the creeds, the Augsburg Confession, and the Small Catechism. The Missouri-related Evangelical Lutheran Church of Brazil has 207,000 members, and there are smaller Lutheran churches in Argentina, Bolivia, Chile, El Salvador, Guyana, and other countries.

German Lutherans who did not accept the imposed union of Lutheran and Reformed churches in Prussia emigrated in 1838 and 1841 to Australia. They laid the foundations of what became in 1966 the Evangelical Lutheran Church in Australia, which has a clear commitment to the whole *Book of Concord*. It has close to 100,000 members.

One should not forget, however, that there was an emigration of German Lutherans in the eighteenth and nineteenth centuries to eastern Europe. They were invited to settle in Russia, Hungary, Slovakia, Romania, and Yugoslavia. During and after World War II most of the descendants of these ethnic Lutheran groups were forced to return to Germany or they emigrated to other continents. This history has left, for example, the once rather large German-speaking Evangelical Church of the Augsburg Confession in Romania (Transylvania) with only 17,000 members today. A large group of ethnic German Lutherans did remain in the Soviet Union, where their church life was suppressed but their faith was kept alive by laypeople. During the last years of the Soviet Union and after its dissolution Lutheran congregations assembled again and formed the Evangelical Lutheran Church in Russia and Other States with a membership of about 250,000. The "resurrection" of this church is a moving witness to Christian faithfulness.

3. Expansion of Lutheranism through Mission

Lutheran mission agencies in Europe and North America entered the world scene mainly in the second half of the nineteenth century and often in close connection with the colonial expansion of European nations in Africa and Asia. The work of Lutheran mission societies, and of mission societies from the United Churches in Germany, led to the establishment of Lutheran churches, which became independent in the 1960s. The confessional subscription of these churches usually reflects that of the churches from which their missionaries came. All these churches have accepted Holy Scripture, the creeds, the Augsburg Confession, and the Small Catechism as their confessional basis. In a few cases, this basis is broadened by reference to the other documents in the *Book of Concord*. An important exception is Indonesia, where the missionaries came mainly from the mission societies of the United Churches in Germany. They used the Small Catechism, but the 1930 church order of the Protestant Christian Batak Church (HKBP) referred only to Holy Scripture. In the 1940s a confessional stance was needed because of its relation to other churches and of the growing influence of sects, other religions, and religious nationalism. A new confession that sought to respond to this situation while remaining faithful to the main conviction of the Lutheran Reformation was accepted by the Synod of the HKBP in 1951. The Lutheran World Federation (LWF) considered this confession compatible with the

Lutheran confessional tradition, and the HKBP was accepted into membership of the LWF in 1952.

Several of the Lutheran churches in Africa and Asia belong to the most rapidly growing churches within the Lutheran family. In Africa the largest church is the Evangelical Lutheran Church in Tanzania with 2.5 million members, followed by the Ethiopian Evangelical Church Mekane Yesus with over 2 million members, the Malagasy Lutheran Church (1.5 million), the Lutheran churches in South Africa (886,000), Namibia (655,000), Cameroon (206,000), Zaire (136,000), Zimbabwe (100,000), and several smaller churches. In Asia the largest Lutheran presence is in Indonesia, where the eight member churches of the LWF have 2.4 million members. Ten Lutheran churches in India have 1.3 million members, and the two Lutheran churches in Papua, New Guinea, have 910,000 members. There are 84,700 Lutherans in Malaysia, 41,500 in Hong Kong, 32,500 in Japan, and smaller churches exist in Bangladesh, Jordan, Korea, Myanmar, Philippines, Taiwan, and Thailand.

◆

The Confessions: Bond and Commitment in the Lutheran Communion

The Lutheran confessions exercised an essential function not only in the expansion of Lutheranism and the establishment of Lutheran churches in Europe, North and South America, Africa, and Asia, but also in the mutual discovery of these churches, the establishment of closer relations, and the development of a sense of a worldwide communion of Lutheran churches.

In the nineteenth century several other families of churches began to form their confessional organizations and structures for mutual exchange and common discussion. For example, the Lambeth Conference of all Anglican bishops met for the first time in 1867, and the World Alliance of Reformed Churches was founded in 1875. Compared to these traditions the Lutheran churches of the world initiated forms of closer relations and cooperation relatively late. In 1923 the very modestly organized Lutheran World Convention (LWC) was founded at Eisenach in Germany. It was the first world meeting of Lutherans, even though only a few participants came from Africa and Asia. In the deliberations of the LWC the Lutheran confessions were repeatedly recognized as the foundation of this emerging fellowship of churches. At Eisenach a doctrinal basis was introduced into the constitution of the LWC that acknowledged Holy Scripture as the only source and infallible norm of doctrine and practice, and the confessions of the Lutheran Church, especially the Unaltered Augsburg Confession and the Small Catechism, as the pure exposition of the Word of God. Thus the confessions became the rallying point of Lutherans worldwide.

Lutheran emergency aid and newly established contacts after World War II led to the foundation of the Lutheran World Federation (LWF) at its first assembly in Lund, Sweden, in 1947. The LWF, too, based its bond of fellowship on the common faith confessed in the Lutheran confessions and affirmed this in its doctrinal basis, which it took over from the LWC. The LWF stated cautiously in its constitution, however, that the LWF "shall be a free association of Lutheran churches" in order to guard the full autonomy of its member churches and to avoid the impression that a "super-church" was intended. Through the assemblies, meetings, commissions, consultations, visits, and exchanges organized by its staff in Geneva, Switzerland, the LWF serves its member churches by undertaking theological studies and by supporting church relations, mission involvement, world service, development aid, involvement of women and youth, and its Institute for Ecumenical Research at Strasbourg, France. Through these and other means the LWF has helped to strengthen relationships among Lutheran churches, furthered their ecumenical commitment, and enabled their common service and witness in response to the challenges of our time and world.

The confessions have been a constant point of reference in the work of the Lutheran World Federation. Two examples illustrate this. Since around 1970 the LWF has become one of the most active partners in the growing number of international bilateral theological dialogues between Christian World Communions (confessional families). Such dialogues have been and are undertaken between the LWF and the Roman Catholic Church, the Orthodox Churches, the Anglican Communion, the World Alliance of Reformed Churches, the World

Methodist Council, the Baptist World Alliance, and the Seventh-day Adventist Church. In these conversations the Lutheran position is presented and interpreted on the basis of the biblical witness, the confessions, and present theological insights. It is important that in such dialogues the participants are able to refer to authoritative statements of their church and not just present their own ideas. In addition, in the work of the LWF the original ecumenical character and aim of the Lutheran confessions was rediscovered and thus experienced as an impetus and encouragement for involvement in these dialogues and in other ecumenical activities.

In a similar way the confessions provided guidance when the fellowship of Lutheran churches faced contemporary problems, for example, the challenge of racism in the form of apartheid in South Africa. There the white and black Lutheran churches were kept apart by institutionalized apartheid. In response to this situation the Sixth Assembly of the LWF at Dar-es-Salaam in 1977 stated:

> The Lutheran churches are confessional churches. Their unity and mutual recognition are based upon the acknowledgment of the Word of God and therefore of the fundamental Lutheran confessional writings, particularly the Augsburg Confession, as normative. . . . Churches which have signed the confessions of the church thereby commit themselves to show through their daily witness and service that the gospel has empowered them to live as the people of God.

The resolution also asserts that political systems may become so perverted and oppressive that "it is consistent with the confessions to reject them and work for change. We especially appeal to our white member churches in Southern Africa to recognize that the situation in Southern Africa constitutes a *status confessionis**. This means that, on the basis of faith and in order to manifest the unity of the church, churches should publicly and unequivocally reject the existing apartheid system" (*In Christ—A New Community*, 179–80).

The bilateral dialogues, this apartheid resolution, and the growing fellowship among Lutheran churches generally prepared the way for a change in the self-understanding of the LWF and the communion of Lutheran churches it serves. Because of their unity in the right proclamation of the gospel and the administration of the sacraments in accordance with the gospel (CA 7), which is affirmed by their common adherence to the Lutheran confessions, the Lutheran churches saw themselves increasingly as a worldwide Lutheran communion. Accordingly, the constitution of the LWF was changed at the Eighth Assembly of the LWF in Curitiba, Brazil, in 1990. The formulation according to which the LWF is a "free association of Lutheran churches" was now replaced by the statement that the "LWF is a communion of churches which confess the triune God, agree in the proclamation of the Word of God and are united in pulpit and altar fellowship." As of 1998 the LWF has 122 member churches representing about 57.6 million Lutherans in the world. Together they gratefully recognize their confessional heritage and contemporary commitment as an inspiration and guidance for their *koinonia* in faith, life, and witness.

Questions for Discussion and Further Study

1. List some of the essential elements of Lutheran identity.
2. Describe the place and role of the Lutheran confessions in the formation of your own church and in its constitutional and liturgical texts.
3. In what sense are the confessions for the worldwide Lutheran Communion a bond of fellowship and a commitment to ecumenical involvement?

G. G.

Chapter One: Setting the Stage: The Reformation in Historical Context

1. See Eike Wolgast, *Hochstift und Reformation*, 83–110, 197–207.

2. LW 31:75.

Chapter Two: The Development of Lutheranism

1. Luther is reported to have added: "Here I stand; I cannot do otherwise. God help me. Amen." On this speech, see Scott Hendrix, *Luther and the Papacy*, 132–33.

2. LW 45:70–71 (*Sincere Admonition by Martin Luther to All Christians to Guard against Insurrection and Rebellion*, early 1522).

3. LW 38:67 (Report of the Marburg Colloquy by the Nuremberg reformer, Andrew Osiander).

4. LW 38:88.

5. LW 49:343.

6. LW 49:354.

7. LW 40:271.

8. *Die evangelischen Kirchenordnungen*, VI/1/2, 965.

9. *BC* 338.1.

10. Hausmann (1478/79–1538) was the first superintendent in Zwickau and later introduced the Reformation to Anhalt-Dessau. See *OER* 2:214–15.

11. LW 53:64–65, 68.

12. Wengert, "Wittenberg's Earliest Catechism."

13. FC 7.12–16.

14. SA 2, 4.7. The divine right of papal authority had been the major point of contention between Luther and Eck at the Leipzig Debate of 1519.

15. Gleason, *Gasparo Contarini*,140–49.

16. Gleason, *Gasparo Contarini*, 229–30.

17. For a precise summary of the current situation of Lutheranism in southern and eastern Europe with historical perspective, see Günther Gassmann, "Lutherische Kirchen," in *TRE*, 21:599–616.

18. The nonelectoral (or Albertine) lands of Saxony were ruled until his death by Duke George, who remained an opponent of the Reformation. Its chief cities were Dresden and Leipzig, where the Reformation had been introduced in 1539 under Duke Henry. Duke Moritz, who became Elector Moritz in 1547, was the first son of Henry.

19. German and Latin texts of the Augsburg Interim are printed in *Das Augsburger Interim von 1548*, ed. Joachim Mehlhausen.

20. A good analysis of this complicated process and how it led to intra-Lutheran controversies is given by Joachim Mehlhausen, "Der Streit über die Adiaphora," in *Bekenntnis und Einheit der Kirche*, 105–28.

21. The German text is printed in CR 7:258–64 (no. 4433); however, the articles on justification and good works, which were taken over from an earlier document, are printed in CR 7:48–62. English translation of the whole in Jacobs, *Book of Concord*, 2:260–72.

22. The diet at Naumburg and the accusation that Lutherans were confused play a significant role in Jacob Andreae's preface to the *Book of Concord* (*BC* 6–8).

23. Which version of the Augsburg Confession Calvin subscribed to and whether he physically signed it are unclear from the sources. For an overview of the matter, see Brian Gerrish, "Strasbourg Revisited: The Augsburg Confession in A Reformed Perspective," in *The Augsburg Confession in Ecumenical Perspective*, 132–37.

24. For the text of these sermons and a fuller description of the road to concord, see Kolb, *Andreae and the Formula of Concord*.

25. Kolb, *Andreae and the Formula of Concord*, 61–62.

26. For the story of the Philippists in Saxony and of the Crypto-Calvinist controversy, see Luther D. Peterson, "Philippists," in *OER* 3:255–62.

Chapter Four: The Lutheran Confession: The Structure of the Faith

1. LW 32:112.

2. LW 44:135.

3. LW 44:135.

4. *Enchiridion Symbolorum*, 364, *1501, and 366, *1507.

5. Luther vividly recounts this experience in the preface to the 1545 edition of his collected Latin writings; LW 34:336–38.

6. In his lectures Luther made some use of Augustine's treatise *The Letter and the Spirit* (based on 2 Cor 3:5b: "For the letter kills, but the Spirit gives life"), but the relationship that he established between law and grace was his own. See Leif Grane, *Modus loquendi theologicus*, 46–52.

7. LW 31:364.

8. *Melanchthon: Selected Writings*, 144.

9. LW 40:274.

10. On the 1527 controversy, its prelude and its aftermath, see Wengert, *Law and gospel*.

11. LW 40:295–96.

12. The text of the Formula actually makes this assertion about Sacramentarians but certainly has Zwingli and his followers in mind. Using Luther's own words, the Solid Declaration (FC-SD 8.38–43) specifically rejects Zwingli's use of *alloeosis*, his term for a mere rhetorical and not a real exchange of the properties of both natures of Christ.

13. *Freedom of a Christian*, in LW 31:344.

Chapter Five: The Lutheran Confessions: The Christian Community

1. "Accedit verbum ad elementum et fit sacramentum, etiam ipsum tamquam visibile verbum." *In Joannis Evangelium Tractatus* 80.3, in PL 35:1840.

2. LW 36:4–126, especially 18: "To begin with, I must deny that there are seven sacraments, and for the present maintain there are but three: baptism, penance, and the bread. All three have been subjected to a miserable captivity by the Roman curia, and the church has been robbed of all her liberty."

3. LW 37:161–372.

4. LW 38:287–319.

5. For the text see *The Leuenberg Agreement and Lutheran-Reformed Relationships*, 1989.

6. *A Common Calling*, 1993.

7. *Lutherans and Catholics in Dialogue III*, 187–98.

8. Lutheran/Roman Catholic International Commission, *The Eucharist* (Geneva: LWF, 1980).

9. See part 3 of Martin Luther, *On the Councils and the Church* (1539), in LW 41:143–78.

10. Compare the famous statement by Cyprian of Carthage (d. 258): "One cannot have God as father if one has not the church as mother." *De ecclesiae catholicae unitate* 6, OECT, ed. Bévenot, 66.

11. Compare another famous phrase from Cyprian: "Outside the church there is no salvation." *Epistula* 73.21.2, in *Saint Cyprian Correspondence*, ed. Bayard, 2:275.

Chapter Six: The Lutheran Confessions: The Christian Life

1. Reu, *The Augsburg Confession*, 119.

2. *The Judgment of Martin Luther on Monastic Vows* (1521), in LW 44:243–400.

3. Immenkötter, *Der Reichstag zu Augsburg und die Confutatio*, 92.

4. WA 43:461.11–13.

5. WA 43:460.25–28.

6. CR 92:370.6–9. Zwingli's view was criticized by Luther and by Urbanus Rhegius; this criticism is probably behind the remark in *BC* 29, n.3, which claims "the reformers" placed Zwingli in the same Pelagian camp with scholastic theologians.

7. Immenkötter, 46–47.

8. Reu, 101.

9. Augustine, *On Grace and Free Will* 6.13, in NPNF 5:449. Latin text in PL 44:889.

10. Immenkötter, 61–62.

11. *Melanchthon on Christian Doctrine: Loci Communes 1555*, 60.

12. Luther, *Babylonian Captivity of the Church* (LW 36:253); and *Melanchthon on Christian Doctrine: Loci Communes 1555*, 60.

13. Luther comments on the Seventh Commandment ("Do not steal"): "A person steals not only when a strongbox or a pocket is robbed, but when that person takes advantage of a neighbor at market, in a grocery shop, butcher stall, wine and beer cellar, workshop, and, in short, wherever business is transacted and money is exchanged for goods and labor" (LC 1.224). Further: "Beware how you deal with the poor, of whom there are many now. . . . [The cries of the poor] will reach God . . . who will not leave them unavenged" (LC 1.246–47).

14. *Lutheran Book of Worship*, 1978, 56.

15. LW 31:368.

16. LW 31:297–306.

17. LW 44:21–114.

18. See Luther's comment on Gal 3:12 in LW 26:272.

19. LW 31:371.

20. LW 35:370.

21. *Eine kurze Form der zehn Gebote, eine kurze Form des Glaubens, eine kurze Form des Vaterunsers 1520*, in Clemen 2,39.9–25.

22. Articles 198–202 in Reu, 108.

23. Leif Grane argues that the formulations "should bring forth" in the German text (*bringen soll*) and "is bound to bring forth" in the Latin text (*debeat . . . parere*) are more typical of Melanchthon's theology and a slight departure from the way in which Luther views works as the spontaneous product of faith (Grane, *Die Confessio Augustana*, 65). That is unlikely, however, since Luther uses the same term in *Freedom of a Christian* to explain the relationship between faith and works. There Luther writes: "Although Christians are thus free from all works, they ought (*debet*) in this liberty to empty themselves. . . and to serve, help, and in every way deal with the neighbor" (LW 31:366). For Luther this "ought" means both spontaneity and obligation, just as he argues in the catechism that the Ten Commandments should be obeyed and yet spontaneously are kept when the first of them is obeyed. No less than

Melanchthon, Luther emphasizes that good works are both necessary and inevitable in the Christian life.

24. In the Latin text Melanchthon bolsters this explanation by citing once more a patristic text allegedly by Ambrose, *The Calling of the Gentiles*, now thought to have been written by Prosper of Aquitaine (d. after 455). See Altaner-Stuiber, *Patrologie*, 451.

25. Melanchthon probably knew that the verse he cited in support of this main point (John 15:5: "Apart from me you can do nothing") was cited against Pelagius in canon 5 of the Council of Carthage (418). See *Enchiridion symbolorum*, 84, #227.

26. Immenkötter, 63.

27. Sample texts are cited by Paul Tschackert, *Die Entstehung der lutherischen und der reformierten Kirchenlehre*, 516.

28. *Enchiridion symbolorum*, 380, #1574. Between 1565 and 1573 one of the Formula's authors, Martin Chemnitz, had published a four-volume critique of Trent's decrees.

29. His treatise *Wider den newen Taufforden* ("Against the New Baptizing Order," Augsburg, 1527) was directed specifically at Denck. On Denck see *OER* 1:469–70.

30. To the Pelagians, Augustine retorts, "It is God's own gifts that God crowns, not your merits." Augustine, *On Grace and Free Will* 6.15, in NPNF 5:450. Latin text in PL 44:89–91.

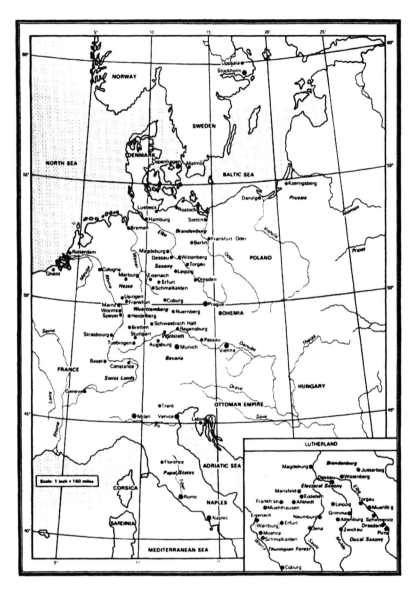

Central Europe at the time of the Reformation
from Erwin Weber, From Luther to 1580: A Pictorial Account

I. Martin Luther & Philip Melanchthon	II. The Reformation	III. The Confessions
1517 Ninety-five Theses		
1518 PM arrives in Wittenberg		
1519 ML debates John Eck at Leipzig. PM present and writes report		
1520 ML: 4 treatises: Babylonian Captivity, Christian Freedom, To the Christian Nobility, Good Works		
1521 Edict of Worms outlaws ML	1521 Diet and Edict of Worms	
1521 PM: *Loci communes* (1st edition)	1521 Rapid spread of evangelical movement	
1522 March: ML returns to Wittenberg; eight sermons challenge Karlstadt		
1525 ML marries Katharina von Bora; *De servo arbitrio* against Erasmus	1525 Revolution of 1525 ("Peasants' War"); Thomas Müntzer executed	
	1525 First "Anabaptists" in Zurich	
1526 ML: German Mass	1526 First Diet of Speyer (each estate free to adopt the evangelical movement)	
1526 Lord's Supper controversy begins		
1527 ML & PM: *Instruction for Visitors of Parish Pastors in Electoral Saxony*		
1529 ML & PM at Marburg Colloquy	1529 Second Diet of Speyer (Evangelicals protest renewal of Edict of Worms)	1529 ML: Catechisms
	1529 Marburg Colloquy (Philip of Hesse)	1529 Marburg, Schwabach, Torgau Articles
1530 ML at Coburg while PM in Augsburg at Diet; correspondence	1530 Diet of Augsburg	1530 John Eck's 404 Articles
		1530 PM: Augsburg Confession read in presence of Emperor Charles V on June 25

1530	August: Confutation of the Roman theologians at Augsburg
1530	September 22: Edict of Augsburg
1531	PM: Apology of the Augsburg Confession. Response to Confutation
1536	Wittenberg Concord with Bucer over the presence of Christ in the Supper
1537	ML: Smalcald Articles requested by Elector John Frederick of Saxony
1537	PM: Treatise on the Power and Primacy of the Pope. Considered addendum to the CA
1540	PM: Altered CA (*Variata*)

1532	PM: Romans commentary
1531	Ulrich Zwingli dies in battle
1531	Formation of the Smalcald League
1534	Anabaptist kingdom at Münster
1536	Pope Paul III calls council to convene in Mantua in May 1537
1537	Diet of Smalcald (February-March)
1540	Charles V calls for religious colloquies (Hagenau, Worms, Regensburg)
1541	Colloquy at Regensburg fails to reconcile evangelicals and Catholics
1541	Calvin returns as reformer to Geneva
1547	Council of Trent opens
1547	Smalcald War. Charles V defeats Smalcald League, captures Wittenberg

1539	ML: The Councils and the Church
1540	PM meets John Eck again at Worms religious colloquy
1546	ML dies in Eisleben; eulogies by PM and Bugenhagen
1547	PM, Katharina Luther, and children flee capture of Wittenberg

1548   Adiaphorist Controversy over the Interim leads to Gnesio-Lutheran vs. Philippist debates

1557   Religious Colloquy at Worms intensifies Lutheran disagreement

1568   Jacob Andreae and Martin Chemnitz initiate drive for Lutheran unity

1573   Jacob Andreae: "Six Christian Sermons"

1573   Elector August of Saxony joins drive

1576   Torgau Book

1577   Bergen Book = Solid Declaration Andreae prepares Epitome for princes

1580   June 25: *BC* published in Dresden

1548   Augsburg Interim imposes religious compromise that favors Catholics

1555   Peace of Augsburg gives legal sanction to all adherents of the CA

1556   Charles V abdicates and retires

1563   Council of Trent closes

1563   Palatinate becomes Calvinist; Heidelberg Catechism

1564   Calvin dies in Geneva

1555   PM edits final German edition of *Loci*

1557   PM attends last religious colloquy at Worms (Lutheran disunity)

1560   PM dies in Wittenberg. Interred close to ML in Castle Church

Abelard, Peter (1079–1142). Versatile medieval theologian in France whose writings encouraged critical reflection on the faith, provoked controversies, and shaped scholastic thought.

adiaphora. Literally "indifferent matters." Rites and practices imposed by the Interims in 1548 that Melanchthon and others considered to be indifferent, that is, not able to undermine the gospel, while Gnesio-Lutherans held that such matters were not indifferent in a period of persecution or *status confessionis.*

Agricola, John (1492–1566). Theologian who questioned the place of the law in Lutheran teaching and instigated the Antinomian controversies.

Agricola, Michael (1510–1557). Leading Lutheran reformer, translator, and shaper of church life in Finland.

Albert of Mainz (1490–1545). German archbishop who reported Luther's criticism of indulgences (Ninety-five Theses, 1517) to Rome.

Altered Augsburg Confession (1540). Melanchthon's reworking of certain articles in the 1530 Augsburg Confession that later Lutherans rejected. Often called by the Latin word for "altered": *Variata.*

Ambrosiaster. Name coined for the author of a fourth-century commentary on the Pauline epistles that had been falsely attributed to Ambrose of Milan.

Amsdorf, Nicholas von (1483–1565). Early colleague of Luther and Melanchthon who became a reformer in Magdeburg and a leader of the Gnesio-Lutheran party.

Anabaptists. Literally "rebaptizers." Pejorative name given to those Christians in the sixteenth century who practiced believers' baptism of those already baptized as infants.

Andreae, Jacob (1528–1590). Lutheran theologian from southern Germany who led the campaign for Lutheran unity and was a main author of the Formula of Concord (1577).

Anselm of Canterbury (c. 1033–1109). Medieval monk and theologian who became archbishop of Canterbury; famous for his treatises that gave rational grounds for articles of faith.

Antichrist. The concept of a powerful antagonist of Christ who would threaten the church at the end of time (based on 1 John 2:4 and 2 John 2); the identification of the Antichrist with the papacy by some medieval groups anticipated its use by Luther and other reformers.

antinomian. Literally "against the law." Pejorative name given to John Agricola and others who feared that teaching the commandments to Christians would undermine the gospel.

Apostolic Tradition (c. 215). An informative description of liturgy and polity in the early church at Rome probably written by the presbyter and theologian Hippolytus (c. 170–c. 236).

Aquinas, Thomas (c. 1224–1274). Medieval scholastic theologian, member of the Dominican order, and author of the comprehensive *Summa Theologiae*.

Aristotle (384–322 BC). Greek philosopher whose work served as the foundation of medieval scholastic theology that the reformers criticized.

Arius (d. 336). Priest in Alexandria who tried to safeguard the unity of God by teaching that the Son was subordinate to the Father; his teaching (called Arianism) was rejected as heretical in favor of the Son being "of the same essence" as the Father.

Athanasius (c. 296–373). Bishop of Alexandria whose persistent campaign against the teachings of Arius led to the triumph of the trinitarian doctrine of God formulated at Nicea in 325 and confirmed at Constantinople in 381.

Augsburg, Edict of (1530). Decree that ended the Diet of Augsburg by giving evangelical cities and territories until April 15, 1531, to return to the faith and practice of the Roman Church.

Augsburg, Peace of (1555). Political settlement of the German Reformation that gave legal recognition to adherents of the Augsburg Confession (Lutherans).

August of Saxony (1526–1586). As elector in the 1570s, he played a decisive role in the process of Lutheran unity that led to the adoption of the *Book of Concord* (1580).

Augustine (354–430). North African bishop of Hippo and most influential theologian of Western Christianity; he was avidly read and debated during the Reformation. Favorite theologian of the young Luther, who belonged to the order named after him: Order of the Hermits of St. Augustine.

Basel, Council of (1431–1449). Controversial council of the late medieval church that attempted to assert conciliar authority and to carry out the reforming mandates of its predecessor at Constance.

Berengar of Tours (c. 1010–1088). Medieval theologian criticized and censured for his symbolic view of the presence of Christ in the Lord's Supper.

Biel, Gabriel (c. 1410–1495). Late medieval scholastic theologian who belonged to the Nominalist school and was studied by the young Luther.

Bora, Katharina von (1499–1552). Former Cistercian nun from a Saxon noble family who married Luther in 1525 and managed the family's large household in the former Augustinian monastery.

both kinds. From the Latin *sub utraque specie* ("under both kinds"). Reference to both elements of the Eucharist, bread and wine, which the evangelical movement demanded that laity receive—in opposition to the practice of withholding the cup from the laity.

Brenz, John (1499–1570). Lutheran reformer of southwestern Germany and defender of the doctrine of ubiquity.

Briessmann, John (1488–1549). Lutheran reformer and theologian in East Prussia and the Baltic region.

Bucer, Martin (1491–1551). Leading reformer and theologian in Strasbourg who diligently pursued evangelical unity in Germany before spending the last three years of his life in England.

Bugenhagen, John (1485–1558). Theologian and pastor in Wittenberg who wrote and implemented church orders in northern Germany and in Denmark. Often called Pomeranus because he was from Pomerania in north Germany.

Bullinger, Heinrich (1504–1575). Swiss reformer and long-term successor of Zwingli in Zurich who alongside Calvin defined the theology of the Reformed churches.

Calvin, John (1509–1564). French reformer of Geneva, author of the *Institutes of the Christian Religion,* and shaper of Reformed Protestantism also referred to as Calvinism.

canon law. The body of ecclesiastical law consisting of the pronouncements of bishops, popes, and councils that gradually acquired authority in Western Christianity and existed in several collections by 1500.

canon of the Mass. The prayer of consecration in the eucharistic liturgy that contains the words of institution and was criticized by reformers for its use of sacrificial language.

catholic/Catholic. From the Greek word for "universal." Uncapitalized, it designates the historic, orthodox mainstream of Christianity whose doctrine was defined by the ecumenical councils and creeds. Most reformers, not just Lutherans, appealed to this catholic tradition and believed that they were in continuity with it. Capitalized, it designates historically the opponents of the evangelical movement who remained loyal to the bishop of Rome; especially after the Council of Trent it came to mean the Roman Catholic Church.

celibacy, clerical. Requirement that clergy remain unmarried; it was formally enacted by the medieval Roman Church but abolished by Protestants at the time of the Reformation.

Chalcedon, Council of (451). The fourth ecumenical council; against the teachings of Nestorius and Eutyches it defined the way of speaking properly about the union of two distinct natures, divine and human, in the one person of Christ.

Chemnitz, Martin (1522–1586). Lutheran theologian and pastor in Braunschweig, a primary author of the Formula of Concord, and critic of the Council of Trent.

chiliasm. From the Greek word for "thousand." See **millennialism.**

Christian III (1503–1559). Devout Lutheran king of Denmark and Norway who established the Reformation in those lands.

Chrysostom, John (354–407). Theologian and patriarch of Constantinople renowned for his personal holiness, reforming zeal, and his preaching (Chrysostom is Greek for "golden-mouthed").

church orders. Term used for the constitutions adopted by cities and territories during the Reformation that governed doctrine, worship, polity, education, and finances in their new evangelical churches.

Chytraeus, David (1531–1600). Lutheran theologian, professor at the University of Rostock, and coauthor of the Formula of Concord.

communicatio idiomatum. Literally "communication of properties." Christological term affirmed by Chalcedon that defines how the two natures of Christ share the properties of those natures with each other and with the person of Christ.

Invoked by Lutherans to explain how the human nature of Christ can be present with the divine nature in the Lord's Supper.

concomitance. Eucharistic teaching by the Council of Constance that both the body and the blood of Christ are contained in each of the elements, bread or wine, and that laity receiving only the bread consequently receive the entire Christ.

concupiscence. Inordinate desire arising from the senses that remains active following baptism and that Lutheran reformers considered to be authentic sin against the opinion of some medieval theologians.

Confutation, Roman. Response to the Augsburg Confession written by Roman theologians and read at the Diet of Augsburg on August 3, 1530. Melanchthon's Apology is a rebuttal of the confutation.

Consensus Tigurinus (1549). Latin for "Zurich Agreement." An agreement on the sacraments drafted by Calvin and Bullinger in Zurich in 1549 that rejected the real bodily presence and defined Reformed doctrine.

Constance, Council of (1414–1418). Important council of the late medieval church that ended the papal schism of Western Christianity and mandated ongoing reform.

Constantinople, First Council of (381). The second ecumenical council; it amplified the faith of Nicea in a creed known as the Nicene (officially the Niceno-Constantinopolitan) Creed ascribed to this council.

Contarini, Gasparo (1483–1542). Devout and scholarly Italian cardinal who served as papal legate to the Regensburg religious colloquy in 1541.

corpus doctrinae. Literally "body of doctrine." A collection of authoritative theological writings considered normative for Christian teaching in a particular area. The *Book of Concord* became the most widely accepted such collection for Lutheran cities, territories, and lands.

Counter-Reformation. A term formerly used for sixteenth-century Roman Catholic reform as a whole but now applied to Catholic reform only insofar as it rejected and reacted to the Protestant Reformation.

Crypto-Calvinism. A pejorative term applied by Gnesio-Lutherans to other Lutherans whom they accused of believing in a spiritual rather than a bodily presence of Christ in the Lord's Supper.

***Decretum Gratiani* (c. 1140).** Over four thousand texts concerning matters of church discipline compiled by the Italian scholar Gratian with a view toward harmonizing their discrepancies; it became the first body of canon law.

Denck, Hans (c. 1500–1527). Early Anabaptist leader in southern Germany whose spiritualist theology was probably one object of condemnation in the Augsburg Confession.

Donatists. Fourth-century schismatic church in North Africa that claimed a pure line of clerical succession untainted by ordinations performed by bishops who had lapsed during persecution or by their successors; vigorously opposed by Augustine and condemned in 411.

Duns Scotus, John (c. 1265–1308). Influential Franciscan philosopher and scholastic theologian between Thomas Aquinas and the Nominalists who anticipated the latter on some issues, like God's freedom to order salvation however God willed.

Eck, John (1486–1543). Incisive Roman theologian who faced Luther at the Leipzig Debate in 1519 and continued to oppose Melanchthon, the Augsburg Confession, and the entire evangelical movement until his death.

enthusiasts. English word for *Schwärmer*, Luther's German label for both radical and Roman theologians who granted equal or superior authority to extrascriptural revelation through the Holy Spirit over against the external Word of God.

Epicureans. Followers of Epicurus (342–270 B.C.), a Greek philosopher who valued the senses and taught that the goal of life was pleasure in the sense of freedom from fear and pain.

Erasmus of Rotterdam, Desiderius (c. 1467–1536). Famous Christian humanist of the north European Renaissance who came out in opposition to the Reformation by attacking Luther's view of the enslaved will.

Eunomius (d. 394). Arian bishop in Asia Minor whose opposition to the doctrine that the Son was of the same essence as the Father was rejected by orthodox theologians and implicitly by the Council of Constantinople (381).

evangelical. From the Greek word for "gospel" and its German derivative. Original designation for the early reformers and their supporters that is still used in German-speaking areas for non-Roman and non-Orthodox Christians. Replaced by "Protestant" in many English-speaking lands; historically unrelated to twentieth-century evangelical movements.

ex opere operato. Literally "by the work performed." Scholastic phrase meaning that the validity and efficacy of the sacraments depend on the grace-conferring power of the rites themselves and not on the merits of the recipient or the minister. Criticized by reformers for neglecting the importance of the recipient's faith.

Exsurge Domino (1520). The papal bull, issued by Pope Leo X in 1520, that threatened Luther with excommunication.

facere quod in se est. Literally "to do what is in oneself," or to do one's best. Phrase used by scholastic theologians to describe the human effort that would merit God's grace; rejected by Lutheran and Reformed theologians.

Fifth Lateran Council (1512–1517). Convened in opposition to the antipapal Council of Pisa, Lateran V passed some reform measures and reasserted papal over conciliar authority on the eve of the Reformation.

filioque. Literally "and from the Son." Western insertion into the text of the third article of the Niceno-Constantinopolitan Creed regarding the procession of the Holy Spirit; it contributed to the schism (1054) between Eastern and Western Christianity.

Flacius Illyricus, Matthias (1520–1575). Controversial Lutheran theologian from Croatia who studied and taught at Wittenberg before opposing Melanchthon on the Interims and becoming a leader of the Gnesio-Lutheran movement.

Florence, Council of (1438–1445). Part of the council that originated at Basel; it sought the reunion of Rome with the Eastern (Orthodox) Churches and sanctioned the number of seven sacraments in a decree of 1439.

Fourth Lateran Council (1215). Important medieval council that defined the doctrine of transubstantiation and set the requirement of annual confession for all Christians.

Frederick of Saxony (1463–1525). Founder of the University of Wittenberg and Luther's prince and patron. As one of the electors of the Holy Roman Emperor, Frederick used his princely power to protect Luther and the early evangelical movement after they were outlawed in the empire.

Gerson, Jean (1363–1429). French medieval theologian and chancellor of the University of Paris who was read by the young Luther and esteemed by the reformers for his spiritual and pastoral insights.

Gnesio-Lutherans. From the Greek for "genuine or pure" Lutherans. Pejorative term applied to those Lutherans who opposed the Interims and, led by Flacius and von Amsdorf, sought to uphold Luther's theology against compromises that they thought were made by Philip Melanchthon and his supporters, whom they dubbed Philippists.

Gregory of Rimini (c. 1300–1358). Italian theologian at the University of Paris and leader of the Augustinian order whose theology may have influenced Luther.

Gropper, John (1503–1559). Conciliatory German Catholic theologian and reformer in Cologne who conceived the notion of a twofold justification included in the Regensburg Book drafted by him and Martin Bucer.

Heidelberg Catechism (1563). First Reformed catechism written in Germany when the territory of the Palatinate became Calvinist.

Hussites. Followers of John Hus (c. 1372–1415), the Bohemian (Czech) reformer who was executed at the Council of Constance. They are sometimes called Utraquists because they asserted the right of laity to receive both kinds (*sub utraque specie*) in the Eucharist.

indelible character *(character indelebilis)*. Medieval concept of a permanent sacramental character that is imprinted on the soul by baptism, confirmation, and ordination, thus making these sacraments unrepeatable.

Interims (Augsburg and Leipzig, 1548). Attempts by Emperor Charles V after the defeat of the Smalcald League to reimpose Catholic rites and practices on evangelical territories of Germany that led to vigorous controversies among Lutherans over adiaphora.

Jesuits. See **Society of Jesus** (1540).

John Frederick of Saxony (1503–1554). Son of John and nephew of Frederick who presided as elector of Saxony over the expansion of the Smalcald League from 1532 until its defeat in 1547. After forfeiting the electoral title and Wittenberg to Duke Moritz, he ruled the shrunken duchy of Saxony from his court in Weimar, pursuing a Gnesio-Lutheran policy.

John of Saxony (1468–1532). Brother of Frederick who became elector of Saxony at Frederick's death in 1525 and advanced the evangelical cause in visitations, the Diet of Augsburg (1530), and the Smalcald League.

Jonas, Justus (1493–1555). Lutheran reformer and colleague of Luther and Melanchthon in Wittenberg who translated some of their most important Latin works into German, including the Apology.

Karlstadt, Andrew Bodenstein von (c. 1480–1541). Luther's faculty colleague who was displaced from leadership of the evangelical movement by Luther's return to Wittenberg in 1522; his disagreements with Luther over theology and procedure provided the first impulses toward defining a Lutheran movement.

keys, power of the. Ecclesiastical power of discipline and governance based on Matt 16:19 and 18:18, limited by Luther to the binding and loosing of sin (SA 3, 7) and especially to absolution as a means of applying the gospel (SA 3, 4).

Körner, Christoph (1518–1594). Professor of theology at Frankurt an der Oder in Brandenburg and coauthor of the Formula of Concord in 1577.

Lombard, Peter (c. 1100–1160). Paris theologian who wrote the *Four Books of Sentences,* which became the standard medieval textbook of theology.

Lutheran Orthodoxy. The age of Lutheran theology in Europe from the Formula of Concord (1577) to the end of the seventeenth century marked by comprehensive treatments of doctrine, like the *Loci theologici* of John Gerhard (1582–1637).

Major, George (1502–1574). German Lutheran theologian in Wittenberg who was a supporter of Melanchthon in the intra-Lutheran controversies, one of which, over the necessity of good works, bears his name.

manducatio oralis. Literally "oral eating." A phrase used in arguments for the real bodily presence to indicate that a communicant receives ("eats") the body and blood of Christ even if that communicant does not have faith and contrition.

Manichaeism. Dualistic system of thought originating in third-century Persia that attracted Christian adherents like Augustine (temporarily) but was rejected because its myth of salvation contradicted the unitary biblical view of creation, sin, evil, and redemption.

Marburg Colloquy (1529). Meeting of evangelical theologians from Germany and Switzerland called by Philip of Hesse at Marburg in an unsuccessful attempt to settle differences over the presence of Christ in the Lord's Supper.

Melanchthon, Philip (1497–1560). German humanist scholar and Lutheran theologian in Wittenberg, younger colleague of Luther and, after him, the most important Lutheran leader. Wrote three confessional documents: Augsburg Confession, Apology, and Treatise on the Power and Primacy of the Pope.

meritum de condigno. A scholastic term for the kind of human merit, earned in a state of grace, that deserves the reward of eternal salvation.

meritum de congruo. A scholastic term for the kind of human merit, earned prior to receiving grace, which receives justification by God's gracious reckoning despite not being fully worthy of doing so.

millennialism. From the Latin word for "thousand." Belief in a thousand-year earthly reign of Christ based on Rev 20:4-6 and expected by some Christians as the outcome of movements like the sixteenth-century Reformation.

Moritz of Saxony (1521–1553). Became elector of Saxony in 1547 after siding with Emperor Charles V against the Smalcald League but then resisted Charles's efforts to impose the Augsburg Interim on Saxony and led the revolt of princes that issued in the Peace of Augsburg.

Müntzer, Thomas (c. 1491–1525). Evangelical pastor, teacher, and theologian who became convinced that the Reformation was the inauguration of the kingdom of God on earth and died as the revolutionary leader of the peasant army at Frankenhausen in 1525.

Musculus, Andreas (1514–1581). Professor of theology at Frankfurt an der Oder, superintendent of the church in Brandenburg, and coauthor of the Formula of Concord (1577).

Nantes, Edict of (1598). Articles signed by King Henry IV of France that granted limited civil and religious rights to French Protestants until it was revoked in 1685.

Neoplatonism. Greek philosophical system from the third century that exercised an important influence on Christian theologians like Augustine and Dionysius the Pseudo-Areopagite (c. 500).

Nicea, Council of (325). The first ecumenical council; it rejected the views of Arius by declaring the Son to be of the same essence as the Father in an early form of what is known as the Nicene Creed.

Nicholas of Cusa (1401–1464). German cardinal, philosopher, and theologian who participated in the Council of Basel and wrote a comprehensive proposal for the reform of church and empire.

Ninety-five Theses (1517). Latin statements critical of indulgences and the pope's prerogative in regard to them. Written by Luther for an academic debate, they instead ignited the Reformation and led to irreconcilable conflict between Luther and the Roman curia.

Nominalism. School of medieval philosophy and theology in which Luther was trained. It argued for the primacy of divine revelation and for the freedom of God to establish the order of salvation as a covenant between God and human beings.

Novatian. Third-century Roman presbyter who protested the lax treatment of Christians who had wavered under persecution; his followers formed a small schismatic church similar to the North African Donatists.

Osiander, Andrew (1496–1552). Lutheran reformer of Nuremberg who went to East Prussia at the time of the Interims and whose teaching on the righteousness of Christ instigated a controversy that was settled in FC 3.

Paschasius Radbertus (c. 790–860). Theologian and monk at Corbie in France whose works include a controversial treatise on the Eucharist.

patristic. Literally "of the fathers." Term applied to the works and teachings of Christian writers, traditionally called fathers of the church, beginning in the second century and extending to the end of the eighth century.

Paul of Samosata. Third-century bishop of Antioch condemned by the synod of Antioch (268) for allegedly denying the full divinity of Christ.

Peasants' War (1525); also **Revolution of 1525**. A widespread social and political revolt, concentrated in southern and central Germany, that used the Bible and the reformers' appeal to Christian freedom as justification for a new Christian social order. Opposed by Catholic and evangelical authorities who defeated several armies, including the one led by Thomas Müntzer at Frankenhausen in 1525.

Pelagius (c. 350–c. 418). British ascetic teacher in Rome who argued that the fall did not prevent human beings from taking responsibility, even with the help of grace, for their salvation. Augustine rejected the views of Pelagius and of his disciple Caelestius as a threat to salvation by grace alone and condemned Pelagians as heretical.

penance, sacrament of. The late medieval practice of this sacrament, formally consisting of contrition, confession, and satisfaction, was criticized by reformers for turning confession into interrogation and for making absolution secondary.

Petri, Laurentius (1499–1573). Younger brother of Olaus and first Lutheran archbishop in Sweden; he oversaw the adoption of the evangelical church ordinance two years before his death.

Petri, Olaus (1493–1552). Lutheran reformer of Sweden who shaped church life through his pastorate in Stockholm and through important writings like his Swedish translation of the New Testament and his Swedish manual of liturgy.

Philip of Hesse (1504–1567). Protestant prince and coleader of the Smalcald League, who sought unity among evangelical theologians but whose leadership was neutralized by the scandal surrounding his bigamy in 1540.

Philippists. Pejorative term applied to the supporters of Philip Melanchthon and his theology by the Gnesio-Lutherans, who thought Melanchthon had betrayed Luther's theology and the principles of the evangelical movement, especially on the issue of adiaphora.

Protestant. A name sometimes given to evangelical cities and territories in Germany after the imperial Diet of Speyer in 1529, when they protested the repeal of a 1526 decision that allowed them to ignore the Edict of Worms (1521) against Luther and to proceed with the Reformation in their jurisdictions. In the English-speaking world the term gradually came to be used mainly of non-Roman Catholic and non-Orthodox Christians.

real bodily presence. Phrase often used to describe the distinct Lutheran insistence on the presence of the human as well as of the divine nature of Christ in the Lord's Supper.

receive, reception. Official terminology for the acceptance of doctrines, pronouncements, and confessions into the tradition of a particular church or group of churches.

Regensburg Book. A set of conciliatory theological articles, known especially for its statement on a twofold justification, that were discussed by evangelical and Catholic theologians at the colloquy of Regensburg in 1541 but were unable to provide a basis for agreement.

Revolution of 1525. See Peasants' War.

Rhegius, Urbanus (1489–1541). Prolific Lutheran reformer and theologian in Augsburg who after 1530 became superintendent of the church in Lower Saxony and helped to establish the Reformation in cities and territories of northern Germany.

Sacramentarians. Literally those who believe in the external sign (*sacramentum*) but not the inner reality (*res*) of the sacraments. Pejorative name applied by Lutherans (e.g., in FC 8) to those theologians who did not hold a real bodily presence of Christ in the Lord's Supper.

scholastic. Literally "of the schools." Term applied to theology as it came to be taught in the cathedral schools and universities of the Middle Ages. Citing Scripture, philosophy (especially Aristotle), and patristic writings, scholastic theologians debated propositions and each other, forming their own schools of thought such as Nominalism.

Schwenckfeld, Caspar von (1490–1561). Silesian nobleman and spiritualist reformer who rejected a real bodily presence of Christ in the Eucharist and imposed a moratorium on celebrating the sacrament for his followers, who eventually formed a separate Schwenckfeldian church.

Second Helvetic Confession (1566). Definitive and influential confession of the Swiss Reformed churches written by Heinrich Bullinger.

Selnecker, Nicholas (1530–1592). German Lutheran theologian, pastor, and musician in Leipzig who worked closely with Jacob Andreae and Martin Chemnitz to produce the Formula of Concord and gain support for it.

Smalcald League (1530). A political alliance of evangelical cities and territories formed in December 1530 at the town of Smalcald in Thuringia in reaction to the Edict of Augsburg.

Society of Jesus. A religious order of the Roman Catholic Church founded by Ignatius Loyola (c. 1491–1556) and his companions, approved by the pope in 1540, and devoted to pastoral ministry and to mission.

sola scriptura. Literally "by Scripture alone." Lutheran principle of the authority of Scripture that claims that Scripture is the supreme authority for Christian faith and is to be followed when other authorities conflict with it or with one another.

status confessionis. Originally *casus confessionis* in FC 10.2. Literally "a state or case of confession." A condition in which the faith is so threatened that Christians must take a confessional stand on the matter at stake.

Staupitz, John von (c. 1469–1524). Late medieval theologian and official of the Augustinian order who influenced Luther theologically and pastorally and was his predecessor as professor of biblical studies at the University of Wittenberg.

Strigel, Viktorin (1524–1569). German theologian and supporter of Melanchthon who was accused by Gnesio-Lutherans of synergism because of his opposition to Flacius on sin and the human will. His views forced the precise and balanced discussions of these topics in FC 1 and 2.

synergism. From the Greek for "working together." Term applied to cooperation of the human will with divine grace in the process of salvation. Generally opposed by theologians in the Augustinian tradition and by Gnesio-Lutherans in the synergistic controversy. Carefully discussed and defined in FC 2.

Tauler, John (c. 1300–1361). German Dominican preacher and theologian whose sermons, containing themes of inwardness, detachment, and receptivity, were read by Luther.

Transubstantiation. Philosophical explanation adopted by the Fourth Lateran Council (1215) of how the bread and wine of the Eucharist become the body and blood of Christ: the internal substance of bread and wine is transformed into body and blood while their external features (accidents) retain the properties of bread and wine.

Trent, Council of (1545–1563). Council of the Roman Church that enacted important reforms and defined Catholic teaching on doctrines such as justification and the sacraments in contrast to the views of the Protestant Reformation.

ubiquity. From the Latin word for "everywhere." Argument for the bodily presence of Christ in the Lord's Supper based on the union of his two natures: since the divinity of Christ can be everywhere, the humanity of Christ can also be everywhere, including in the sacrament.

Unity of the Brethren. *Unitas fratrum*, known also as Bohemian or Moravian brethren. Radical group of Hussites who became a vibrant church that survived persecution in Bohemia to become the ancestor of Moravians, the Evangelical Church of the Czech Brethren, and the Czechoslovak Hussite Church.

Utraquists. See **Hussites.**

Valentinians. Followers of Valentinus (d. c. 165), a theologian from Egypt, whose teaching was condemned by the church fathers as gnostic heresy.

Variata (1540). See **Altered Augsburg Confession.**

Vasa, Gustav (1496–1560). Swedish king sympathetic to the Reformation who allowed a national church, independent of the papacy, to become the Lutheran Church of Sweden.

via moderna. Literally the "modern way." Another designation for Nominalism, over against the "old way," which referred to the theology of Thomas Aquinas and others that was based on philosophical realism.

visitations. Inspection tours of parishes carried out by clergy and public officials in both Protestant and Catholic territories in order to assess the condition of congregational teaching and practice.

Westphal, Joachim (1510–1574). Gnesio-Lutheran theologian in Hamburg and prominent antagonist of Calvin and Melanchthon who participated in several intra-Lutheran controversies.

William of Ockham (c. 1285–c. 1349). English Franciscan philosopher and theologian, regarded as a chief representative of Nominalism, who was censured by the church and sided with the spiritual wing of his order against the papacy.

Wittenberg Concord (1536). Agreement on the mode of Christ's presence in the Lord's Supper that was reached by evangelical theologians from south Germany, under the leadership of Martin Bucer, and Lutheran theologians in Wittenberg.

Worms, Edict of (1521). Official proclamation of the imperial convention (Diet of Worms) that outlawed Luther and his supporters in the Holy Roman Empire.

Zwingli, Ulrich (1484–1531). Reformer of Zurich and initiator of Reformed Protestantism who clashed with Lutherans over the presence of Christ in the Lord's Supper.

Zwinglians. Supporters of Ulrich Zwingli and of his theology, sometimes referred to in Lutheran documents in the sense of Sacramentarians.

Sources and Reference

Altaner, Berthold; and Stuiber, Alfred. *Patrologie*. 7th ed. Freiburg: Herder, 1996.

Das Augsburger Bekenntnis Deutsch 1530–1980. Revidierter Text. Ed. Günther Gassmann. 6th ed. Göttingen: Vandenhoeck & Ruprecht, 1988.

Das Augsburger Interim von 1548: Deutsch und Lateinisch. Ed. Joachim Mehlhausen. Neukirchen-Vluyn: Neukirchener Verlag, 1970.

Die Bekenntnisschriften der evangelisch-lutherischen Kirche. 6th ed. Göttingen: Vandenhoeck & Ruprecht, 1967.

Bente, Friedrich. *Historical Introductions to the Book of Concord*. St. Louis: Concordia, 1965.

Bibliography of the Lutheran Confessions. Ed. David Daniel and Charles Arand. Sixteenth Century Bibliography 28. St. Louis: Center for Reformation Research, 1988.

Book of Concord, or The Symbolical Books of the Evangelical Lutheran Church. 2 vols. Ed. Henry Eyster Jacobs. Philadelphia: General Council Publication Board, 1919.

A Common Calling. The Report of the Lutheran-Reformed Committee for Theological Conversations, 1988–1992. Minneapolis: Augsburg, 1993.

Concordia Triglotta: The Symbolical Books of the Evangelical Lutheran Church. Ed. Friedrich Bente. St. Louis: Concordia, 1921.

Die Confutatio der Confessio Augustana vom 3. August 1530. Ed. Herbert Immenkötter. Rev. ed. Münster: Aschendorff, 1981.

Cyprian of Carthage. *De Lapsis and De Ecclesiae Catholicae Unitate*. Ed. and trans. Maurice Bévenot. OECT. Oxford: Clarendon, 1971.

Enchiridion symbolorum definitionum et declarationum de rebus fidei et morum. Ed. H. Denzinger and A. Schönmetzer. 34th ed. Freiburg in Breisgau: Herder, 1967.

Die evangelischen Kirchenordnungen des XVI. Jahrhunderts. Ed. Emil Sehling, VI/1/2. Tübingen: Mohr (Siebeck), 1957.

La foi des églises luthériennes: Confessions et catéchismes. Ed. André Birmelé and Marc Lienhard. Paris: Éditions du Cerf; Geneva: Labor et Fides, 1991.

Green Lowell C.; with Froehlich, Charles D. *Melanchthon in English: New Translations into English with a Registry of Previous Translations*. St. Louis: Center for Reformation Research, 1982.

In Christ—A New Community. The Proceedings of the Sixth Assembly of the Lutheran World Federation, Dar-es-Salaam, Tanzania, June 13–25, 1977. Ed. Arne Sovik. Geneva: LWF, 1977.

Leuenberg Agreement and Lutheran-Reformed Relationships. Ed. William G. Rusch and Daniel F. Martensen. Minneapolis: Augsburg Fortress Press, 1989.

Loci Communes of Philip Melanchthon. Trans. Charles Leander Hill. Boston: Meador, 1944.

Lutheran Book of Worship. Minneapolis: Augsburg; Philadelphia: Board of Publication, Lutheran Church in America, 1978.

Lutheran/Roman Catholic International Commission, *The Eucharist.* Geneva: LWF, 1980.

Lutherans and Catholics in Dialogue, I–III. Minneapolis: Augsburg, n.d.

Luther's Works, American Edition. 55 vols. St. Louis: Concordia; Philadelphia: Fortress Press, 1955–1986.

Melanchthon on Christian Doctrine: Loci Communes 1555. Trans. and ed. Clyde Manschreck. Grand Rapids: Baker, 1982.

Melanchthon: Selected Writings. Trans. Charles Leander Hill. Minneapolis: Augsburg, 1962.

Oxford Dictionary of the Christian Church. Ed. F. L. Cross and E. A. Livingstone. 3d ed. Oxford and New York: Oxford Univ. Press, 1997.

Oxford Encyclopedia of the Reformation. Ed. Hans J. Hillerbrand. 4 vols. New York and Oxford: Oxford Univ. Press, 1996.

Reu, J. Michael. *The Augsburg Confession: A Collection of Sources.* Chicago: Wartburg, 1930.

Saint Cyprien Correspondance. 2 vols. Ed. Louis Bayard. Paris: Société d'édition "Les belles lettres," 1925.

Urkunden und Aktenstücke zur Geschichte von Martin Luthers Schmalkaldischen Artikeln (1536–1574). Ed. Hans Volz. Berlin: Walter de Gruyter, 1957.

Interpretations of the Confessions and Commentaries

Allbeck, Willard D. *Studies in the Lutheran Confessions.* Philadelphia: Muhlenberg, 1952.

Fagerberg, Holsten. *A New Look at the Lutheran Confessions 1529–1537.* St. Louis: Concordia, 1972.

Grane, Leif. *Die Confessio Augustana.* Göttingen: Vandenhoeck & Ruprecht, 1970.

Grane, Leif. *The Augsburg Confession.* Minneapolis: Fortress Press, 1987.

Gritsch, Eric; and Jenson, Robert. *Lutheranism: The Theological Movement and Its Confessional Writings.* Philadelphia: Fortress Press, 1976.

Maurer, Wilhelm. *Historical Commentary on the Augsburg Confession.* Philadelphia: Fortress Press, 1986.

Peters, Christian. *Apologia Confessionis Augustanae: Untersuchungen zur Textgeschichte einer lutherischen Bekenntnisschrift (1530–1584).* Stuttgart: Calwer, 1997.

Pöhlmann, Horst Georg; Austad, Torleif; and Krüger, Friedhelm. *Theologie der Lutherischen Bekenntnisschriften.* Munich: Chr. Kaiser; Gütersloh: Gütersloher Verlagshaus, 1996.

Mildenberger, Friedrich. *Theology of the Lutheran Confessions.* Philadelphia: Fortress Press, 1983.

Russell, William R. *Luther's Theological Testament: The Schmalkald Articles.* Minneapolis: Fortress Press, 1995.

Schlink, Edmund. *Theology of the Lutheran Confessions.* Philadelphia: Muhlenberg, 1961.

Wenz, Gunther. *Theologie der Bekenntnisschriften der evangelisch-lutherischen Kirche.* 2 vols. Berlin and New York: Walter de Gruyter, 1996–1998.

Confessional History and Theology

450th Anniversary Augsburg Confession. Sixteenth Century Journal 11:3 (1980).

Anderson, Niels Knud. *Confessio Hafniensis: Den kobenhavnske Bekendelse af 1530.* Copenhagen: G. E. C. Gads, 1954.

The Augsburg Confession in Ecumenical Perspective. Ed. Harding Meyer. LWF Report 6/7. Geneva: LWF, 1980.

Bekenntnis und Einheit der Kirche: Studien zum Konkordienbuch. Ed. Martin Brecht and Reinhard Schwarz. Stuttgart: Calwer, 1980.

Burgess, Joseph A. *The Role of the Augsburg Confession: Catholic and Lutheran Views.* Philadelphia: Fortress Press, 1980.

Campbell, Ted A. *Christian Confessions: A Historical Introduction.* Louisville: Westminster John Knox, 1996.

The Church and the Confessions: The Role of the Confessions in the Life and Doctrine of the Lutheran Churches. Ed. Vilmos Vajta and Hans Weissgerber. Philadelphia: Fortress Press, 1963.

Cochrane, Arthur. "The Act of Confession-Confessing." *Sixteenth Century Journal* 8:4 (1977) 61–83.

Confessions and Catechisms of the Reformation. Ed. Mark Noll. Grand Rapids: Baker, 1991.

Dingel, Irene. *Concordia und Kontroverse: Das Ringen um konfessionelle Pluralität und bekenntnismässige Einheit im Spiegel der öffentlichen Diskussionen um Konkordienformel und Konkordienbuch.* Gütersloh: Gütersloher Verlagshaus, 1996.

Discord, Dialogue, and Concord: Studies in the Lutheran Reformation's Formula of Concord. Ed. Lewis W. Spitz and Wenzel Lohff. Philadelphia: Fortress Press, 1977.

Forde, Gerhard. *Justification by Faith: A Matter of Death and Life.* Minneapolis: Fortress Press, 1982.

Formula of Concord Quadricentenntial Essays. Sixteenth Century Journal 8:4 (1977).

Hauschild, Wolf-Dieter. "Corpus Doctrinae und Bekenntnisschriften. Zur Vorgeschichte des Konkordienbuches," in *Bekenntnis und Einheit der Kirche* (see above), 235–52.

Jungkuntz, Theodore. *Formulators of the Formula of Concord.* St. Louis: Concordia, 1977.

Kaufmann, Thomas. *Universität und lutherische Konfessionalisierung.* Gütersloh: Gütersloher Verlagshaus, 1997.

Kolb, Robert. *Andreae and the Formula of Concord: Six Sermons on the Way to Lutheran Unity.* St. Louis: Concordia, 1977.

Kolb, Robert. *Luther's Heirs Define His Legacy: Studies on Lutheran Confessionalization.* Aldershot (UK) and Brookfield, Vt.: Ashgate (Variorum), 1996.

Die lutherische Konfessionalisierung in Deutschland. Ed. Hans-Christoph Rublack. Gütersloh: Gerd Mohn, 1992.

Lutheran Identity. Final Report of the Study Project: "The Identity of the Lutheran Churches in the Context of the Challenges of our Time." Strasbourg: Institute for Ecumenical Research, 1977.

Pfnür, Vinzenz. *Einig in der Rechtfertigungslehre?* Wiesbaden: Fritz Steiner, 1970.

Schmauk, Theodore E.; and Benze, C. Theodore. *The Confessional Principle and the Confessions of the Lutheran Church.* Philadelphia: General Council Publication Board, 1911.

Schmid, Heinrich. *The Doctrinal Theology of the Evangelical Lutheran Church.* 4th ed. Trans. Charles A. Hay and Henry E. Jacobs. Philadelphia: Lutheran Publication Society, 1899.

Tschackert, Paul. *Die Entstehung der lutherischen und der reformierten Kirchenlehre samt ihren innerprotestantischen Gegensätzen.* Göttingen: Vandenhoeck & Ruprecht, 1979.

Wengert, Timothy J. *Law and Gospel: Philip Melanchthon's Debate with John Agricola of Eisleben over Poenitentia.* Grand Rapids: Baker, 1997.

Wengert, Timothy J. "Wittenberg's Earliest Catechism." *LQ* 7 (1993) 247–60.

History and Theology of Lutheranism

Anderson, N. K. "The Reformation in Scandinavia and the Baltic Countries." *The New Cambridge Modern History,* 2: *The Reformation 1520–1559.* Ed. G. R. Elton. 2d ed. Cambridge: Cambridge Univ. Press, 1990, 144–71.

Althaus, Paul. *The Ethics of Martin Luther.* Trans. Robert C. Schultz. Philadelphia: Fortress Press, 1972.

Althaus, Paul. *The Theology of Martin Luther.* Trans. Robert C. Schultz. Philadelphia: Fortress Press, 1966.

Bachmann, E. Theodore; and Bachmann, Mercia Brenne. *Lutheran Churches in the World: A Handbook.* Minneapolis: Augsburg Fortress Press, 1989.

Bergendoff, Conrad. *Olavus Petri and the Ecclesiastical Transformation in Sweden.* Philadelphia: Fortress Press, 1965.

Betts, R. R. "Poland, Bohemia, and Hungary." *The New Cambridge Modern History,* 2: *The Reformation 1520–1559.* Ed. G. R. Elton. 2d ed. Cambridge: Cambridge Univ. Press, 1990, 198–222.

Bornkamm, Heinrich. *Luther in Mid-Career 1521–1530.* Trans. E. Theodore Bachmann. Philadelphia: Fortress Press, 1983.

Braaten, Carl E. *Principles of Lutheran Theology.* Philadelphia: Fortress Press, 1983.

Braaten, Carl E.; and Jenson, Robert W. *The Catholicity of the Reformation.* Grand Rapids and Cambridge (UK): Eerdmans, 1996.

Brady, Thomas A., Jr. *Protestant Politics: Jacob Sturm (1489–1553) and the German Reformation.* Atlantic Highlands, N.J.: Humanities Press, 1995.

Brecht, Martin. *Martin Luther.* 3 vols. Philadelphia and Minneapolis: Fortress Press, 1985–1992.

Ebeling, Gerhard. *Luther: An Introduction to His Thought.* Trans. R. A. Wilson. Philadelphia: Fortress Press, 1972.

Edwards, Mark U., Jr. *Luther and the False Brethren.* Stanford: Stanford Univ. Press, 1975.

Forell, George W. *Martin Luther, Theologian of the Church: Collected Essays.* Word & World Supplement Series 2. Ed. William R. Russell. St. Paul: Luther Seminary, 1994.

Gassmann, Günther. "Lutherische Kirchen." *TRE* 21:599–620.

Grane, Leif. *Modus loquendi theologicus: Luthers Kampf um die Erneuerung der Theologie (1515–1518).* Leiden: E. J. Brill, 1975.

Grell, Ole Peter. "Scandinavia," in *The Reformation in National Context.* Ed. R. Scribner, R. Porter, and M. Teich. Cambridge: Cambridge Univ. Press, 1994, 111–30.

von Hase, Hans Christoph. *Die Gestalt der Kirche Luthers: Der casus confessionis im Kampf des Matthias Flacius gegen das Interim von 1548.* Göttingen: Vandenhoeck & Ruprecht, 1940.

Heininen, Simo. *Die finnischen Studenten in Wittenberg 1531–1552.* Helsinki: Luther-Agricola Gesellschaft, 1980.

Hendrix, Scott. *Luther and the Papacy: Stages in a Reformation Conflict.* Philadelphia: Fortress Press, 1981.

Hendrix, Scott. *Tradition and Authority in the Reformation.* Aldershot (UK) and Brookfield, Vt: Ashgate (Variorum), 1996.

Immenkötter, Herbert. *Der Reichstag zu Augsburg und die Confutatio.* Münster: Aschendorff, 1979.

Kolb, Robert. *Confessing the Faith: Reformers Define the Church, 1530–1580.* St. Louis: Concordia, 1991.

Kolb, Robert. *For All the Saints: Changing Perceptions of Martyrdom and Sainthood in the Lutheran Reformation.* Macon: Mercer Univ. Press, 1987.

Kolb, Robert. *Nikolaus von Amsdorf (1483–1565): Popular Polemics in the Preservation of Luther's Legacy.* Nieuwkoop: De Graaf, 1978.

Lau, Franz; and Bizer, Ernst. *Reformationsgeschichte Deutschlands bis 1555.* 2d ed. Göttingen: Vandenhoeck & Ruprecht, 1969.

Lindberg, Carter. *Beyond Charity: Reformation Initiatives for the Poor.* Minneapolis: Fortress Press, 1993.

Lindberg, Carter. *The European Reformations.* Oxford and Cambridge, Mass.: Blackwell, 1996.

Lohse, Bernhard. "Dogma und Bekenntnis in der Reformation: Von Luther bis zum Konkordienbuch." *Handbuch der Dogmengeschichte, 2.* Ed. Carl Andresen and Adolf Martin Ritter. 2d ed. Göttingen: Vandenhoeck & Ruprecht, 1998, 1–164.

Lohse, Bernhard. *Luthers Theologie in ihrer historischen Entwicklung und in ihrem systematischen Zusammenhang.* Göttingen: Vandenhoeck & Ruprecht, 1995.

Luther and Melanchthon in the History and Theology of the Reformation. Ed. Vilmos Vajta. Philadelphia: Muhlenberg, 1961.

Lutheran Church Past and Present. Ed. Vilmos Vajta. Minneapolis: Augsburg, 1977.

zur Mühlen, Karl-Heinz. "Die Einigung über den Rechtfertigungsartikel auf dem Regensburger Religionsgespräch von 1541—eine verpasste Chance?" *ZThK* 76 (1979): 331–59.

Nischan, Bodo. *Prince, People, and Confession: The Second Reformation in Brandenburg.* Philadelphia: University of Pennsylvania Press, 1994.

Raitt, Jill. *Shapers of Religious Traditions in Germany, Switzerland, and Poland, 1560–1600.* New Haven and London: Yale Univ. Press, 1981.

Roberts, Michael. *The Early Vasas: A History of Sweden 1523–1611.* Cambridge: Cambridge Univ. Press, 1968.

The Scandinavian Reformation: From Evangelical Movement to Institutionalisation of Reform. Ed. Ole Peter Grell. Cambridge: Cambridge Univ. Press, 1995.

Scheible, Heinz. "Luther and Melanchthon." *LQ* 4 (1990) 317–39.

Scheible, Heinz. *Melanchthon: Eine Biographie.* Munich: C. H. Beck, 1997.

Schwarz Lausten, Martin. *Biskop Niels Palladius: Et Bidrag til den Danske Kirkes Historie 1550–1560.* Copenhagen: G. E. C. Gads, 1968.

Smith, Ralph. *Luther, Ministry, and Ordination Rites in the Early Reformation Church.* New York: Peter Lang, 1996.

Spitz, Lewis W.; and Kolb, Robert. "Lutheranism." *OER* 2:467–73.

Wicks, Jared, S.J. "Abuses under Indictment at the Diet of Augsburg 1530." *Theological Studies* 41:2 (1980) 253–301.

Wolgast, Eike. *Hochstift und Reformation* (Stuttgart: Franz Steiner, 1995).

Printed in the United States
209678BV00003B/1-120/P